UPGRADING
AND
REPAIRING PCs
TECHNICIAN'S PORTABLE

REFERENCE

SECOND EDITION

 Sco ... ark Edward Soper

Upgrading and Repairing PCs Technician's Portable Reference, Second Edition

Copyright© 2001 by Que

International Standard Book Number: 0-7897-2454-5

Library of Congress Catalog Card Number: 00-104012

Printed in the United States of America

First Printing: October 2000

02   01   00   4   3   2   1

Trademarks

Warning and Disclaimer

Associate Publisher
Greg Wiegand

Senior Acquisitions Editor
Jill Byus Schorr

Senior Development Editor
Rick Kughen

Managing Editor
Thomas F. Hayes

Project Editor
Karen S. Shields

Copy Editor
Megan Wade

Technical Editor
Mark Reddin

Proofreader
Jeanne Clark

Indexer
Mary SeRine

Interior Design
Kevin Spear

Cover Design
Karen Ruggles

Layout Technicians
Heather Hiatt Miller
Stacey Richwine-DeRome

Contents at a Glance

Contents

3 BIOS Configurations and Upgrades 69

4 SCSI and IDE Hard Drives and Optical Drives 93

About the Authors

Scott Mueller is president of Mueller Technical Research, an international research and corporate training firm. Since 1982, MTR has specialized in the industry's longest running, most in-depth, accurate, and effective corporate PC hardware and technical training seminars, maintaining a client list that includes Fortune 500 companies, the U.S. and foreign governments, and major software and hardware corporations, as well as PC enthusiasts and entrepreneurs. His seminars have been presented to thousands of PC support professionals throughout the world.

Scott Mueller has developed and presented training courses in all areas of PC hardware and software. He is an expert in PC hardware, operating systems, and data-recovery techniques. For more information about a custom PC hardware or data-recovery training seminar for your organization, contact Lynn at

Mueller Technical Research
21 Spring Lane
Barrington Hills, IL 60010-9009
Phone: (847) 854-6794
Fax: (847) 854-6795
Internet: scottmueller@compuserve.com
Web: http://www.m-tr.com

Scott has many popular books, articles, and course materials to his credit, including *Upgrading and Repairing PCs*, which has sold more than 2 million copies, making it by far the most popular PC hardware book on the market today.

If you have questions about PC hardware, suggestions for the next edition of the book, or any comments in general, send them to Scott via email at scottmueller@compuserve.com.

When he is not working on PC-related books or teaching seminars, Scott can usually be found in the garage working on performance projects. This year a Harley Road King with a Twin-Cam 95ci Stage III engine continues as the main project (it's amazing how something with only two wheels can consume so much time and money <g>), along with a modified 5.7L '94 Impala SS and a 5.9L Grand Cherokee (hotrod SUV).

Mark Edward Soper is president of Select Systems and Associates, Inc., a technical writing and training organization that has been in business since 1989. Select Systems specializes in revealing the hidden power and features in PCs, their hardware, and their software. Select Systems has developed training courses and manuals for computer training firms and industrial, manufacturing, and media clients in print, HTML, and Adobe Acrobat formats.

Mark has taught computer troubleshooting and other technical subjects to thousands of students from Maine to Hawaii since 1992. He is an A+ Certified hardware technician and a Microsoft Certified Professional. He has been writing technical documents since the mid-1980s, and has contributed to several other Que books, including *Upgrading and Repairing PCs, 11th and 12th Editions*; *Upgrading and Repairing Networks, 2nd Edition*; and *Special Edition Using Windows Millennium Edition*. Mark co-authored the original edition of this book, and his first books on A+ Certification will be published after the revised A+ Certification Exams are released at the end of 2000. Watch for details about these and other book projects at the newly improved Que Web site at www.mcp.com.

For more information about customized technical reference and training materials, contact

Select Systems and Associates, Inc.
1100 W. Lloyd Expy #104
Evansville, IN 47708
Phone: (812) 421-1170
Fax: (812) 426-6138

Email: mesoper@selectsystems.com
Web: http://www.selectsystems.com

Mark has been writing for major computer magazines since 1990, with more than 125 articles in publications such as *SmartComputing*, *PCNovice*, *PCNovice Guides*, and the *PCNovice Learning Series*. His early work was published in *WordPerfect Magazine*, *The WordPerfectionist*, and *PCToday*. Many of Mark's articles are available in back issue or electronically via the World Wide Web at www.smartcomputing.com. Select Systems maintains a subject index of all Mark's articles at http://www.selectsystems.com.

When he's not sweating out a writing deadline, Mark enjoys life with his wife, Cheryl, a children's librarian who is also a published writer. Their children (now 21, 20, 20, and 18) are all computer users, keeping him busy with their questions, and he also provides computer support to his local church. Mark still finds time to watch, photograph, and (occasionally) ride trains. He's using his years of experience with photography and computers to build a personal image archive, and he has also created archiving programs for a local university.

Mark welcomes your comments and suggestions about this book. Send them to mesoper@selectsystems.com.

About the Technical Editor

Mark Reddin, MCSE, A+, is a Microsoft Certified Systems Engineer and an A+ Certified PC technician. In addition to his work as a Que technical editor, Mark provides consulting services for NT systems and business networks. He has enjoyed using computers at the hobbyist level since the days of the Atari 400. This interest led to a professional level of involvement and, after dabbling in programming, he discovered networking. He achieved his first certification from Microsoft in early 1998 and has worked as a configuration technician for a computer reseller as well as an NT specialist and general networking contractor.

Acknowledgments

Mark would like to thank the following people: Scott Mueller, whose *Upgrading and Repairing PCs* has been on his "short list" of great computer books for more than 10 years and whose latest edition provided much of the material for this book; Jill Byus Schorr and Rick Kughen at Que, whose encouragement and guidance have helped make this book a success; Cheryl, who never stopped believing that I could write; and God, who gives all of us talents and abilities and cheers us on as we develop them.

Tell Us What You Think!

As the reader of this book, *you* are our most important critic and commentator. We value your opinion and want to know what we're doing right, what we could do better, what areas you'd like to see us publish in, and any other words of wisdom you're willing to pass our way.

As the associate publisher for this book, I welcome your comments. You can fax, email, or write me directly to let me know what you did or didn't like about this book—as well as what we can do to make our books stronger.

When you write, please be sure to include this book's title and authors as well as your name and phone or fax number. I will carefully review your comments and share them with the authors and editors who worked on the book.

Fax: 317-581-4666

Email: hardware@mcp.com

Mail: Macmillan USA
         201 West 103rd Street
         Indianapolis, IN 46290

Introduction

If you're a computer repair technician or student, you know just how crucial it is to have concise, yet detailed, technical specifications at your fingertips. It can mean the success or failure of your job.

Unfortunately, most detailed hardware books are far too large to tote around in a briefcase, book bag, or in your back pocket—where you need them.

Upgrading and Repairing PCs: Technician's Portable Reference is the exception. This concise book provides just the information you need to upgrade or repair your PC, without weighing you down.

Although you should consider this book to be a companion to Scott Mueller's best-selling opus, *Upgrading and Repairing PCs*, you'll also find that it stands quite well on its own. While much of the information is in the mother book, much of what is found here is presented in a boiled-down, easy-to-digest reference that will help you get the job done quickly and efficiently. You'll also find that this portable reference contains some information not found in the main book—information that is specially geared to help the technician in the field.

I recommend that you keep *Upgrading and Repairing PCs, 12th Edition* (ISBN 0-7897-2303-4) on your desk or workbench and *Upgrading and Repairing PCs: Technician's Portable Reference* with your toolkit, so it's ready to go with you anytime—whether it's to a customer job site or a class.

Chapter 1

General Technical Reference

PC Subsystem Components Quick Reference

The following table lists the major PC subsystems and how they are configured. Use this table as a shortcut to the most likely place(s) to look for problems with these subsystems. Then, go to the appropriate chapter for more information.

Table 1.1 Major PC Subsystems and Where to Configure Them			
Subsystem	**Components**	**How Configured and Controlled**	**See Chapters for Details**
Motherboard	CPU, RAM, ROM, expansion slots, BIOS	Jumper blocks (CPU) BIOS (all others plus CPU on some systems)	2, 3
I/O ports	Serial	BIOS and operating system	3, 6
	Parallel	BIOS and operating system	3, 7
	USB	BIOS and operating system drivers	3, 8
	PS/2 mouse	MB jumper blocks or BIOS	3, 9
	Keyboard	BIOS	3, 9
I/O devices	Modem	Driver software	6
	Sound card	Driver software	10
Input devices	Keyboard, mouse, trackball, touchpad	BIOS Driver software	9 9
	Scanner	Driver software	7
Standard mass storage	Floppy	BIOS	5
	IDE	BIOS and jumper blocks	4
Add-on mass storage	CD-ROM, Zip, LS-120, other removable media	Jumper blocks and driver software	4
	SCSI	Jumper blocks and add-on BIOS card or driver software	4

Table 1.1 Major PC Subsystems and Where to Configure Them Contiuned			
Subsystem	Components	How Configured and Controlled	See Chapters for Details
	Tape backup	Jumper blocks and tape backup software	4, 5
Display	Video card and monitor	BIOS (basic features), operating system (advanced features)	10
Power supply	(same)	Autoselected voltage or slider switch on unit; on/off switch	2

The Motherboard and Its Components

Figure 1.1 shows a typical motherboard with its major components labeled as it would appear before installation in a system.

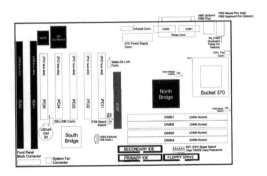

Figure 1.1   A typical ATX motherboard (overhead view).

Figure 1.2 shows the ports on a typical ATX motherboard as they would be seen from the rear of the system.

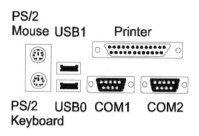

Figure 1.2   Ports on the rear of a typical ATX motherboard.

Understanding Bits, Nibbles, and Bytes

The foundation of all memory and disk size calculations is the *byte*. When storing plain-text data, a byte equals one character.

Data can also be stored or transmitted in portions of a byte. A *bit* equals 1/8 of a byte, or, in other words, a byte equals eight bits. A *nibble* equals 1/2 of a byte, or four bits. Thus, two nibbles equal one byte. Keep the difference between bits and bytes in mind as you review the table of standard capacity abbreviations and meanings.

Standard Capacity Abbreviations and Meanings

Use the following table to translate megabytes, gigabytes, and the other abbreviations used to refer to memory and disk space into their decimal or binary values.

Unfortunately, some parts of the computer industry use the decimal values, while others use the binary values. Typically, hard disk and other drive manufacturers rate their products in decimal megabytes or gigabytes. On the other hand, the ROM BIOS on most (but not all) systems and the MS-DOS and Windows FDISK programs use binary megabytes or gigabytes, thus creating an apparent discrepancy in disk capacity. RAM is virtually always calculated using binary values.

Table 1.2   Standard Abbreviations and Meanings

Abbreviation	Description	Decimal Power	Decimal Value	Binary Power	Binary Value
Kbit or Kb	Kilobit	10^3	1,000	2^{10}	1,024
K or KB	Kilobyte	10^3	1,000	2^{10}	1,024
Mbit or Mb	Megabit	10^6	1,000,000	2^{20}	1,048,576
M or MB	Megabyte	10^6	1,000,000	2^{20}	1,048,576
Gbit or Gb	Gigabit	10^9	1,000,000,000	2^{30}	1,073,741,824
G or GB	Gigabyte	10^9	1,000,000,000	2^{30}	1,073,741,824
Tbit or Tb	Terabit	10^{12}	1,000,000,000,000	2^{40}	1,099,511,627,776
T or TB	Terabyte	10^{12}	1,000,000,000,000	2^{40}	1,099,511,627,776

> **Note**
>
> For other conversion and reference tables, see the Technical
> Reference (found on the CD-ROM) of *Upgrading and Repairing
> PCs, Twelfth Edition.*

Glossary of Essential Terms

Table 1.3   Terms and Their Definitions

Term	Definition
ACPI	Advanced configuration and power interface; power management for all types of computer devices.
AGP	Accelerated graphics port; a fast dedicated slot interface between the video adapter or chipset and the motherboard chipset North Bridge; developed by Intel. AGP is 32 bits wide; runs at 66MHz; and can transfer 1, 2, or 4 bits per cycle (1x, 2x, and 4x modes).
APM	Advanced power management; power management for hard drives and monitors.
ATAPI	AT attachment-packet interface; modified version of IDE that supports removable media and optical drives that use software drivers. Can coexist on the same cable with IDE hard drives.
Beep code	A series of one or more beeps used by the system BIOS to report errors. Beep codes vary by BIOS brand and version.
BIOS	Basic input/output system; a chip on the system board that controls essential devices, such as the keyboard, basic video display, floppy and hard drives, and memory.
Cluster	Also called *allocation unit*; the minimum disk space actually used by a file when it is stored; this size increases with larger drives due to the limitations of the FAT size.
Color depth	How many colors a video card can display at a given resolution; the higher the resolution, the more RAM required to display a given color depth.
COM	Communication port; also called *serial* port.
Combo slot	Also called *shared slot*; a pair of slots that share a single card bracket; only one of the two slots can be used at a time.
Compact flash	A type of flash memory device.
CPU	Central processing unit; the "brains" of a computer.
CRT	Cathode-ray tube; conventional TV-like picture tube display technology used on most desktop monitors.
Data bus	The connection that transmits data between the processor and the rest of the system. The width of the data bus defines the number of data bits that can be moved in to or out of the processor in one cycle.
DCC	Direct cable connection; Windows 9x/Me/2000 program that enables computers to link up through parallel or serial ports; Windows NT 4.0 supports serial port linkups only.

Table 1.3   Terms and Their Definitions Continued

Term	Definition
Device Manager	Tab in the System Properties sheet for Windows 9x/2000/Me that enables you to view, change the configuration of, and remove system and add-on devices.
DFP	Digital flat panel; an early digital monitor standard replaced by DVI.
DIMM	Dual inline memory module; leading type of memory device from late 1990s to present; current versions have 168 edge connectors.
DMA	Direct memory access; data transfer method used by some devices to bypass the CPU and go directly to and from memory; some ISA devices require the use of a specific DMA channel.
DNS	Domain name system; matches IP addresses to Web site and Web server names.
DPMS	Display Power Management Standard; the original power management standard for monitors.
Drive geometry	Combination of heads, sectors per track, and cylinders used to define an IDE drive in the system BIOS CMOS setup program. When a drive is moved to another system, the same drive geometry and translation settings must be used to enable the new system to read data from the drive.
DVD	Digital versatile disc; the emerging standard for home video and also a popular add-on for computers.
DVI	Digital video interface; the current digital monitor standard.
ECC	Error correcting code. A method of error correction; a type of system memory or cache that is capable of detecting and correcting some types of memory errors without interrupting processing. ECC requires parity-checked memory plus an ECC-compatible motherboard with ECC enabled.
EISA	Enhanced Industry Standard Architecture; a 32-bit version of ISA developed in 1989; found primarily in older servers; obsolete, but can be used for ISA cards.
FAT	File allocation table; on-disk directory that lists filenames, sizes, and locations of all clusters in a file. The size of the FAT limits the size of the drive.
FAT-16	16-bit FAT supported by MS-DOS and Windows 95/95 OSR 1.x; drive letter limited to 2.1GB.
FAT-32	32-bit FAT supported by Windows 95 OSR 2.x/98/Me; drive letter limited to 2.1TB.
FCC ID	Identification number placed on all computer hardware to certify it's approved by the Federal Communications Commission. Use this number to locate drivers for some boards.
Firmware	"Software on a Chip"; general term for BIOS code on motherboards and in devices such as modems, printers, and others.
Flash BIOS	BIOS/firmware on systems or devices that can be updated through software.
Flash memory	Memory device whose contents can be changed electrically, but doesn't require electrical power to retain its contents; used in digital cameras and portable music players.

Table 1.3   Terms and Their Definitions Continued

Term	Definition
HomePNA	Home Phoneline Networking Alliance; a trade group that develops standards for networking over telephone lines within a home or small office.
Host-based	A type of printer in which the computer processes the image data; these printers are cheaper but less versatile than those containing a page-description or printer command language.
Hub	Device that accepts multiple connections, such as USB, 10BASE-T, and 10/100 or Fast Ethernet hubs.
I/O port	Input/output port; used to communicate to and from motherboard or add-on devices. All devices require one or more I/O port address ranges, which must be unique to each device.
ICS	Internet connection sharing; a feature on Windows 98SE, Windows 2000, and Windows Me that enables one computer to share its Internet connection with other Windows computers, including Win95 and Win98 original versions.
IDE	Integrated Drive Electronics; also called *AT Attachment*. The 40-pin interface used on most hard drives, CD-ROMs, and internal versions of LS-120 SuperDisk and Iomega Zip drives. Drives must be jumpered as master, slave, or single.
IEEE-1284	A series of parallel-port standards that include EPP and ECP high-speed bi-directional modes.
IEEE-1394	Also called *i.Link* and *FireWire*; a very high-speed, direct-connect interface for high-performance storage, digital video editing, and scanning devices.
IPX/SPX	Standard protocols used on NetWare 3.x/4.x networks.
IRQ	Interrupt request line; used by devices to request attention from the CPU.
ISA	Industry Standard Architecture; a slot standard developed by IBM in 1981 for 8-bit cards; enhanced by IBM in 1984 for 16-bit cards; now obsolete, although most systems have one or two on board.
KDE	K Desktop Environment; a popular GUI for Linux.
LAN	Local area network.
LBA	Logical block addressing; a BIOS-based method of remapping the normal drive geometry to overcome the 504-megabyte/528.5-million-byte limit imposed by normal IDE drive designs. Can also be implemented by add-on cards or software drivers.
LCD	Liquid crystal display; flat-panel display technology used on notebook and advanced desktop computers.
Legacy	Non plug-and-play (PnP) card; also can refer to serial and parallel ports.
Local Bus	A series of high-speed slot standards (VL-Bus, PCI, and AGP) for video that bypass the slow ISA bus.
Loopback	A method of testing ports that involves sending data out and receiving data back through the same port; implemented with loopback plugs that loop send lines back to receive lines.
LPT	Line printer port; also called *parallel* port.
LS-120	Also called *SuperDisk*; a 3.5" drive and disk made by Imation (originally 3M) with 120MB capacity. Drive can also read/write/format standard 1.44MB 3.5" media.

Table 1.3	Terms and Their Definitions Continued
Term	**Definition**
MCA	Micro Channel Architecture; a 16/32-bit slot standard developed by IBM in 1987 for its PS/2 models. Never became popular outside IBM circles; obsolete and incompatible with any other standard.
Memory bank	Amount of memory (in bits) equal to the system bus of a specific CPU. The number of memory modules to achieve a memory bank on a given system varies with the CPU and the memory types the system can use.
Memory stick	A type of flash memory device developed by Sony for use in its camera and electronic products.
Mwave	A series of IBM-made multifunction cards that combine sound and modem functions.
NetBEUI	Microsoft version of NetBIOS network protocol; can be used for small, non-routable workgroup networks.
NIC	Network interface card; connects your computer to a LAN (local area network).
Parity	A method of error checking in which an extra bit is sent to the receiving device to indicate whether an even or odd number of binary 1 bits was transmitted. The receiving unit compares the received information with this bit and can obtain a reasonable judgment about the validity of the character. Parity checking was used with many early memory chips and SIMMs, but is now used primarily in modem and serial port configuration.
Parity error	An error displayed when a parity check of memory reveals incorrect values were stored; the system halts and all unsaved work is lost.
PC Card	Current term for former PCMCIA card standard used in notebook computers.
PC/AT	Systems using an 80286 or better CPU; these have a 16-bit or wider data bus.
PC/XT	Systems using an 8088 or 8086 CPU; these have an 8-bit data bus.
PCI	Peripheral Component Interconnect; a 32/64-bit slot standard developed by Intel in 1992; 32-bit version used in all PCs from mid-1990s onward for most add-on cards; 64-bit version found in some servers.
PCL	Printer Control Language; a series of printer control commands and routines used by Hewlett-Packard on its LaserJet printers.
PCMCIA	Personal Computer Memory Card International Association; original term for what are now called *PC Cards*; primarily used in notebook computers. Some use PCMCIA/PC Card to avoid confusion with regular add-on cards for desktop computers.
PDL	Page Description Language; general term for any set of printer commands, such as PCL or PostScript.
Peer server	Computer that can be used as a client and also shares printers, folders, and drives with other users.
PIO	Programmed input/output; a series of IDE data-transfer rates that enable faster data throughput. Both the drive and interface must support the same PIO mode for safety.
PnP	Plug-and-Play; the combination of add-on device, BIOS, and operating system (OS) that enables the OS to detect, install software for, and configure the device. PnP is supported by Windows 9x/Me/2000.
POST	Power on self test; a test performed by the system BIOS during system startup.

Table 1.3	Terms and Their Definitions Continued
Term	**Definition**
PostScript	Adobe's sophisticated printer language used in laser and inkjet printers designed for graphic arts professionals.
QIC	Quarter-Inch Committee; the standards body responsible for most tape drive standards used by PC clients and small network servers.
QIC-EX	Extra-capacity cartridges developed for some QIC, QIC-Wide, and Travan drives by Verbatim.
Register size	Number of bits of data the CPU can process in a single operation.
Resolution	Combination of horizontal and vertical pixels in an image; larger monitors support higher resolutions.
ROM BIOS	Read-only memory BIOS; older BIOS chips that were socketed and could be updated only by being physically replaced.
RS-232	Diverse serial port standard with many different device-specific pinouts; supports both 9-pin and 25-pin ports.
Scan codes	Hexadecimal codes transmitted by the keyboard when keys are struck; must be converted to ASCII for display onscreen.
SCSI	Small computer system interface; a family of high-performance interfaces used on high-speed hard drives, optical drives, scanners, and other internal and external devices. Each device must have a unique ID number.
SIMM	Single Inline Memory Module; common type of memory device from late 1980s to mid-1990s; can have 30 or 72 edge connectors.
SmartMedia	A type of flash memory device.
SoundBlaster	Creative Labs' longtime family of sound cards; the *de facto* standard for DOS-based audio.
TCP/IP	Transmission Control Protocol/Internet Protocol; the protocol of the World Wide Web and the Internet.
Travan	A family of tape drives and media developed from QIC and QIC-Wide standards by Imation (originally 3M).
UART	Universal Asynchronous Receive/Transmit chip; the heart of a serial port or hardware-based modem.
UDMA	Ultra DMA; a series of IDE data transfer rates that use DMA for even faster performance. Most effective when combined with bus-mastering hard disk host adapter driver software.
USB	Universal Serial Bus; a high-speed, hub-based interface for pointing, printing, and scanning devices.
UTP	Unshielded twisted-pair cable, such as Category 5 used with 10/100 Ethernet.
v.90	Current 56Kbps high-speed, dial-up modem standard; replaced x2 and K56flex.
v.92	New version of v.90 due in late 2000; supports call waiting and faster uploading.
VESA	Video Electronic Standards Association; trade group of monitor and video card makers that develops various display and power management standards.
VGA	Video graphics adapter; a family of analog display standards that support 16 or more colors and 640×480 or higher resolutions.

Table 1.3	Terms and Their Definitions Continued
Term	**Definition**
VL-Bus	VESA Local-Bus; a slot standard based on ISA that added a 32-bit connector to ISA slots in some 486 and early Pentium models; obsolete, but can be used for ISA cards.
Windows keys	Keys beyond the normal keyboard's 101 keys that perform special tasks in Windows 9x/NT4/2000/Me.
WINS	Windows Internet Naming Service; matches IP addresses to computers on a Windows network.
x86	All processors that are compatible with Intel CPUs from the 8086/88 through the newest Pentium IIIs and Celerons. Can refer to both Intel and non-Intel (AMD, VIA/Cyrix) CPUs.

PC99 Color Standards

Table 1.4	PC99 Color Coding Standards for Ports
Port Type	**Color**
Analog VGA (DB15)	Blue
Audio line in	Light blue
Audio line out	Lime green
Digital monitor (DFP)	White
IEEE-1394 (i.Link, FireWire)	Grey
Microphone	Pink
MIDI/game port	Gold
Parallel port	Burgundy
Serial Port	Teal or turquoise
Speaker out (subwoofer)	Orange
Right-to-left speaker	Brown
USB	Black
Video out	Yellow
SCSI, network, telephone, modem, and so on	None
PS/2 Keyboard	Purple
PS/2 Mouse	Green

Hexadecimal/ASCII Conversions

Use Table 1.5 to look up the various representations for any character you see onscreen or want to insert into a document. You can use the Alt+keypad numbers to insert any character into an ASCII document you create with a program such as Windows Notepad or MS-DOS's Edit.

Table 1.5	Hexadecimal/ASCII Conversions				
Dec	**Hex**	**Octal**	**Binary**	**Name**	**Character**
0	00	000	0000 0000	blank	
1	01	001	0000 0001	happy face	☺
2	02	002	0000 0010	inverse happy face	☻
3	03	003	0000 0011	heart	♥
4	04	004	0000 0100	diamond	♦
5	05	005	0000 0101	club	♣
6	06	006	0000 0110	spade	♠
7	07	007	0000 0111	bullet	•
8	08	010	0000 1000	inverse bullet	◘
9	09	011	0000 1001	circle	o
10	0A	012	0000 1010	inverse circle	o
11	0B	013	0000 1011	male sign	♂
12	0C	014	0000 1100	female sign	♀
13	0D	015	0000 1101	single note	♪
14	0E	016	0000 1110	double note	♫
15	0F	017	0000 1111	sun	☼
16	10	020	0001 0000	right triangle	►
17	11	021	0001 0001	left triangle	◄
18	12	022	0001 0010	up/down arrow	↕
19	13	023	0001 0011	double exclamation	‼
20	14	024	0001 0100	paragraph sign	¶
21	15	025	0001 0101	section sign	§
22	16	026	0001 0110	rectangular bullet	■
23	17	027	0001 0111	up/down to line	↨
24	18	030	0001 1000	up arrow	↑
25	19	031	0001 1001	down arrow	↓
26	1A	032	0001 1010	right arrow	→
27	1B	033	0001 1011	left arrow	←
28	1C	034	0001 1100	lower left box	∟
29	1D	035	0001 1101	left/right arrow	↔
30	1E	036	0001 1110	up triangle	▲
31	1F	037	0001 1111	down triangle	▼
32	20	040	0010 0000	space	Space
33	21	041	0010 0001	exclamation point	!
34	22	042	0010 0010	quotation mark	"
35	23	043	0010 0011	number sign	#

Table 1.5	Hexadecimal/ASCII Conversions Continued				
Dec	**Hex**	**Octal**	**Binary**	**Name**	**Character**
36	24	044	0010 0100	dollar sign	$
37	25	045	0010 0101	percent sign	%
38	26	046	0010 0110	ampersand	&
39	27	047	0010 0111	apostrophe	'
40	28	050	0010 1000	opening parenthesis	(
41	29	051	0010 1001	closing parenthesis	)
42	2A	052	0010 1010	asterisk	*
43	2B	053	0010 1011	plus sign	+
44	2C	054	0010 1100	comma	,
45	2D	055	0010 1101	hyphen or minus sign	-
46	2E	056	0010 1110	period	.
47	2F	057	0010 1111	slash	/
48	30	060	0011 0000	zero	0
49	31	061	0011 0001	one	1
50	32	062	0011 0010	two	2
51	33	063	0011 0011	three	3
52	34	064	0011 0100	four	4
53	35	065	0011 0101	five	5
54	36	066	0011 0110	six	6
55	37	067	0011 0111	seven	7
56	38	070	0011 1000	eight	8
57	39	071	0011 1001	nine	9
58	3A	072	0011 1010	colon	:
59	3B	073	0011 1011	semicolon	;
60	3C	074	0011 1100	less-than sign	<
61	3D	075	0011 1101	equal sign	=
62	3E	076	0011 1110	greater-than sign	>
63	3F	077	0011 1111	question mark	?
64	40	100	0100 0000	at sign	@
65	41	101	0100 0001	capital A	A
66	42	102	0100 0010	capital B	B
67	43	103	0100 0011	capital C	C
68	44	104	0100 0100	capital D	D
69	45	105	0100 0101	capital E	E
70	46	106	0100 0110	capital F	F
71	47	107	0100 0111	capital G	G
72	48	110	0100 1000	capital H	H

Table 1.5		Hexadecimal/ASCII Conversions Continued			
Dec	**Hex**	**Octal**	**Binary**	**Name**	**Character**
73	49	111	0100 1001	capital I	I
74	4A	112	0100 1010	capital J	J
75	4B	113	0100 1011	capital K	K
76	4C	114	0100 1100	capital L	L
77	4D	115	0100 1101	capital M	M
78	4E	116	0100 1110	capital N	N
79	4F	117	0100 1111	capital O	O
80	50	120	0101 0000	capital P	P
81	51	121	0101 0001	capital Q	Q
82	52	122	0101 0010	capital R	R
83	53	123	0101 0011	capital S	S
84	54	124	0101 0100	capital T	T
85	55	125	0101 0101	capital U	U
86	56	126	0101 0110	capital V	V
87	57	127	0101 0111	capital W	W
88	58	130	0101 1000	capital X	X
89	59	131	0101 1001	capital Y	Y
90	5A	132	0101 1010	capital Z	Z
91	5B	133	0101 1011	opening bracket	[
92	5C	134	0101 1100	backward slash	\
93	5D	135	0101 1101	closing bracket	]
94	5E	136	0101 1110	caret	^
95	5F	137	0101 1111	underscore	_
96	60	140	0110 0000	grave	`
97	61	141	0110 0001	lowercase A	a
98	62	142	0110 0010	lowercase B	b
99	63	143	0110 0011	lowercase C	c
100	64	144	0110 0100	lowercase D	d
101	65	145	0110 0101	lowercase E	e
102	66	146	0110 0110	lowercase F	f
103	67	147	0110 0111	lowercase G	g
104	68	150	0110 1000	lowercase H	h
105	69	151	0110 1001	lowercase I	i
106	6A	152	0110 1010	lowercase J	j
107	6B	153	0110 1011	lowercase K	k
108	6C	154	0110 1100	lowercase L	l
109	6D	155	0110 1101	lowercase M	m
110	6E	156	0110 1110	lowercase N	n

Table 1.5		Hexadecimal/ASCII Conversions Continued			
Dec	**Hex**	**Octal**	**Binary**	**Name**	**Character**
111	6F	157	0110 1111	lowercase O	o
112	70	160	0111 0000	lowercase P	p
113	71	161	0111 0001	lowercase Q	q
114	72	162	0111 0010	lowercase R	r
115	73	163	0111 0011	lowercase S	s
116	74	164	0111 0100	lowercase T	t
117	75	165	0111 0101	lowercase U	u
118	76	166	0111 0110	lowercase V	v
119	77	167	0111 0111	lowercase W	w
120	78	170	0111 1000	lowercase X	x
121	79	171	0111 1001	lowercase Y	y
122	7A	172	0111 1010	lowercase Z	z
123	7B	173	0111 1011	opening brace	{
124	7C	174	0111 1100	vertical line	|
125	7D	175	0111 1101	closing brace	}
126	7E	176	0111 1110	tilde	~
127	7F	177	0111 1111	small house	Δ
128	80	200	1000 0000	C cedilla	Ç
129	81	201	1000 0001	u umlaut	ü
130	82	202	1000 0010	e acute	é
131	83	203	1000 0011	a circumflex	â
132	84	204	1000 0100	a umlaut	ä
133	85	205	1000 0101	a grave	à
134	86	206	1000 0110	a ring	å
135	87	207	1000 0111	c cedilla	ç
136	88	210	1000 1000	e circumflex	ê
137	89	211	1000 1001	e umlaut	ë
138	8A	212	1000 1010	e grave	è
139	8B	213	1000 1011	I umlaut	ï
140	8C	214	1000 1100	I circumflex	î
141	8D	215	1000 1101	I grave	ì
142	8E	216	1000 1110	A umlaut	Ä
143	8F	217	1000 1111	A ring	Å
144	90	220	1001 0000	E acute	É
145	91	221	1001 0001	ae ligature	æ
146	92	222	1001 0010	AE ligature	Æ
147	93	223	1001 0011	o circumflex	ô

Dec	Hex	Octal	Binary	Name	Character
148	94	224	1001 0100	o umlaut	ö
149	95	225	1001 0101	o grave	ò
150	96	226	1001 0110	u circumflex	û
151	97	227	1001 0111	u grave	ù
152	98	230	1001 1000	y umlaut	ÿ
153	99	231	1001 1001	O umlaut	Ö
154	9A	232	1001 1010	U umlaut	Ü
155	9B	233	1001 1011	cent sign	¢
156	9C	234	1001 1100	pound sign	£
157	9D	235	1001 1101	yen sign	¥
158	9E	236	1001 1110	Pt	₧
159	9F	237	1001 1111	function	ƒ
160	A0	240	1010 0000	a acute	á
161	A1	241	1010 0001	I acute	í
162	A2	242	1010 0010	o acute	ó
163	A3	243	1010 0011	u acute	ú
164	A4	244	1010 0100	n tilde	ñ
165	A5	245	1010 0101	N tilde	Ñ
166	A6	246	1010 0110	a macron	ā
167	A7	247	1010 0111	o macron	ō
168	A8	250	1010 1000	opening question mark	¿
169	A9	251	1010 1001	upper-left box	⌐
170	AA	252	1010 1010	upper-right box	¬
171	AB	253	1010 1011	1/2	½
172	AC	254	1010 1100	1/4	¼
173	AD	255	1010 1101	opening exclamation	¡
174	AE	256	1010 1110	opening guillemets	«
175	AF	257	1010 1111	closing guillemets	»
176	B0	260	1011 0000	light block	▒
177	B1	261	1011 0001	medium block	▓
178	B2	262	1011 0010	dark block	█
179	B3	263	1011 0011	single vertical	│
180	B4	264	1011 0100	single right junction	┤
181	B5	265	1011 0101	2 to 1 right junction	╡
182	B6	266	1011 0110	1 to 2 right junction	╢
183	B7	267	1011 0111	1 to 2 upper-right	╖
184	B8	270	1011 1000	2 to 1 upper-right	╕
185	B9	271	1011 1001	double right junction	╣

Table 1.5   **Hexadecimal/ASCII Conversions Continued**

Table 1.5 Hexadecimal/ASCII Conversions Continued

Dec	Hex	Octal	Binary	Name	Character
186	BA	272	1011 1010	double vertical	‖
187	BB	273	1011 1011	double upper-right	╗
188	BC	274	1011 1100	double lower-right	╝
189	BD	275	1011 1101	1 to 2 lower-right	╜
190	BE	276	1011 1110	2 to 1 lower-right	╛
191	BF	277	1011 1111	single upper-right	┐
192	C0	300	1100 0000	single lower-left	└
193	C1	301	1100 0001	single lower junction	┴
194	C2	302	1100 0010	single upper junction	┬
195	C3	303	1100 0011	single left junction	├
196	C4	304	1100 0100	single horizontal	─
197	C5	305	1100 0101	single intersection	┼
198	C6	306	1100 0110	2 to 1 left junction	╞
199	C7	307	1100 0111	1 to 2 left junction	╟
200	C8	310	1100 1000	double lower-left	╚
201	C9	311	1100 1001	double upper-left	╔
202	CA	312	1100 1010	double lower junction	╩
203	CB	313	1100 1011	double upper junction	╦
204	CC	314	1100 1100	double left junction	╠
205	CD	315	1100 1101	double horizontal	═
206	CE	316	1100 1110	double intersection	╬
207	CF	317	1100 1111	1 to 2 lower junction	╧
208	D0	320	1101 0000	2 to 1 lower junction	╨
209	D1	321	1101 0001	1 to 2 upper junction	╤
210	D2	322	1101 0010	2 to 1 upper junction	╥
211	D3	323	1101 0011	1 to 2 lower-left	╙
212	D4	324	1101 0100	2 to 1 lower-left	╘
213	D5	325	1101 0101	2 to 1 upper-left	╒
214	D6	326	1101 0110	1 to 2 upper-left	╓
215	D7	327	1101 0111	2 to 1 intersection	╫
216	D8	330	1101 1000	1 to 2 intersection	╪
217	D9	331	1101 1001	single lower-right	┘
218	DA	332	1101 1010	single upper-right	┌
219	DB	333	1101 1011	inverse space	█
220	DC	334	1101 1100	lower inverse	▄
221	DD	335	1101 1101	left inverse	▌
222	DE	336	1101 1110	right inverse	▐

Table 1.5	Hexadecimal/ASCII Conversions Continued				
Dec	**Hex**	**Octal**	**Binary**	**Name**	**Character**
223	DF	337	1101 1111	upper inverse	■
224	E0	340	1110 0000	alpha	α
225	E1	341	1110 0001	beta	β
226	E2	342	1110 0010	Gamma	Γ
227	E3	343	1110 0011	pi	π
228	E4	344	1110 0100	Sigma	Σ
229	E5	345	1110 0101	sigma	σ
230	E6	346	1110 0110	mu	μ
231	E7	347	1110 0111	tau	τ
232	E8	350	1110 1000	Phi	Φ
233	E9	351	1110 1001	theta	θ
234	EA	352	1110 1010	Omega	Ω
235	EB	353	1110 1011	delta	δ
236	EC	354	1110 1100	infinity	∞
237	ED	355	1110 1101	phi	φ
238	EE	356	1110 1110	epsilon	ε
239	EF	357	1110 1111	intersection of sets	∩
240	F0	360	1111 0000	is identical to	≡
241	F1	361	1111 0001	plus/minus sign	±
242	F2	362	1111 0010	greater/equal sign	≥
243	F3	363	1111 0011	less/equal sign	≤
244	F4	364	1111 0100	top half integral	⌠
245	F5	365	1111 0101	lower half integral	⌡
246	F6	366	1111 0110	division sign	÷
247	F7	367	1111 0111	approximately	≈
248	F8	370	1111 1000	degree	°
249	F9	371	1111 1001	filled-in degree	•
250	FA	372	1111 1010	small bullet	·
251	FB	373	1111 1011	square root	√
252	FC	374	1111 1100	superscript n	^{n}
253	FD	375	1111 1101	superscript 2	^{2}
254	FE	376	1111 1110	box	■
255	FF	377	1111 1111	phantom space	ˇ

Chapter 2

System Components and Configuration

Processors and Their Data Bus Widths

Table 2.1	Processors and Their Data Bus Widths
Processor	**Data Bus Width**
Intel 8088	8-bit
Intel 8086	16-bit
Intel 286	16-bit
Intel 386SX	16-bit
Intel 386DX	32-bit
Intel 486SLC	16-bit[4]
Intel 486DLC	32-bit[4]
Intel 486 (all SX/DX series)	32-bit
Intel 5X86	32-bit[5, 6]
Intel Pentium	64-bit
AMD K5	64-bit[1]
Intel Pentium MMX	64-bit
AMD K6	64-bit[1]
Cyrix 6x86	64-bit[3]
Cyrix 6x86MX	64-bit[3]
Cyrix MII	64-bit[2]
Cyrix III	64-bit[7]
Intel Pentium Pro	64-bit
Intel Pentium II	64-bit
Intel Celeron	64-bit
Intel Pentium III	64-bit
Pentium II Xeon	64-bit
Intel Pentium III Xeon	64-bit
AMD Athlon	64-bit
AMD Duron	64-bit[8]
Intel Itanium	64-bit[9]
Intel Willamette	64-bit[10]

1. *Pin-compatible with Pentium.*

2. *Cyrix is now a division of VIA; pin-compatible with Pentium.*

3. *Designed by Cyrix, produced for Cyrix by IBM. Chips might be marked as "Cyrix" or "IBM"; pin-compatible with Pentium.*

4. *Designed by Cyrix, produced by Texas Instruments and others. Chips might be marked as "Cyrix" or "Texas Instruments." Despite names, 486SLC was similar to 386SX, and 486DLC was similar to 386DX.*

5. *Used as an upgrade to 486SX/DX-based systems.*

6. *Different internally from AMD's chip, but also used as an upgrade to 486SX/DX-based systems.*

7. *Pin-compatible with Intel Celeron.*

8. *Uses new Socket A technology.*

9. *Future CPU model; will be capable of running new 64-bit instructions as well as 32-bit Windows instructions; previously code-named "Merced."*

10. *Future CPU model; is designed to run 32-bit Windows instructions.*

Differences Between PC/XT and AT Systems

Systems that feature an 8-bit memory bus are called *PC/XT* systems after the pioneering IBM PC and IBM PC/XT. As you can see in Table 2.2, the differences between these systems and descendents of the IBM AT (16-bit memory bus and above) are significant. All modern systems fall into the AT category.

Table 2.2 Differences Between PC/XT and AT Systems		
System Attributes PC/XT Type	8-Bit	16-, 32-, 64-Bit AT Type
Supported processors	All x86 or x88	286 or higher
Processor modes	Real	Real, Protected, Virtual Real[2]
Software supported	16-bit only	16- or 32-bit[2]
Bus slot width	8-bit	16-, 32-[1], and 64-bit[4]
Slot type	ISA only	ISA, EISA[1], MCA, PC-Card, Cardbus[3], VL-Bus[3], PCI[3], AGP[4]
Hardware interrupts	8 (6 usable)	16 (11 usable)
DMA channels	4 (3 usable)	8 (7 usable)
Maximum RAM	1MB	16MB/4GB[1] or more
Floppy controller speed	250 Kbit/sec	250, 300, 500, and 1,000 Kbit/sec
Standard boot drive	360KB or 720KB	1.2M, 1.44MB, and 2.88MB
Keyboard interface	Unidirectional	Bidirectional
CMOS memory/clock	None standard	MC146818-compatible
Serial-port UART	8250B	16450/16550A or better

1. *Requires 386DX-based system or above*

2. *Requires 386SX-based system or above*

3. *Requires 486SX-based system or above*

4. *Requires Pentium-based system or above*

Intel and Compatible Processor Specifications

See Tables 2.3 and 2.4 to help determine the features of any CPU you encounter. It might be necessary to remove the heat sink or fan to see the processor markings on an older system, but many recent systems display CPU identification and speeds at startup.

Table 2.4 shows the major Pentium-class CPUs made by companies other than Intel. The newest versions of these processors can often be used to upgrade an older Pentium—as long as proper voltage and system configuration information can be provided, either through adjusting the motherboard/BIOS settings or by purchasing an upgrade-type processor with third-party support.

Footnotes for both tables follow Table 2.4.

Table 2.3   Intel Processor Specifications

Processor	CPU Clock	Voltage	Internal Register Size	Data Bus Width
8088	1x	5v	16-bit	8-bit
8086	1x	5v	16-bit	16-bit
286	1x	5v	16-bit	16-bit
386SX	1x	5v	32-bit	16-bit
386SL	1x	3.3v	32-bit	16-bit
386DX	1x	5v	32-bit	32-bit
486SX	1x	5v	32-bit	32-bit
486SX2	2x	5v	32-bit	32-bit
487SX	1x	5v	32-bit	32-bit
486DX	1x	5v	32-bit	32-bit
486SL[2]	1x	3.3v	32-bit	32-bit
486DX2	2x	5v	32-bit	32-bit
486DX4	2–3x	3.3v	32-bit	32-bit
486Pentium OD	2.5x	5v	32-bit	32-bit
Pentium 60/66	1x	5v	32-bit	64-bit
Pentium 75-200	1.5–3x	3.3-3.5v	32-bit	64-bit
Pentium MMX	1.5–4.5x	1.8–2.8v	32-bit	64-bit
Pentium Pro	2–3x	3.3v	32-bit	64-bit
Pentium II	3.5–4.5x	1.8–2.8v	32-bit	64-bit
Celeron	3.5–4.5x	1.8–2.8v	32-bit	64-bit
Celeron A	3.5–7x	1.8–2v	32-bit	64-bit
Pentium II PE[3]	3.5–6x	1.6v	32-bit	64-bit
Pentium II Xeon	4–4.5x	1.8–2.8v	32-bit	64-bit
Pentium III Slot1	4.5–7.5x	1.8–2v	32-bit	64-bit
Pentium III PGA370	4–7x	1.8–2v	32-bit	64-bit
Pentium III Xeon	5–6.5x	varies	32-bit	64-bit

Max. Memory	Level 1 Cache	L1 Cache Type	L2 Cache	L2 Cache Speed	Special Features
1MB	—	—	—	—	—
1MB	—	—	—	—	—
16MB	—	—	—	—	—
16MB	—	—	—	Bus	—
16MB	0KB¹	WT	—	Bus	—
4GB	—	—	—	Bus	—
4GB	8KB	WT	—	Bus	—
4GB	8KB	WT	—	Bus	—
4GB	8KB	WT	—	Bus	FPU
4GB	8KB	WT	—	Bus	FPU
4GB	8KB	WT	—	Bus	FPU Opt.
4GB	8KB	WT	—	Bus	FPU
4GB	16KB	WT	—	Bus	FPU
4GB	2x16KB	WB	—	Bus	FPU
4GB	2x8KB	WB	—	Bus	FPU
4GB	2x8KB	WB	—	Bus	FPU
4GB	2x16KB	WB	—	Bus	FPU, MMX
64GB	2x8KB	WB	256KB, 512KB, 1MB	Core	FPU
64GB	2x16KB	WB	512KB	1/2 Core	FPU, MMX
64GB	2x16KB	WB	0KB	—	FPU, MMX
64GB	2x16KB	WB	128KB	Core	FPU, MMX
64GB	2x16KB	WB	256KB	Core	FPU, MMX
64GB	2x16KB	WB	512KB, 1MB, 2MB	Core	FPU, MMX
64GB	2x16KB	WB	512KB	1/2 Core	FPU, SSE
64GB	2x16KB	WB	256KB	Core	FPU, SSE
64GB	2x16KB	WB	512KB, 1MB, 2MB	Core	FPU, SSE

Table 2.4   Intel-Compatible Pentium-Class Processors

Processor	CPU Clock	Voltage	Internal Register Size	Data Bus Width	Max. Memory
AMD K5	1.5–1.75x	3.5v	32-bit	64-bit	4GB
AMD K6	2.5–4.5x	2.2–3.2v	32-bit	64-bit	4GB
AMD K6-2	2.5–6x	1.9–2.4v	32-bit	64-bit	4GB
AMD K6-3	3.5–4.5x	1.8–2.4v	32-bit	64-bit	4GB
AMD Athlon (nee K7)	5–10x[10]	1.6–1.8v	32-bit	64-bit	8TB
AMD Athlon, with perform-ance enhancing cache (PEC) (code name "Thunderbird")	5–10x[10]	1.8v	32-bit	64-bit	8TB
AMD Duron[9] "Thunderbird"	6x–7.5x[10]	1.6–1.8v	32-bit	64-bit	8TB
Cyrix 6x86	2x	2.5–3.5v	32-bit	64-bit	4GB
Cyrix 6x86MX/MII	2–3.5x	2.2–2.9v	32-bit	64-bit	4GB
VIA Cyrix III	2.5–7x	2.2v	32-bit	64-bit	4GB
Nexgen Nx586	2x	4v	32-bit	64-bit	4GB
IDT Winchip	3–4x	3.3–3.5v	32-bit	64-bit	4GB
IDT Winchip2/2A	2.33–4x	3.3–3.5v	32-bit	64-bit	4GB
Rise mP6	2–3.5x	2.8v	32-bit	64-bit	4GB

FPU = Floating-Point unit (internal math coprocessor)

WT = Write-through cache (caches reads only)

WB = Write-back cache (caches both reads and writes)

Bus = Processor external bus speed (motherboard speed)

Core = Processor internal core speed (CPU speed)

MMX = Multimedia extensions, 57 additional instructions for graphics and sound processing

3DNow = MMX plus 21 additional instructions for graphics and sound processing

SSE = Streaming SIMD (Single Instruction Multiple Data) Extensions, MMX plus 70 additional instructions for graphics and sound processing

1. *The 386SL contains an integral-cache controller, but the cache memory must be provided outside the chip.*

2. *Intel later marketed SL Enhanced versions of the SX, DX, and DX2 processors. These processors were available in both 5v and 3.3v versions and included power-management capabilities.*

3. *The Enhanced mobile PII has an on-die L2 cache similar to the Celeron.*

Level 1 Cache	L1 Cache Type	Level 2 Cache	L2 Cache Speed	Special Features	Similar to[4]
16+8KB	WB	—	Bus	FPU	Pentium
2x32KB	WB	—	Bus	FPU, MMX	Pentium MMX
2x32KB	WB	—	Bus	FPU, 3DNow	Pentium MMX
2x32KB	WB	256KB	Core	FPU, 3DNow	Pentium MMX
2x64KB	WB	512KB[6]	1/3[7] Core	FPU, 3DNow	Pentium III[8]
2x64KB	WB	256KB	Core	FPU, 3DNow	Pentium III
2x64KB	WB	64KB	Core	FPU, 3DNow	Athlon PEC
16KB	WB	—	Bus	FPU	Pentium
64KB	WB	—	Bus	FPU, MMX	Pentium MMX
64KB	WB	256KB	Core		
2x16KB	WB	—	Bus	FPU	Pentium[5]
2x32KB	WB	—	Bus	FPU, MMX	Pentium MMX
2x32KB	WB	—	Bus	FPU, 3DNow	AMD K6-2
2x8KB	WB	—	Bus	FPU, MMX	Pentium MMX

4. *These processors physically fit into the same Socket 7 used by Intel Pentium 75MHz and above models except as noted, but might require special chipsets or BIOS settings for best operation. Check with motherboard and chip mfr. before installing them in place of your existing Pentium-class chip.*

5. *Pentium-class performance, but unique, non-standard pinout.*

6. *Cache size for initial shipments (3rd Q 1999). Athlon designed it to allow cache sizes up to 8MB.*

7. *Athlon's cache interface is designed to handle variable speed ratios, so later versions can run L2 cache more quickly.*

8. *Athlon uses new AMD Slot A, physically similar to Slot 1 but with a different electrical pinout.*

9. *Duron and "Thunderbird" versions of Athlon use new Socket A.*

10. *Clock Multipliers listed based on 100MHz system bus (FSB) speeds; although Athlon and Duron use 200MHz bus, memory for these systems runs at PC100 or PC133 speeds, depending on the processor model.*

Use Tables 2.5 and 2.6 to help determine which processors *may* fit in place of your existing CPU. Note that a replacement CPU must have the same pinout, the same electrical requirements, and be compatible with your motherboard. Many vendors sell upgrade-compatible processor versions, which have been modified from their original forms by adding a voltage regulator and other support options.

Table 2.5   Intel and Compatibles 486/Pentium-Class CPU Socket Types and Specifications

Socket Number	Pins	Pin Layout	Voltage	Supported Processors
Socket 1	169	17×17 PGA	5v	486 SX/SX2, DX/DX2[1], DX4 OverDrive
Socket 2	238	19×19 PGA	5v	486 SX/SX2, DX/DX2[1], DX4 OverDrive, 486 Pentium OverDrive
Socket 3	237	19×19 PGA	5v/3.3v	486 SX/SX2, DX/DX2, DX4, 486 Pentium OverDrive, AMD 5x86, Cyrix 5x86
Socket 4	273	21×21 PGA	5v	Pentium 60/66, OverDrive
Socket 5	320	37×37 SPGA	3.3/3.5v	Pentium 75-133, OverDrive
Socket 6[2]	235	19×19 PGA	3.3v	486 DX4, 486 Pentium OverDrive
Socket 7	321	37×37 SPGA	VRM	Pentium 75-233+, MMX, OverDrive, AMD K5/K6, Cyrix M1, VIA Cyrix MII
Socket 8	387	dual pattern SPGA	Auto VRM	Pentium Pro
PGA370	370	37×37 SPGA	2.0v	Celeron, Pentium III, VIA Cyrix III
Slot 1	242	Slot	Auto VRM	Pentium II/III, Celeron
Slot 2	330	Slot	Auto VRM	Pentium II Xeon/ Pentium III Xeon
Slot A	242	Slot	Auto VRM	AMD Athlon (K7) SECC
Socket A	462	SPGA	Auto VRM	AMD Duron/AMD Athlon PGA

1. Non-overdrive DX4 or AMD 5x86 also can be supported with the addition of an aftermarket 3.3v voltage-regulator adapter.

2. Socket 6 was a paper standard only and was never actually implemented in any systems.

PGA = Pin Grid Array.

SPGA = Staggered Pin Grid Array.

VRM = Voltage Regulator Module.

Table 2.6 lists the fastest processors you can install according to the socket type in your system. Note that newer socket designs allow faster processors, but that the bus speed and clock multiplier settings of your motherboard are also limiting factors for some CPU types.

Table 2.6	Maximum Processor Speeds by Socket
Socket Type	**Fastest Processor Supported**
Socket 1	5x86-133MHz with 3.3v adapter
Socket 2	5x86-133MHz with 3.3v adapter
Socket 3	5x86-133MHz
Socket 4	Pentium OverDrive 133MHz
Socket 5	Pentium MMX 233MHz or AMD K6 with 2.8v adapter
Socket 7	AMD K6-2 up to 550MHz, K6-III up to 500MHz
Socket 8	Pentium Pro OverDrive (333MHz Pentium II performance)
Slot 1	Celeron 400MHz (66MHz bus)
Slot 1	Pentium III 850MHz (100MHz bus)
Slot 1	Pentium III 1.0GHz (133MHz bus)
Slot 2	Pentium III Xeon 550MHz (100MHz bus)
Slot 2	Pentium III Xeon 866MHz (133MHz bus)
Socket 370	Celeron 600MHz (66MHz bus)
Socket 370	Pentium III 933MHz (100MHz bus)
Slot A	1GHz AMD Athlon (K7) (200MHz bus), 1GHz AMD Athlon PEC (Thunderbird)
Socket A	750MHz AMD Duron (200MHz bus), 1GHz AMD Athlon PEC (Thunderbird)

Troubleshooting Processor Problems

Table 2.7 provides a general troubleshooting checklist for processor-related PC problems.

Table 2.7 Troubleshooting Processor-Related Problems

Problem Identification	Possible Cause	Resolution
System is dead, no cursor, no beeps, or no fan.	Power cord failure.	Plug in or replace power cord. Power cords can fail even though they look fine.
	Power supply failure.	Replace the power supply. Use a known, good spare for testing.
	Motherboard failure.	Replace motherboard. Use a known, good spare for testing.
	Memory failure.	Remove all memory except one bank and retest. If the system still won't boot, replace bank 1.
System is dead, no beeps, or locks up before POST begins.	All components either not installed or incorrectly installed.	Check all peripherals, especially memory and graphics adapter.
		Reseat all boards and socketed components, such as CPUs and memory modules.
System beeps on startup, fan is running, no cursor onscreen.	Improperly seated or failing graphics adapter.	Reseat or replace graphics adapter. Use known, good spare for testing.
Locks up during or shortly after POST.	Poor heat dissipation.	Check CPU heat sink/fan; replace if necessary, using one with a higher capacity.
		Use thermal paste between fan/heatsink and CPU as directed by heatsink and CPU vendors.
	Improper voltage settings.	Set motherboard for proper core processor voltage.
	Wrong motherboard bus speed.	Set motherboard for proper speed.
	Wrong CPU clock multiplier.	Jumper motherboard for proper clock multiplier.
Improper CPU identification during POST.	Old BIOS.	Update BIOS from manufacturer.
	Board not configured properly.	Check manual and jumper board according to proper bus and multiplier settings.
		If board is jumperless, adjust bus and multiplier in BIOS.

Table 2.7	**Troubleshooting Processor-Related Problems Continued**	
Problem Identification	**Possible Cause**	**Resolution**
Operating system will not boot.	Poor heat dissipation.	Check CPU fan; replace if necessary. May need higher capacity heat sink and thermal paste.
	Improper voltage settings.	Jumper motherboard for proper core voltage.
	Wrong motherboard bus speed.	Jumper motherboard or adjust BIOS settings to correct speed.
	Wrong CPU clock multiplier.	Jumper motherboard or adjust BIOS settings to correct multiplier.
	Applications will not install or run.	Improper drivers or incompatible hardware. Update drivers and check for compatibility issues.
System appears to work but no video is displayed	Monitor turned off or failed.	Check monitor and power to monitor. Replace with known-good spare for testing.

If, during POST, the processor is not identified correctly, your motherboard settings might be incorrect or your BIOS might need to be updated. Check that the motherboard is jumpered or configured correctly for the processor that you have, and make sure that you have the latest BIOS for your motherboard.

If the system seems to run erratically after it warms up, try setting the processor to a lower speed. If the problem goes away, the processor might be defective or overclocked.

Many hardware problems are really software problems in disguise. Be sure you have the latest BIOS for your motherboard and the latest drivers for your peripherals. Also, it helps to use the latest version of your given operating system because, normally, fewer problems will occur.

Note

For more information about processors, see Chapter 3 of *Upgrading and Repairing PCs, 12th Edition,* also published by Que.

Motherboard Form Factors

Although many PC users have extended the life span of their systems by changing the CPU, any system that will be kept for a long time could be a candidate for a motherboard replacement. Use the following charts to determine whether your system uses one of these standard form factors, which will allow you the choice of many vendors for a replacement. A replacement motherboard provides you with these benefits:

- Access to faster, more advanced CPUs

- "Free" updated BIOS with support for large hard drives; Y2K; and boot from LS-120, Zip, and CD-ROM drives

- Newer I/O features, such as USB ports, UDMA-66 hard disk interfacing, and AGP video

Baby-AT Motherboard

Until mid-1996, this descendent of the original IBM/XT motherboard was the dominant design. Even though limited numbers of these motherboards are still available for use with both Pentium-class and Pentium II/III/Celeron processors, the lack of built-in ports and cooling problems make this an obsolete design. If you are trying to upgrade a system that uses this motherboard design, consider purchasing a new ATX-style case, power supply, and motherboard. In addition, you should consider moving the CPU, RAM, drives, and cards from your existing system to the new box (see Figure 2.1).

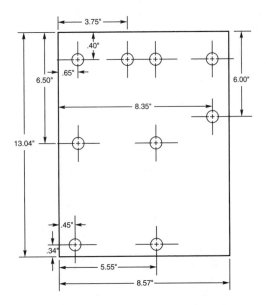

Figure 2.1   Baby-AT motherboard form factor dimensions.

LPX Motherboard

Since 1987, many low-cost systems have used variations on this layout, which features a single slot used for a riser card. The expansion cards for video, audio, and so forth are connected to the riser card, not the motherboard. Most LPX systems use riser cards that mount the expansion slots parallel to the motherboard; some use a T-shaped riser card that keeps the expansion slots at their normal upright position. Additionally, most LPX systems have built-in video, audio, and other I/O ports. Unfortunately, because its details were never standardized, it is virtually impossible to upgrade. Systems with this motherboard are essentially disposable (see Figure 2.2).

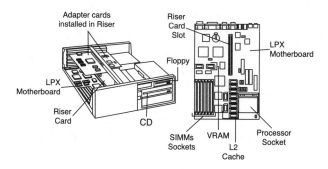

Figure 2.2 Typical LPX system chassis and motherboard.

ATX Motherboard

Since mid-1996, the ATX motherboard has become the standard for most systems using non-proprietary motherboards (see Figure 2.3). Similar to Baby-AT, it's also an industry standard, and similar to LPX, it features built-in ports. Compared to both, though, it offers much greater ease of upgrading and servicing. ATX motherboards are rotated 90 degrees when compared to Baby-ATs and also use a different power supply for advanced power management features. Because of their built-in ports and differences in layout, ATX motherboards require an ATX case. ATX cases can also be used for Baby-AT motherboards, though. Figure 2.3 shows a full-size ATX layout; however, several smaller versions now exist, including mini-ATX, micro-ATX, and flex-ATX.

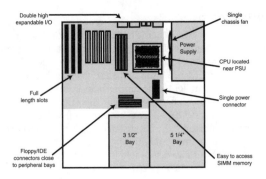

Figure 2.3   ATX system chassis layout and features.

NLX Motherboard

The replacement for the old LPX low-profile motherboard is the NLX motherboard (see Figure 2.4). NLX also features built-in ports and a riser card, but its standard design means that replacement motherboards should be easier to purchase than those for LPX systems. A major advantage of NLX systems is that the motherboard is easy to remove for servicing through a side panel, a feature that makes NLX-based systems popular as corporate network client PCs.

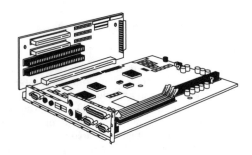

Figure 2.4   NLX motherboard and riser combination.

Which Motherboard Is Which?

Use Table 2.8 to help determine whether a system is a Baby-AT, an LPX, an ATX, or an NLX-based system.

Table 2.8	Comparison of Major Motherboard Form Factors				
	Baby-AT	**LPX**	**ATX/ Micro ATX**[1]	**NLX**	**WTX**
Ports built into chassis	No	Yes	Yes	Yes	No[2]
Riser card	No	Yes	No	Yes	No
Single row of ports at rear	N/A	Yes	No	No	No
Two rows of ports at rear	N/A	No	Yes	Yes	No[3]
Slots on both sides of riser card	N/A	Opt	N/A	No	N/A
Riser card location on MB	N/A	Middle	N/A	Side near power supply	N/A

1. MicroATX motherboards can fit into ATX cases, but have fewer slots and are designed for socketed, rather than slot-based, processors. They also usually feature onboard audio and video, both of which are usually optional on ATX motherboards.

2. WTX supports a FlexSlot design, which uses a single modified PCI slot for all standard ports.

3. The layout of ports on the rear of a FlexSlot resembles the layout on the rear of an ATX or a MicroATX motherboard, but they are vertically oriented because they are attached to a FlexSlot. See www.wtx.org for more information.

PC99 Color-Coding for Ports

Microsoft and Intel have developed the following standardized color-coding of connectors for computers compliant with the PC99 design standards. Use Table 2.9 to help you match non–color-coded peripherals with the correct external ports.

> **Note**
>
> Some systems, especially those built before 1999, might use a proprietary color scheme for ports.

Check the inside front and back covers of this book for pictures of these ports. For color samples, see the following Web site:

http://www.pcdesguide.com/documents/pc99icons.htm

Table 2.9	PC99 Color-Coding Standards for Ports
Port Type	**Color**
Analog VGA (DB15)	Blue
Audio line in	Light blue
Audio line out	Lime green
Digital monitor	White

Table 2.9 PC99 Color-Coding Standards for Ports Continued	
Port Type	**Color**
IEEE-1394 (i.Link, FireWire)	Grey
Microphone	Pink
MIDI/Gameport	Gold
Parallel port	Burgundy
Serial port	Teal or turquoise
Speaker out (subwoofer)	Orange
Right-to-left speaker	Brown
USB	Black
Video out	Yellow
SCSI, network, telephone, modem, and so on	None

Power Supplies

Power supplies actually convert high-voltage AC (alternating current) into low-voltage DC (direct current) for use by PCs. Power supplies come in several form factors, and they also feature various motherboard connectors to correspond with the newer motherboard designs on the market. Table 2.10 illustrates which power supplies are most likely to be used with various motherboards.

Table 2.10 Matching Power Supplies and Motherboards		
Motherboard Form Factor	**Most Common PS Form Factor Used**	**Other PS Form Factors Used**
Baby-AT	LPX style	Baby-AT, AT/Tower, or AT/Desk
LPX	LPX style	None
ATX	ATX style	None
MicroATX	ATX style	SFX style
NLX	ATX style	None

LPX Versus ATX Power Supplies

Some motherboards are designed to handle either LPX or ATX power supplies. The ATX is the preferred design because it provides the lower voltage needed by today's CPUs, offers foolproof installation, and also provides better cooling than older designs.

Table 2.11 compares two of the more common power supply form factors used in computers today, and Figure 2.5 shows an LPX power supply.

Table 2.11	Comparing ATX and LPX Power Supplies		
Power Supply Type	**Voltage Output**	**Motherboard Power Connectors**	**Other Features Notes**
LPX	5v, 12v	2–6 pins each (P8/P9)	Easy to reverse the plug due to poor keying
ATX	3.3v, 5v, 12v	1–20 pins	Keyed to go in only one way; allows hibernation via operating system or keyboard command

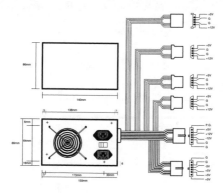

Figure 2.5   LPX form factor power supply.

Table 2.12 breaks down the typical LPX power supply connector.

Caution

To get the cables oriented correctly, keep the ground wires (black) next to each other. Although most connectors are keyed to prevent improperly plugging them in, some connectors can easily be inserted incorrectly. This will cause your motherboard to be destroyed the first time you switch on the power and could possibly cause a fire.

Table 2.12   Typical LPX Power Supply Connections

Connector	Voltage	Standard Color/Notes
P8-1	Power_Good (+5v)	Orange
P8-2	+5v	Red
P8-3	+12v	Yellow
P8-4	-12v	Blue
P8-5	Ground (0)	Black
P8-6	Ground (0)	Black
P9-1	Ground (0)	Black
P9-2	Ground (0)	Black
P9-3	-5v	White
P9-4	+5v	Red
P9-5	+5v	Red
P9-6	+5v	Red

Power Connectors for the Drive(s)

The connectors shown in Table 2.13 might not be labeled, but they easily can be distinguished by the four-wire cable and color-coding. The same colors are used for drive power connectors on ATX power supplies. Figure 2.6 shows an ATX power supply.

Table 2.13   ATX Power Supply Color Coding

Connector	Voltage	Standard Color/Notes
P10-1	+12v	Yellow
P10-2	Ground (0)	Black
P10-3	Ground (0)	Black
P10-4	+5v	Red

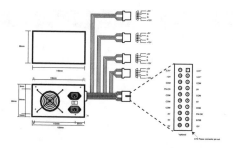

Figure 2.6   ATX form factor power supply used with both ATX and NLX systems. The pinout for the motherboard power is shown at lower right. Note the single square pin used for keying.

Table 2.14 shows the pinout for the ATX motherboard power connector.

Table 2.14	ATX Motherboard Power Supply Connections				
Color	**Signal**	**Pin**	**Pin**	**Signal**	**Color**
Orange	+3.3v	11	1	+3.3v	Orange
Blue	-12v	12	2	+3.3v	Orange
Black	GND	13	3	GND	Black
Green	PS_On	14	4	+5v	Red
Black	GND	15	5	GND	Black
Black	GND	16	6	+5v	Red
Black	GND	17	7	GND	Black
White	-5v	18	8	Power_Good	Grey
Red	+5v	19	9	+5VSB (Standby)	Purple
Red	+5v	20	10	+12v	Yellow

Quick-Reference Chart for Troubleshooting Power Supplies

Table 2.15	Troubleshooting Power Supplies	
Symptom	**Cause(s)**	**Tests and Solution(s)**
Overheating.	Inadequate system cooling	Check ventilation around system; clean system internally; check for missing slot covers.
	Higher load on system in watts than power supply rating	Replace power supply with higher rated unit.

Table 2.15	Troubleshooting Power Supplies Continued	
Symptom	**Cause(s)**	**Tests and Solution(s)**
System reboots itself.	Incorrect power level on Power_Good; can indicate overloaded power supply or otherwise bad unit	Use DC-voltage digital multimeter (DMM) to test P8-1 (orange wire) on LPX and older power supplies or Pin 8 (gray wire) on ATX and newer power supplies; rated voltage is +5v; acceptable is +3.0v to +6.0v.
		Replace failed power supply with higher rated unit.
Fan turns for only a moment and then stops.	Wrong voltage (PS set to 220/230v in U.S.)	Turn off system; reset PS to correct voltage (110/115v in U.S.) and restart. Using 220/230v power on a PS set for 110/115v will destroy it!
	Dead short in system	Short can be caused by loose screws, failed hard drives, or add-on cards.
		Turn off and unplug system; disconnect hard drive and see whether system starts. If system still fails, plug in drive and remove add-on card; repeat until each card and drive has been checked; also check Y-adapter cables because bad cables can cause shorts.
		Replace faulty component(s).

> **Note**
>
> For more information on power supplies, wattage ratings, and testing, see Chapter 21 of *Upgrading and Repairing PCs, 12th Edition*, published by Que.

Memory Types

RAM (random access memory) provides the work area that processors use to create and modify data. While RAM was sometimes found on expansion boards on old XT-class and early AT-class systems, all standard 486-based and Pentium-class systems have their memory modules attached to the motherboard.

Memory modules come in two major forms: SIMMs and DIMMs. *SIMM* stands for single-sided inline memory module, and *DIMM* stands for dual-sided inline memory module. These terms refer to the pin configurations used on the module, rather than the location of the memory chips on the module.

The following features are common to all SIMMs:

- Pins numbered from left to right
- Same pins on both sides of the module

> **Tip**
>
> Note that all dimensions for both SIMMs and DIMMs in the following figures are in both inches and millimeters (in parentheses).

30-Pin SIMM

The 30-pin SIMM is the oldest type of memory module still in use (see Figure 2.7). It was popular on 386-based and early 486-based systems, but became obsolete with the rise of Pentium-class 64-bit CPUs. Although its capacities are extremely small compared to more modern memory designs, its unpopularity since the early 1990s makes the 30-pin SIMM the most expensive memory type per megabyte. If you are still supporting systems that use this type of module, look for sources of used memory or replace the motherboard with one that uses newer, 72-pin SIMM or DIMM memory instead of buying new 30-pin modules.

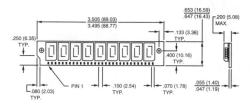

Figure 2.7 A typical 30-pin SIMM. The one shown here is 9-bit, although the dimensions would be the same for 8-bit.

72-Pin SIMM

The 72-pin SIMM was the most popular for a number of years, but has now been superseded on newer systems by DIMM modules. 72-pin SIMMs are commonly found on late-model 486-based systems, most Pentiums, and most early Pentium-compatible systems. Because these modules are also becoming very expensive per megabyte, try to salvage or swap memory to populate older systems rather than purchase new. 72-pin SIMMs can be either fast-page or extended data out (EDO). 486-class systems can use only fast-page SIMMs, but Pentium-class systems that use SIMMs can use either type. Fast-page and EDO SIMMs should not be mixed. Some systems require BIOS configuration to optimize performance if you install EDO memory (see Figure 2.8).

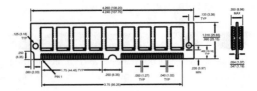

Figure 2.8   A typical 72-pin SIMM, although the dimensions would be the same for 32-bit.

DIMMs

DIMMs became popular with the rise of the Pentium II/III/Celeron family of processors—AMD's Athlon series—and can also be found on many late-model Pentium and "Super Socket 7" motherboards used with AMD K6-series and Cyrix 6x86MX/MII processors (see Figure 2.9). DIMMs are the most popular and fastest type of memory module in widespread use. Most DIMMs are Synchronous DRAM (SDRAM). On motherboards with both SIMM and DIMM sockets, SDRAMs cannot be used in conjunction with SIMMs, but the relatively rare EDO DIMMs can be used along with EDO SIMMs.

The following features are common to all DIMMs:

- Three edge connectors of varying widths for positive keying

- Different pinouts on each side of the DIMM

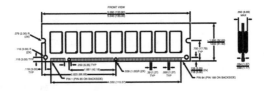

Figure 2.9   A typical 168-pin DIMM. The one shown here is 72-bit, although the dimensions would be the same for 64-bit.

RDRAM

The *RDRAM*, or *Rambus DRAM*, is a radical new memory design that is slowly appearing in high-end PC systems that use Intel chipsets. RDRAM differs from previous memory devices in that it provides multiple high-speed (800MHz), narrow-channel (16-bit–wide) data transfers to and from a 128-bit memory bus instead of the slower (100MHz or 66MHz), 32-bit or 64-bit data transfers of SDRAM and previous memory types.

RDRAM modules are called *RIMMs (Rambus Inline Memory Module)*, and any unused RIMM slots on a motherboard must be filled with a continuity module to permit a continuous high-speed data pathway through the RIMMs (see Figure 2.10). Each RIMM represents multiple memory banks, and thus a single RIMM at a time can be added to a system—much the way installation of DIMMs works, although the memory types are not interchangeable.

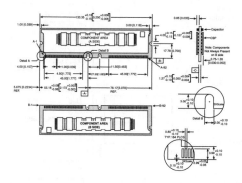

Figure 2.10   Typical RDRAM bus layout, showing two RIMMs and one continuity module installed.

DDR SDRAM

Double Data Rate (DDR) SDRAM memory is an improved version of standard SDRAM in which data is transferred twice as fast. Instead of doubling the actual clock rate, DDR memory achieves the doubling in performance by transferring twice per transfer cycle—once at the leading (falling) and once at the trailing (rising) edge of the cycle. This is similar to the way RDRAM operates and effectively doubles the transfer rate, even though the same overall clock and timing signals are used.

DDR SDRAM is supported by many of the newest server chipsets and provides a design alternative to the more radical RDRAM. The DDR Consortium—an industry panel consisting of Fujitsu, Ltd.; Hitachi, Ltd.; Hyundai Electronics Industries Co.; Mitsubishi Electric Corp.; NEC Corp.; Samsung Electronics Co.; Texas Instruments, Inc.; and Toshiba Corp.—undertook official standardization of DDR.

DDR-SDRAM uses a new DIMM module design with 184 pins. Figure 2.11 shows the DDR SDRAM DIMM.

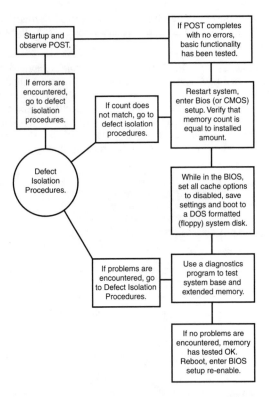

Figure 2.11   184-pin DDR (Double Data Rate) SDRAM DIMM.

DDR DIMMs are rated for either PC200 (100MHz x 2) or PC266 (133MHz x 2) operation and normally run on 2.5 volts. They are basically an extension of the PC100 and PC133 DIMMs redesigned to support double clocking, where data is sent on each clock transition (twice per cycle) rather than once per cycle as is standard with SDRAM.

Parity Versus Non-Parity Memory

Parity-checked RAM uses units of 8 memory bits plus 1 parity bit, for a total of 9 bits. In addition, parity checking uses both the data bits and the parity bit to ensure that memory contents are accurate with each memory access.

Virtually all 386-based and older systems, and most 486-based systems, require parity-checked memory, which can detect, but not correct, memory errors. On the other hand, most Pentium-class and higher systems don't require parity-checked RAM, but will ignore the parity bit(s) if present.

Parity-checked memory *must* be used on systems that require it, and *should* be used on systems that can be configured to use the parity bits, *especially* if the systems support ECC (Error Correction Code) operation, which uses the parity bit as a means of *correcting* a faulty memory bit.

Requirements for ECC Memory Use

ECC requires the following:

- Parity-checked memory modules

- A motherboard chipset that offers ECC support

- ECC support enabled in the BIOS system configuration

ECC operation is recommended for servers and other systems that are performing mission-critical tasks because ECC operation can correct single-bit memory errors. Larger memory errors will cause the system to display an error message and halt.

However, systems using ECC will cost more due to the higher cost of parity-checked RAM. Additionally, system performance is slightly slower due to the extra time involved in ECC operation. Check your motherboard or system documentation to determine whether ECC is an option for your system.

To determine whether a memory module supports parity-checking or ECC, use the following tips.

Using the Divide by 3 Rule to Determine Parity Support

Count the chips on a SIMM or DIMM. If you can divide the number of chips by 3, the module is most likely a parity-checked module. However, some memory manufacturers have created memory modules with fake parity chips; these are referred to as *logic parity* modules.

> **Note**
>
> See *Upgrading and Repairing PCs, 12th Edition*, Chapter 6, for more information about how to detect a logic parity module.

Using the Divide by 9 Rule to Determine Parity Support

A similar "divide by 9" rule can also be used to determine parity checking if you know the number of memory bits in the module. Note in Table 2.16 that the number of bits in parity-checked modules can be divided by 9, but the number of bits in non-parity modules can be divided only by 8.

Table 2.16   SIMM and DIMM Capacities

30-Pin SIMM Capacities

Capacity	Parity SIMM	Non-Parity SIMM
256KB	256KB×9	256KB×8
1MB	1MB×9	1MB×8
4MB	4MB×9	4MB×8
16MB	16MB×9	16MB×8

72-Pin SIMM Capacities

Capacity	Parity SIMM	Non-Parity SIMM
1MB	256KB×36	256KB×32
2MB	512KB×36	512KB×32
4MB	1MB×36	1MB×32
8MB	2MB×36	2MB×32
16MB	4MB×36	4MB×32
32MB	8MB×36	8MB×32
64MB	16MB×36	16MB×32
128MB	32MB×36	32MB×32

168-Pin DIMM Capacities

Capacity	Parity DIMM	Non-Parity DIMM
8MB	1MB×72	1MB×64
16MB	2MB×72	2MB×64
32MB	4MB×72	4MB×64
64MB	8MB×72	8MB×64
128MB	16MB×72	16MB×64
256MB	32MB×72	32MB×64

Expanding Memory on a System

Memory must be added to a system in banks. Simply put, a *bank* of memory is the amount of RAM in bits equal to the data bus width of the computer's CPU (see Table 2.17). Thus, a Pentium's data bus is 64 bits, and a memory module(s) used with a Pentium must have a total width of 64 bits for non-parity memory and 72 bits for parity-checked or ECC memory.

Table 2.17 Memory Bank Widths on Various Systems						
Processor	Data Bus	Memory Bank Size (No Parity)	Memory Bank Size (Parity)	30-Pin SIMMs per Bank	72-Pin SIMMs per Bank	168-Pin SIMMs per Bank
8088	8-bit	8 bits	9 bits	1	n/a	n/a
8086	16-bit	16 bits	18 bits	2	n/a	n/a
286	16-bit	16 bits	18 bits	2	n/a	n/a
386SX, SL, SLC	16-bit	16 bits	18 bits	2	n/a	n/a
386DX	32-bit	32 bits	36 bits	4	1	n/a
486SLC, SLC2	16-bit	16 bits	18 bits	2	n/a	n/a
486SX, DX, DX2, DX4, 5x86	32-bit	32 bits	36 bits	4	1	n/a
Pentium, K5, K6 6x86, 6x86MX, MII	64-bit	64 bits	72 bits	8[1]	2	1
Pentium Pro, PII, PIII, Celeron, Xeon, AMD Athlon, Duron, Intel Itanium	64-bit	64 bits	72 bits	8[1]	2	1

1. *Very few motherboards for these processors actually use this type of memory.*

The number of bits for each bank can be made up of single chips, SIMMs, or DIMMs. Modern systems don't use individual chips; instead, they use only SIMMs or DIMMs. If the system has a 16-bit processor, such as a 386SX, it probably uses 30-pin SIMMs and has two SIMMs per bank. All the SIMMs in a single bank must be the same size and type.

Memory Troubleshooting

Figure 2.12 provides basic steps that enable you to effectively test and troubleshoot your system RAM. First, let's cover the memory testing and troubleshooting procedures.

After you've determined that the system's memory is defective, you need to determine which memory module is at fault. Follow the procedure in Figure 2.13 to isolate the module for replacement.

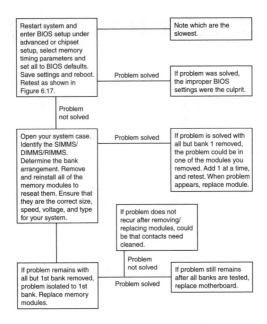

Figure 2.12 Testing and troubleshooting memory.

Memory Usage Within the System

The original PC had a total of 1MB of addressable memory, and the top 384KB of that was reserved for use by the system. Placing this reserved space at the top (between 640KB and 1,024KB instead of at the bottom, between 0KB and 640KB) led to what is often called the *conventional memory barrier*. Systems with more than 1MB of RAM treat the additional RAM as extended memory, beginning at 1MB.

Thus, there is a "hole" in memory usage between 640KB and 1MB. Some standard add-on cards and motherboard devices use part of this memory area for RAM and ROM addresses, leaving the remainder of this space free for additional card usage.

Hardware and Firmware Devices That Use Memory Addresses

The listing of hardware and firmware devices that use memory addresses is relatively short when compared to IRQ, DMA, and I/O port address usage, but it is no less important. No two devices can share a memory address. Table 2.18 shows memory usage in the 640KB–1MB memory range for standard devices.

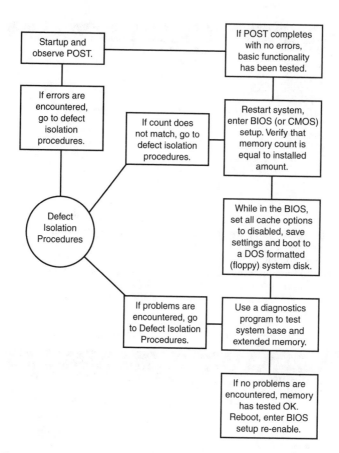

Figure 2.13   Follow these steps if you are still encountering memory errors after completing the steps in Figure 2.12.

Table 2.18	Memory Usage in the 640KB–1MB Range	
Device	**Address Range**	**Notes**
Graphics Mode Video RAM	0A0000–0AFFFF	
Monochrome Text Mode Video RAM	0B0000–0B7FFF	
Color Text Mode Video RAM	0B8000–0BFFFF	
Video ROM for VGA, Super VGA	0C0000–0C7FFF	

Table 2.18   Memory Usage in the 640KB–1MB Range Continued

Device	Address Range	Notes
Unassigned	0C8000–0DFFFF	Available for use by BIOS or RAM chips on add-on cards or by memory managers, such as QEMM or EMM386
Motherboard ROM BIOS extension (IBM PS/2s, most Pentium-class and newer systems)	0E0000–0EFFFF	If not used by BIOS extensions, can be treated as additional unassigned space
Motherboard ROM BIOS (all systems)	0F0000–0FFFFF	

If you are using an add-on card that uses a ROM BIOS chip onboard to overcome IDE hard drive limitations, overcome Y2K date rollover problems, or provide support for bootable SCSI hard drives, the BIOS chips on those cards must be placed in the unassigned memory range listed earlier. If you have two or more add-on cards that use memory address ranges, for best system performance, set the cards to use adjacent memory addresses.

Table 2.19 shows the typical memory uses for some common IDE and SCSI interface cards that use ROM BIOS chips.

Table 2.19   Memory Addresses Used by Various Adapter Cards

Adapter Type	Onboard BIOS Size	BIOS Address Range
Most XT compatible controllers	8KB	0C8000–0C9FFF
Most AT controllers	None	Drivers in motherboard BIOS
Most standard IDE hard disk adapters	None	Drivers in motherboard BIOS
Most enhanced[1] IDE hard disk adapters	16KB	0C8000–0CBFFF
Some SCSI host adapters	16KB	0C8000–0CBFFF
Some SCSI host adapters	16KB	0DC000–0DFFFF

1. *This type of adapter supplements the motherboard's IDE interface by supporting drives beyond 528MB (decimal) or 504MB (binary), or beyond 8.4GB (decimal) in size. Some of these adapters can also provide Y2K-date rollover support. Cards that combine both functions might use a larger (in KB) BIOS chip.*

Some older network cards also used memory addresses for RAM buffers or for ROM BIOS chips that permit diskless workstations to use a network copy of the operating system for booting. Network cards that use memory addresses are seldom used today.

Using Memory Addresses Beyond 1MB (0FFFFF)

Some older Super VGA cards, notably those from ATI, could also be set to use a 1MB extended memory address starting at 15MB for moving video data. This so-called *memory aperture* technique made the video cards using it faster, but could not be used on systems with 16MB of RAM or above. If you use a video card that uses a fixed memory aperture at 15MB on a system with less than 16MB of RAM, disable the memory aperture feature before you upgrade the RAM beyond 16MB. Some current PCI and AGP video cards also use memory apertures, but at addresses that do not interfere with today's larger amounts of system RAM.

Determining Memory Address Ranges in Use

On a system with Windows 9x, Windows 2000, or Windows Me, use the Device Manager's System Properties sheet to see overall memory address usage (see Figure 2.14).

Use add-on card documentation or a memory viewer,such as those included with AMIDiag, CheckIt, or Microsoft's MSD.EXE, to see memory usage on systems running Windows 3.1 or MS-DOS.

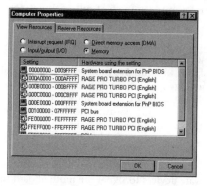

Figure 2.14   A system's upper memory usage as displayed by the Windows 9x Device Manager. Addresses between 000CCFFFF and 000DFFFF in upper memory are available for add-on cards. The ATI video card onboard also uses memory addresses above 1MB for a high-speed memory aperture.

Note

To learn more about memory modules, see Chapter 6 of *Upgrading and Repairing PCs, 12th Edition*, published by Que.

Other Add-On Card Configuration Issues

When a card is installed into an expansion slot or a PCMCIA/PC card device is installed into a PC card slot, the card must use at least one of four hardware resources to be accessible to the system. All add-on cards must use at least an I/O port address range or ranges; most cards use an IRQ (interrupt request line); fewer cards use DMA (Direct Memory Access); and memory addresses are used least of all. Many cards use two or more of these hardware resources.

> **Note**
>
> For more information, see the section "Hardware and Firmware Devices That Use Memory Addresses," earlier in this chapter.

If an add-on card is set to use the same hardware resource as an existing card, it will not work unless that resource is designed to be shared between cards. Although the capability to share IRQs has existed (at least in theory) since the Micro Channel Architecture of the late 1980s, even today the best rule of thumb for adding cards is "each card has its own settings."

Plug-and-Play (PnP) configuration—introduced with Windows 95 and also present with Windows 98, Windows Me, and Windows 2000—is designed to minimize much of the grief of adding cards, but this technology has been in a state of flux since it was introduced. To help you add cards, the following tables of standard settings also list software and hardware tools that can help you find the settings already in use before you install your next card.

IRQs

Interrupt request channels (IRQs), or hardware interrupts, are used by various hardware devices to signal the motherboard that a request must be fulfilled. Most add-on cards use IRQs, and because systems today have the same number of IRQs available with the first IBM PC/AT systems built in 1984, IRQs frequently cause trouble in add-on card installations.

Table 2.20 shows IRQ assignments for 16-bit ISA and 32-bit VL-Bus/PCI expansion slots, listed by priority. Technically speaking, PCI interrupts can be shared, but in practice, many older Pentium systems must use a unique IRQ value for each PCI card, as with ISA and VL-Bus cards.

Table 2.20   16/32-Bit ISA/VL-Bus/PCI Default Interrupt Assignments

IRQ	Standard Function	Bus Slot	Card Type	Recommended Use
0	System timer	No	—	—
1	Keyboard controller	No	—	—
2[1]	Second IRQ controller cascade	No	—	—
8	Real-time clock	No	—	—
9	Available (appears as IRQ 2)	Yes	8-/16-bit	Network Interface Card
10	Available	Yes	16-bit	USB
11	Available	Yes	16-bit	SCSI host adapter
12	Motherboard mouse port available	Yes	16-bit	Motherboard mouse port
13	Math coprocessor	No	—	—
14	Primary IDE	Yes	16-bit	Primary IDE (hard disks)
15	Secondary IDE/ available	Yes	16-bit	Secondary IDE (CD-ROM/ tape)
3[4]	Serial Port 2 (COM 2:)	Yes	8-/16-bit	COM 2:/internal modem
4[3]	Serial Port 1 (COM 1:)	Yes	8-/16-bit	COM 1:
5[2]	Sound/Parallel Port 2 (LPT2:)	Yes	8-/16-bit	Sound card
6	Floppy disk controller	Yes	8-/16-bit	Floppy controller
7	Parallel Port 1 (LPT1:)	Yes	8-/16-bit	LPT1:

1. *The original IBM PC/XT and compatible systems with 8-bit ISA slots did not assign any standard device to IRQ 2. When the 16-bit ISA slot was introduced, along with a second range of IRQs (8–15), this permitted the "cascading" of these interrupts via IRQ 2. Older cards that have IRQ 2 as a setting actually use IRQ 9 instead on 286-based and higher systems.*

2. *On original XT-class systems with 8-bit ISA slots, IRQ 5 was assigned to the hard disk controller card. Even though IRQ 5's "official" assignment is to handle LPT2 on systems with 16-bit ISA slots, only EPP and ECP (IEEE-1284) parallel port modes actually use an IRQ. This permits the use of IRQ 5 for sound cards in most systems without interfering with the use of LPT2.*

3. *Systems with COM 3 default to "sharing" COM 1's IRQ 4. This will cause system lockups in Windows if a serial mouse is used on COM 1 with a modem on COM 3. Use the modem, and the IRQ conflict crashes the system. To avoid problems, set the device using COM 3 to a different IRQ, or disable COM 2 and use COM 2 for the modem.*

4. Systems with COM 4 default to "sharing" COM 2's IRQ 3. This will cause system lockups in Windows if a serial mouse is used on COM 2 with a modem on COM 4. Use the modem, and the IRQ conflict crashes the system. To avoid problems, set the device using COM 4 to a different IRQ, or disable COM 2 and use COM 2 for the modem.

DMA

Direct Memory Access permits high-speed data transfer between I/O devices and memory without CPU management. This method of data transfer boosts performance for devices that use it, but because there is no CPU management, the possibility of data corruption is higher than for non-DMA transfers. Although DMA channels can theoretically be "shared" between devices that are not in use at the same time, this is not a recommended practice.

PCI cards don't use these DMA channels (with the exception of sound cards, which are emulating the ISA-based Sound Blaster or compatibles—the major users of DMA channels today). See Table 2.21.

| | **Table 2.21   16/32-Bit ISA/PCI Default DMA-Channel Assignments** | | | | |
DMA	**Standard Function**	**Bus Slot**	**Card Type**	**Transfer**	**Recommended Use**
0	Available	Yes	16-bit	8-bit	Integrated sound
1	Available	Yes	8-/16-bit	8-bit	8-bit sound
2	Floppy disk controller	Yes	8-/16-bit	8-bit	Floppy controller
3	Available	Yes	8-/16-bit	8-bit	LPT1: in ECP mode
4	1st DMA controller cascade	No	—	16-bit	—
5	Available	Yes	16-bit	16-bit	16-bit sound
6	Available	Yes	16-bit	16-bit	ISA SCSI adapter
7	Available	Yes	16-bit	16-bit	Available

Note that PCI adapters don't use these ISA DMA channels; these are only for ISA cards.

On PC/XT systems with only 8-bit ISA slots, only DMA channels 1–3 are available. DMA channel 2 was used for the floppy controller, as it is today, but channels 1 and 3 were not assigned to standard devices.

Determining Actual IRQ and DMA Usage

Although these tables provide the "official" guidelines for IRQ and DMA usage, these settings might not be true for all systems at all times.

Add-on network, sound, serial, parallel, and SCSI cards can often be moved to different IRQ and DMA channels to work around conflicts. Non-standard settings can be done manually with some cards and is a virtual certainty with PnP cards used with Windows 9x and Windows 2000. Well-designed PnP cards already installed in a system are designed to automatically move to non-conflicting set-tings when less-flexible PnP cards are inserted. Late-model Pentium-class systems using Windows 95 OSR 2.x, Windows 98, Windows 2000, or Windows Me can also use an IRQ holder for PCI steering feature that allows multiple PCI devices to use a single IRQ, if the BIOS is designed to support it.

To view the current IRQ and DMA settings for systems using Windows 9x, use the Device Manager (a tab on the System Properties sheet). View the properties for the "Computer" icon at the top of the device list and you can choose from IRQ, DMA, I/O port, and Memory address information (see Figure 2.15).

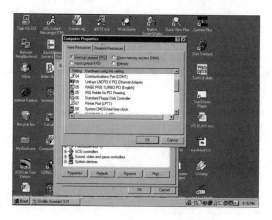

Figure 2.15   The Windows 9x Device Manager and Computer Properties sheet shows IRQs in use; available IRQs are not listed. The IRQ steering fea-ture enables IRQ 5 to be shared between two different PCI-based cards with-out conflicts.

For other operating systems, I recommend an interface card with signal lights for IRQ and DMA usage. The Discovery Card, devel-oped by John Rourke, pioneered this diagnostic category, and many vendors offer cards with this feature. Some vendors combine IRQ/DMA detection with POST code detection or active system testing.

To use an IRQ/DMA card, turn off the system, insert the card into an open slot, and turn on the system. As devices that use an IRQ or a DMA are activated, the corresponding signal light on the card is displayed. Most cards have a reset switch, which enables the card lights to be cleared, allowing you to test for possible conflicts. When combined with information from a system configuration template, this helps provide accurate IRQ and DMA usage information.

I/O Port Addresses

Your computer's I/O ports enable communications between devices and software in your system. They are equivalent to two-way radio channels. If you want to talk to your serial port, you need to know which I/O port (radio channel) it is listening on. Similarly, if you want to receive data from the serial port, you need to listen on the same channel on which it is transmitting.

One confusing issue is that I/O ports are designated by hexadecimal addresses similar to memory addresses. They are not memory; they are ports.

Motherboard and chipset devices are normally set to use I/O port addresses from 0h to FFh, and all other devices use from 100h to FFFFh. Table 2.22 shows motherboard and chipset-based I/O port usage.

Table 2.22 Motherboard and Chipset-Based Device Port Addresses		
Address (Hex)	**Size**	**Description**
0000–000F	16 bytes	Chipset - 8237 DMA 1
0020–0021	2 bytes	Chipset - 8259 interrupt controller 1
002E–002F	2 bytes	Super I/O controller configuration registers
0040–0043	4 bytes	Chipset - Counter/Timer 1
0048–004B	4 bytes	Chipset - Counter/Timer 2
0060	1 byte	Keyboard/Mouse controller byte - reset IRQ
0061	1 byte	Chipset - NMI, speaker control
0064	1 byte	Keyboard/mouse controller, CMD/STAT byte
0070, bit 7	1 bit	Chipset - Enable NMI
0070, bits 6:0	7 bits	MC146818 - Real-time clock, address
0071	1 byte	MC146818 - Real-time clock, data
0078	1 byte	Reserved - Board configuration
0079	1 byte	Reserved - Board configuration
0080–008F	16 bytes	Chipset - DMA page registers
00A0–00A1	2 bytes	Chipset - 8259 interrupt controller 2
00B2	1 byte	APM control port
00B3	1 byte	APM status port
00C0–00DE	31 bytes	Chipset - 8237 DMA 2
00F0	1 byte	Math coprocessor reset numeric error

To find out exactly which port addresses are being used on your motherboard, consult the board documentation or look up the settings in the Windows Device Manager.

Bus-based devices (I/O devices found on the motherboard or on add-on cards) normally use the addresses from 100h on up. Table 2.23 lists the commonly used bus-based device addresses and some common adapter cards and their settings.

Table 2.23	Bus-Based Device Port Addresses	
Address (Hex)	**Size**	**Description**
0130–0133	4 bytes	Adaptec SCSI adapter (alternate
0134–0137	4 bytes	Adaptec SCSI adapter (alternate)
0168–016F	8 bytes	Fourth IDE interface
0170–0177	8 bytes	Secondary IDE interface
01E8–01EF	8 bytes	Third IDE interface
01F0–01F7	8 bytes	Primary IDE/AT (16-bit) hard disk controller
0200–0207	8 bytes	Gameport or joystick adapter
0210–0217	8 bytes	IBM XT expansion chassis
0220–0233	20 bytes	Creative Labs Sound Blaster 16 audio (default)
0230–0233	4 bytes	Adaptec SCSI adapter (alternate)
0234–0237	4 bytes	Adaptec SCSI adapter (alternate)
0238–023B	4 bytes	MS bus mouse (alternate)
023C–023F	4 bytes	MS bus mouse (default)
0240–024F	16 bytes	SMC Ethernet adapter (default)
0240–0253	20 bytes	Creative Labs Sound Blaster 16 audio (alternate)
0258–025F	8 bytes	Intel above board
0260–026F	16 bytes	SMC Ethernet adapter (alternate)
0260–0273	20 bytes	Creative Labs Sound Blaster 16 audio (alternate)
0270–0273	4 bytes	Plug-and-Play I/O read ports
0278–027F	8 bytes	Parallel Port 2 (LPT2)
0280–028F	16 bytes	SMC Ethernet adapter (alternate)
0280–0293	20 bytes	Creative Labs Sound Blaster 16 audio (alternate)
02A0–02AF	16 bytes	SMC Ethernet adapter (alternate)
02C0–02CF	16 bytes	SMC Ethernet adapter (alternate)
02E0–02EF	16 bytes	SMC Ethernet adapter (alternate
02E8–02EF	8 bytes	Serial Port 4 (COM 4)
02EC–02EF	4 bytes	Video, 8514, or ATI standard port
02F8–02FF	8 bytes	Serial Port 2 (COM 2)
0300–0301	2 bytes	MPU-401 MIDI port (secondary)
0300–030F	16 bytes	SMC Ethernet adapter (alternate)
0320–0323	4 bytes	XT (8-bit) hard disk controller
0320–032F	16 bytes	SMC Ethernet adapter (alternate)
0330–0331	2 bytes	MPU-401 MIDI port (default)
0330–0333	4 bytes	Adaptec SCSI adapter (default)
0334–0337	4 bytes	Adaptec SCSI adapter (alternate)

Table 2.23   Bus-Based Device Port Addresses Continued

Address (Hex)	Size	Description
0340–034F	16 bytes	SMC Ethernet adapter (alternate)
0360–036F	16 bytes	SMC Ethernet adapter (alternate)
0366	1 byte	Fourth IDE command port
0367, bits 6:0	7 bits	Fourth IDE status port
0370–0375	6 bytes	Secondary floppy controller
0376	1 byte	Secondary IDE command port
0377, bit 7	1 bit	Secondary floppy controller disk change
0377, bits 6:0	7 bits	Secondary IDE status port
0378–037F	8 bytes	Parallel Port 1 (LPT1)
0380–038F	16 bytes	SMC Ethernet adapter (alternate)
0388–038B	4 bytes	Audio - FM synthesizer
03B0–03BB	12 bytes	Video, Mono/EGA/VGA standard ports
03BC–03BF	4 bytes	Parallel Port 1 (LPT1) in some systems
03BC–03BF	4 bytes	Parallel Port 3 (LPT3)
03C0–03CF	16 bytes	Video, EGA/VGA standard ports
03D0–03DF	16 bytes	Video, CGA/EGA/VGA standard ports
03E6	1 byte	Third IDE command port
03E7, bits 6:0	7 bits	Third IDE status port
03E8–03EF	8 bytes	Serial Port 3 (COM 3)
03F0–03F5	6 bytes	Primary floppy controller
03F6	1 byte	Primary IDE command port
03F7, bit 7	1 bit	Primary floppy controller disk change
03F7, bits 6:0	7 bits	Primary IDE status port
03F8–03FF	8 bytes	Serial Port 1 (COM 1)
04D0–04D1	2 bytes	Edge/level triggered PCI interrupt controller
0530–0537	8 bytes	Windows sound system (default)
0604–060B	8 bytes	Windows sound system (alternate)
0678–067F	8 bytes	LPT2 in ECP mode
0778–077F	8 bytes	LPT1 in ECP mode
0A20–0A23	4 bytes	IBM Token-Ring adapter (default)
0A24–0A27	4 bytes	IBM Token-Ring adapter (alternate)
0CF8–0CFB	4 bytes	PCI configuration address registers
0CF9	1 byte	Turbo and reset control register
0CFC–0CFF	4 bytes	PCI configuration data registers
FF00–FF07	8 bytes	IDE bus master registers
FF80–FF9F	32 bytes	Universal Serial Bus (USB)
FFA0–FFA7	8 bytes	Primary bus master IDE registers
FFA8–FFAF	8 bytes	Secondary bus master IDE registers

Determining Actual I/O Address Ranges in Use

To find out exactly what your devices are using, consult the documentation for the device or look up the device in the Windows 9x Device Manager (see Figure 2.16). Note that some device documentation might list only the starting I/O address and not the full range of addresses used.

Virtually all devices on your system buses use I/O port addresses. Most of these are fairly standardized, meaning you won't often have conflicts or problems with these settings.

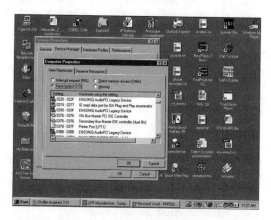

Figure 2.16 The Windows 9x Device Manager lists the starting and ending I/O port addresses for both motherboard-based and add-on card devices.

Troubleshooting Add-on Card Resource Conflicts

The resources in a system are limited. Unfortunately, the demands on those resources seem to be unlimited. As you add more and more adapter cards to your system, you will find that the potential for resource conflicts increases.

Symptoms of a Potential Resource Conflict

- A device transfers data inaccurately.

- Your system frequently locks up.

- Your sound card doesn't sound quite right.

- Your mouse doesn't work.

- Garbage appears on your video screen for no apparent reason.

- Your printer prints gibberish.

- You cannot format a floppy disk.

- The PC starts in Safe mode (Windows 9x/2000/Me).

Spotting Resource Conflicts with Windows 9x/2000/Me

Windows 9x/Me/2000 also show conflicts by highlighting a device in yellow or red in the Device Manager representation. By using the Windows Device Manager, you can usually spot the conflicts quickly (see Figure 2.17).

Keep in mind that many computer viruses can also cause symptoms similar to hardware resource conflicts. Scan your system for viruses before you start working on it.

Recording System Settings

Use a System Configuration Template to record system settings. This sheet is resource-oriented, not device-oriented, to make finding conflicts easier. You can make a printout of the System Summary from the Windows 9x/Me/2000 Device Manager to get a lot of this information. For other operating systems, use the methods listed earlier.

The first system resource map is provided as a model for your use; it lists fixed resources on a modern PC. Add the other resources used on your PC. Note that many high-performance PCI or AGP video cards do use an IRQ, although some motherboard chipsets have a provision for disabling the IRQ usage.

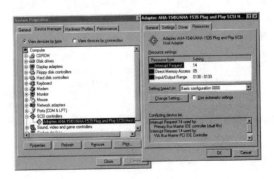

Figure 2.17   The yellow circle next to the Adaptec 154x SCSI card indicates a conflict; view the card resources (right window) to see the conflicting device.

System Resource Map

PC Make and Model: _____

Serial Number: _____

Date: _____

Interrupts (IRQs):	**I/O Port Addresses:**
0 - Timer Circuits _____	040-04B _____
1 - Keyboard/Mouse Controller _____	060 & 064 _____
2 - 2nd 8259 IRQ Controller _____	0A0-0A1 _____
8 - Real-time Clock/CMOS RAM _____	070-071 _____
9 - _____	_____
10 - _____	_____
11 - _____	_____
12 - _____	_____
13 - Math Coprocessor _____	0F0 _____
14 - _____	_____
15 - _____	_____
3 - _____	_____
4 - _____	_____
5 - _____	_____
6 - _____	_____
7 - _____	_____

Devices not using Interrupts:	**I/O Port Addresses:**
Mono/EGA/VGA Standard Ports _____	3B0-3BB _____
EGA/VGA Standard Ports _____	3C0-3CF _____
CGA/EGA/VGA Standard Ports _____	3D0-3DF _____
_____	_____
_____	_____
_____	_____
_____	_____
_____	_____

DMA Channels:

0 - _____

1 - _____

2 - _____

3 - _____

4 - DMA Channel 0-3 Cascade _____

5 - _____

6 - _____

7 - _____

Here's an example of how to fill out the worksheet:

System Resource Map

PC Make and Model: Intel SE440BX-2 _____
Serial Number: 100000 _____
Date: 06/09/99 _____

Interrupts (IRQs):	I/O Port Addresses:
0 - Timer Circuits _____	040-04B_____
1 - Keyboard/Mouse Controller _____	060 & 064 _____
2 - 2nd 8259 IRQ Controller _____	0A0-0A1_____
8 - Real-time Clock/CMOS RAM _____	070-071 _____
9 - SMC EtherEZ Ethernet card _____	340-35F _____
10 - _____	_____
11 - Adaptec 1542CF SCSI Adapter (scanner)	334-337[1] _____
12 - Motherboard Mouse Port _____	060 & 064 _____
13 - Math Coprocessor _____	OFO _____
14 - Primary IDE (hard disk 1 and 2) ____	1F0-1F7, 3F6_____
15 - Secondary IDE (CD-ROM/tape) ____	170-177, 376_____
3 - Serial Port 2 (Modem) _____	3F8-3FF _____
4 - Serial Port 1 (COM1)_____	2F8-2FF _____
5 - Sound Blaster 16 Audio _____	220-233_____
6 - Floppy Controller_____	3F0-3F5 _____
7 - Parallel Port 1 (Printer)_____	378-37F _____

Devices not using interrupts:	I/O Port Addresses:
Mono/EGA/VGA Standard Ports _____	3B0-3BB _____
EGA/VGA Standard Ports_____	3C0-3CF_____
CGA/EGA/VGA Standard Ports _____	3D0-3DF _____
ATI Mach 64 video card additional ports _____	102,1CE-1CF,2EC-2EF _____
Sound Blaster 16 MIDI port_____	330-331 _____
Sound Blaster 16 Game port (joystick)_____	200-207 _____
Sound Blaster 16 FM synthesizer (music) ____	388-38B _____
_____	_____

DMA Channels:

0 - _____
1 - Sound Blaster 16 (8-bit DMA)_____
2 - Floppy Controller _____
3 - Parallel Port 1 (in ECP mode) _____
4 - DMA Channel 0-3 Cascade_____
5 - Sound Blaster 16 (16-bit DMA) _____
6 - Adaptec 1542CF SCSI adapter[1]_____
7 - _____

1. Represents a resource setting that had to be changed to resolve a conflict.

After you've completed your system resource map by recording the current settings for hardware, you're ready to solve conflicts.

Note

Resource use can change whenever PnP or non-PnP hardware is installed or removed, so you should update this chart whenever you add or remove internal hardware.

Resolving Conflicts by Card and Operating System Type

Table 2.24   Guide to Resolving Conflicts

Operating System	Card Type	Notes
Windows 9x/ 2000/Me	PnP	Use Device Manager to change card settings if possible; remove and reinstall card to redetect card and use new settings if card can't be set manually; if new card can't be detected when installed, remove other PnP cards and install new card first.
	Non-PnP	Use Device Manager to see conflicting devices; manually configure cards to non-conflicting settings by changing jumpers, DIP switches, or rerunning configuration programs.
Other operating systems	Any	*When did the conflict first become apparent?* If the conflict occurred after you installed a new adapter card, that new card probably is causing the conflict. If the conflict occurred after you started using new software, chances are good that the software uses a device that is taxing your system's resources in a new way.
		Are two similar devices in your system not working? For example, if your modem, integrated serial ports, or mouse devices that use a COM port do not work, chances are good that these devices are conflicting with each other.
		Have other people had the same problem? And if so, how did they resolve it? Public forums such as those on CompuServe, Internet newsgroups, and America Online are great places to find other users who might be able to help you solve the conflict. Also check vendor forums for help.
		After you research these questions, make one (one!) change to your system configuration, reboot the computer and see whether the problem is now resolved. Repeat with a different setting until the problem is solved.
		Test all components to make sure that "fixing" one component didn't cause a conflict with another.

Expansion Slots

If you want to add network, SCSI, modem, or sound capabilities to an existing system or upgrade your video card, you need to understand expansion slots. Expansion slots act as an extension of the system bus and permit you to connect cards with different features to your system.

ISA

ISA (Industry Standard Architecture) expansion slots are the oldest expansion slot design found in current PCs. 8-bit versions go all the way back to the original IBM PC of 1981. While 8-bit–only ISA slots have faded away, 16-bit ISA slots (introduced with the IBM PC/AT in 1984) are fully pin-compatible with 8-bit ISA cards. See Figures 2.18 and 2.19.

Figure 2.19 shows the orientation and relation of 8-bit and 16-bit ISA bus slots.

EISA—A 32-bit Version of ISA

The EISA (Enhanced ISA) bus was developed from the ISA architecture to provide 32-bit data transfers. The EISA expansion slot (introduced in 1988) is a deeper version of ISA, providing a second, offset row of connectors that allows EISA slots to support ISA cards. Figure 2.20 shows the locations of the pins.

Because of its high cost and limited performance boost over ISA, EISA bus systems have primarily been used for network file servers using 386, 486, and occasionally Pentium-class CPUs.

EISA was introduced as a response to IBM's MicroChannel architecture, which was used primarily on more-advanced models of IBM's PS/2 line from 1987 until the early 1990s. It is now obsolete.

VL-Bus—A Faster 32-Bit Version of ISA

Introduced in 1992, the VL-Bus (VESA Local-Bus) was an improved 32-bit version of ISA designed originally to provide faster video card performance on 486-based systems. This slot design, like EISA, is now obsolete. While most VL-Bus slots were added to an ISA slot, the VL-Bus connector could also be added to an EISA slot. Thus, any VL-Bus slot is also an ISA or an ISA/EISA slot (see Figure 2.21).

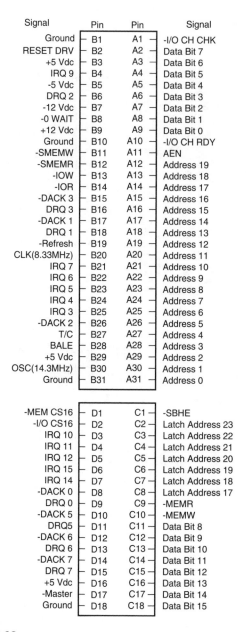

Signal	Pin	Pin	Signal
Ground	B1	A1	-I/O CH CHK
RESET DRV	B2	A2	Data Bit 7
+5 Vdc	B3	A3	Data Bit 6
IRQ 9	B4	A4	Data Bit 5
-5 Vdc	B5	A5	Data Bit 4
DRQ 2	B6	A6	Data Bit 3
-12 Vdc	B7	A7	Data Bit 2
-0 WAIT	B8	A8	Data Bit 1
+12 Vdc	B9	A9	Data Bit 0
Ground	B10	A10	-I/O CH RDY
-SMEMW	B11	A11	AEN
-SMEMR	B12	A12	Address 19
-IOW	B13	A13	Address 18
-IOR	B14	A14	Address 17
-DACK 3	B15	A15	Address 16
DRQ 3	B16	A16	Address 15
-DACK 1	B17	A17	Address 14
DRQ 1	B18	A18	Address 13
-Refresh	B19	A19	Address 12
CLK(8.33MHz)	B20	A20	Address 11
IRQ 7	B21	A21	Address 10
IRQ 6	B22	A22	Address 9
IRQ 5	B23	A23	Address 8
IRQ 4	B24	A24	Address 7
IRQ 3	B25	A25	Address 6
-DACK 2	B26	A26	Address 5
T/C	B27	A27	Address 4
BALE	B28	A28	Address 3
+5 Vdc	B29	A29	Address 2
OSC(14.3MHz)	B30	A30	Address 1
Ground	B31	A31	Address 0

Signal	Pin	Pin	Signal
-MEM CS16	D1	C1	-SBHE
-I/O CS16	D2	C2	Latch Address 23
IRQ 10	D3	C3	Latch Address 22
IRQ 11	D4	C4	Latch Address 21
IRQ 12	D5	C5	Latch Address 20
IRQ 15	D6	C6	Latch Address 19
IRQ 14	D7	C7	Latch Address 18
-DACK 0	D8	C8	Latch Address 17
DRQ 0	D9	C9	-MEMR
-DACK 5	D10	C10	-MEMW
DRQ5	D11	C11	Data Bit 8
-DACK 6	D12	C12	Data Bit 9
DRQ 6	D13	C13	Data Bit 10
-DACK 7	D14	C14	Data Bit 11
DRQ 7	D15	C15	Data Bit 12
+5 Vdc	D16	C16	Data Bit 13
-Master	D17	C17	Data Bit 14
Ground	D18	C18	Data Bit 15

Figure 2.18   Pinouts for the 16-bit ISA bus.

8/16-bit ISA Bus Pinouts.

8-bit PC/XT Connector:

Signal	Pin Numbers		Signal
GROUND	B1	A1	-I/O CHK
RESET DRV	B2	A2	DATA 7
+5 Vdc	B3	A3	DATA 6
IRQ 2	B4	A4	DATA 5
-5 Vdc	B5	A5	DATA 4
DRQ 2	B6	A6	DATA 3
-12 Vdc	B7	A7	DATA 2
-CARD SLCT	B8	A8	DATA 1
+12 Vdc	B9	A9	DATA 0
GROUND	B10	A10	-I/O RDY
-SMEMW	B11	A11	AEN
-SMEMR	B12	A12	ADDR 19
-IOW	B13	A13	ADDR 18
-IOR	B14	A14	ADDR 17
-DACK 3	B15	A15	ADDR 16
DRQ 3	B16	A16	ADDR 15
-DACK 1	B17	A17	ADDR 14
DRQ 1	B18	A18	ADDR 13
-REFRESH	B19	A19	ADDR 12
CLK (4.77MHz)	B20	A20	ADDR 11
IRQ 7	B21	A21	ADDR 10
IRQ 6	B22	A22	ADDR 9
IRQ 5	B23	A23	ADDR 8
IRQ 4	B24	A24	ADDR 7
IRQ 3	B25	A25	ADDR 6
-DACK 2	B26	A26	ADDR 5
T/C	B27	A27	ADDR 4
BALE	B28	A28	ADDR 3
+5 Vdc	B29	A29	ADDR 2
OSC (14.3MHz)	B30	A30	ADDR 1
GROUND	B31	A31	ADDR 0

16-bit AT Connector:

Signal	Pin Numbers		Signal
GROUND	B1	A1	-I/O CHK
RESET DRV	B2	A2	DATA 7
+5 Vdc	B3	A3	DATA 6
IRQ 9	B4	A4	DATA 5
-5 Vdc	B5	A5	DATA 4
DRQ 2	B6	A6	DATA 3
-12 Vdc	B7	A7	DATA 2
-OWS	B8	A8	DATA 1
+12 Vdc	B9	A9	DATA 0
GROUND	B10	A10	-I/O RDY
-SMEMW	B11	A11	AEN
-SMEMR	B12	A12	ADDR 19
-IOW	B13	A13	ADDR 18
-IOR	B14	A14	ADDR 17
-DACK 3	B15	A15	ADDR 16
DRQ 3	B16	A16	ADDR 15
-DACK 1	B17	A17	ADDR 14
DRQ 1	B18	A18	ADDR 13
-REFRESH	B19	A19	ADDR 12
CLK (8.33MHz)	B20	A20	ADDR 11
IRQ 7	B21	A21	ADDR 10
IRQ 6	B22	A22	ADDR 9
IRQ 5	B23	A23	ADDR 8
IRQ 4	B24	A24	ADDR 7
IRQ 3	B25	A25	ADDR 6
-DACK 2	B26	A26	ADDR 5
T/C	B27	A27	ADDR 4
BALE	B28	A28	ADDR 3
+5 Vdc	B29	A29	ADDR 2
OSC (14.3MHz)	B30	A30	ADDR 1
GROUND	B31	A31	ADDR 0

Signal	Pin Numbers		Signal
-MEM CS16	D1	C1	-SBHE
-I/O CS16	D2	C2	LADDR 23
IRQ 10	D3	C3	LADDR 22
IRQ 11	D4	C4	LADDR 21
IRQ 12	D5	C5	LADDR 20
IRQ 15	D6	C6	LADDR 19
IRQ 14	D7	C7	LADDR 18
-DACK 0	D8	C8	LADDR 17
DRQ 0	D9	C9	-MEMR
-DACK 5	D10	C10	-MEMW
DRQ 5	D11	C11	DATA 8
-DACK 6	D12	C12	DATA 9
DRQ 6	D13	C13	DATA 10
-DACK 7	D14	C14	DATA 11
DRQ 7	D15	C15	DATA 12
+5 Vdc	D16	C16	DATA 13
-MASTER	D17	C17	DATA 14
GROUND	D18	C18	DATA 15

Figure 2.19   The 8-bit and 16-bit ISA bus connectors.

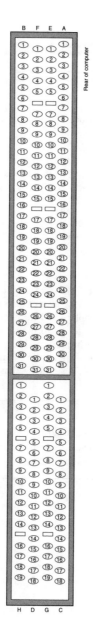

Figure 2.20 The card connector for the EISA bus. The inner connectors were used for the EISA cards, whereas the outer connectors supported 8-bit and 16-bit ISA cards.

Figure 2.21   An example of a VL-Bus slot in an ISA system.

PCI

Intel developed PCI (Peripheral Component Interconnect) in 1992 to eventually replace ISA and its variations. Most PCI slots provide 32-bit transfers, with a 64-bit version of PCI being used in many late-model file servers.

While a number of new "legacy-free" systems offer only PCI slots, most systems you will encounter will also have one or more ISA slots, as in Figure 2.21.

AGP

The latest expansion slot design is AGP (Accelerated Graphics Port), introduced in 1996 to provide faster video performance in a dedicated slot. AGP doesn't replace PCI for general purposes, but AGP video cards offer much faster performance than similar PCI cards, and can also "borrow" from main memory for 3D texturing. Most typical Pentium II/III, Celeron, Athlon, Duron, or Super Socket 7 systems include a single AGP slot as well as a mixture of PCI and ISA slots (see Figure 2.22).

Note
While AGP video is standard on all desktop systems today, it is often implemented on very low-cost systems by means of onboard video rather than an AGP slot.

Table 2.25 provides a visual quick reference for expansion slots found in modern PCs.

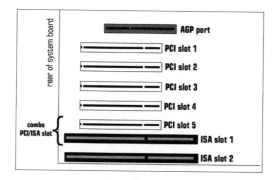

Figure 2.22   The AGP slot is located at the first (inside) slot position on
motherboards with an AGP slot. Note the lack of space between the last PCI
slot and the first ISA slot. This is called a *combo* or *shared* slot; only one of
the slots can actually be used.

Table 2.25	Expansion Slot Quick-Reference Table		
Slot Type	**Bus Speed**	**Bus Width**	**Best Use**
ISA	8.33MHz	8-bit or 16-bit	Modems, serial, parallel ports; will be phased out in early twenty-first century
EISA	8.33MHz	32-bit with EISA cards; compatible with ISA cards	Obsolete for most uses; works well with server-optimized NIC cards
MCA	10MHz	16-bit or 32-bit	Introduced with IBM MicroChannel PS/2s in 1987; obsolete
VL-Bus	25–33MHz typical; can be run up to 40MHz on some systems	32-bit; slot also can be used as ISA	Obsolete; was popular for video cards and IDE hard disk interfaces
PCI	25–33MHz (depends on speed of motherboard)	Most are 32-bit; some 64-bit implementations used on file servers	Video, SCSI, sound, modems; replaced ISA as general-purpose bus
AGP	66MHz	64-bit	Dedicated high-speed video; motherboards can support 1x, 2x, or 4x speeds of AGP cards depending on board design

Chapter 3

BIOS Configurations and Upgrades

What the BIOS Is and What It Does

The BIOS (basic input/output system) chip on the computer's motherboard is designed to provide the essential interfacing between hardware (such as drives, the clock, the CPU, the chipset, and video) and software (the operating system). While video, some SCSI, and a few IDE add-on cards might also have BIOS chips that help manage those devices, whenever I refer to the computer's *BIOS chip*, I mean the one on the motherboard. The BIOS chip is often referred to as the *ROM BIOS*, because in its traditional form it was a read-only memory chip with contents that could not be changed. Later versions could be reprogrammed with an EEPROM programmer, and beginning in the early 1990s, BIOSes using flash memory (*Flash BIOS*) began to appear. Flash BIOSes can be reprogrammed through software, and virtually all BIOSes on Pentium-class machines and beyond are flash upgradable.

Regardless of its form, the BIOS chip on the motherboard is also known as the *system BIOS*.

When a BIOS Update Is Necessary

The following list shows the primary benefits of a ROM BIOS upgrade:

- Adds LS-120 (120MB) floppy drive support (also known as a SuperDrive)

- Adds support for hard drives greater than 8GB

- Adds support for Ultra-DMA/33 or faster IDE hard drives

- Adds support for bootable ATAPI CD-ROM drives

- Adds or improves Plug-and-Play support and compatibility

- Corrects year-2000 and leap-year bugs

- Corrects known bugs or compatibility problems with certain hardware and software

- Adds support for newer types of processors

In general, if your computer is incapable of using all the features of new software or hardware, you might need a BIOS upgrade.

Specific Tests to Determine Whether Your BIOS Needs an Update

To determine whether your BIOS needs to be updated because of hard drive capacity limitations, see Chapter 4, "SCSI and IDE Hard Drives and Optical Drives."

To determine whether your BIOS needs to be updated because of operating system or CPU-upgrade issues, consult the technical-support Web sites for the operating system or CPU upgrade.

If your computer was built before 1999 and you have not performed a BIOS upgrade or loaded year-2000 patches for your operating system and applications, you might have Y2K-related problems with accurate date handling. Because the RTC (Real-Time-Clock) on most computers doesn't track centuries, the system BIOS must accurately add this information before handing the date to the operating system and applications, and the BIOS/RTC must also accurately handle leap years such as 2000 and beyond. A BIOS upgrade is the best way to handle RTC/BIOS issues, but software patches in the AUTOEXEC.BAT or CONFIG.SYS can also be used.

Consult your operating system and application vendors for appropriate solutions, including software updates or replacement versions.

Fixing BIOS Limitations—BIOS Fixes and Alternatives

Use Table 3.1 to determine which options you can follow if a BIOS update isn't possible, depending on the BIOS problem noted.

Table 3.1	Alternatives to BIOS Upgrades		
Problem	**Alternative Fix**	**Benefits of Alternative Fix**	**Limitations of Alternative Fix**
Y2K date rollover	Install Y2K-compliant BIOS card.	Provides hardware solution to non-compliant BIOS; can be combined with fix for hard disk capacity limitations.	Uses an ISA slot; doesn't handle problems with direct access to RTC that might be performed by some operating systems and applications.
	Install Y2K-compliant BIOS and RTC card.	Provides hardware solution for both BIOS and RTC Y2K.	Uses an ISA slot; some versions require that drivers be installed for the operating system in use.
	Install Y2K-compliant TSR or device driver.	Low-cost or free solution that avoids opening system.	Can be bypassed by booting off floppy; might not handle allY2K clock rollover problems; can be removed from boot process; not available for all operating systems.

		Benefits of	Limitations of
Problem	**Alternative Fix**	**Alternative Fix**	**Alternative Fix**

Table 3.1   Alternatives to BIOS Upgrades Continued

Problem	Alternative Fix	Benefits of Alternative Fix	Limitations of Alternative Fix
IDE hard disk capacity limitations	See Chapter 4 for details of these fixes.		
Complete solution	Replace motherboard.	Provides both brand-new BIOS and new motherboard features at a price often just slightly higher than a third-party BIOS upgrade.	System must use standard MB form factor; mix of ISA and PCI/AGP slots might mean some existing cards won't fit because latest motherboards have more PCI than ISA slots; time-consuming hardware install; requires time-consuming redetection and configuration of hardware drivers in operating system.

How BIOS Updates Are Performed

Two different ways of updating a motherboard BIOS are available.

With older systems, a physical *chip swap* (also called a *BIOS chip upgrade*) is necessary. The original BIOS chip is removed, and a new BIOS chip is inserted in its place. The new BIOS must be customized to match the old system's motherboard and chipset, use its existing CPU, and provide the enhanced features specified by the upgrade BIOS manufacturer. The typical cost range is around $60–90 for a single BIOS chip.

With newer systems that have a flash-upgradable BIOS, the update software is downloaded and installed onto a disk, which is used to boot the computer. Then, the new BIOS code is copied to the BIOS chip in a process that takes about 3–5 minutes. If the BIOS update comes from a source *other* than the original system or motherboard maker, it will also cost as much as $90 for the update.

In either case, the system might need to be reconfigured, especially if the new BIOS was physically installed, or if either a chip-based or flash-based BIOS is a different brand of BIOS than the original.

Where BIOS Updates Come From

The best (and cheapest!) place to get a BIOS update is from your motherboard or system vendor. Most major system manufacturers offer free BIOS updates for their systems with flash BIOS chips on their Web sites. For *clone* systems with motherboards from various producers, see the section "Determining Which BIOS You Have" later in this chapter.

A second source for BIOS updates is from one of the following companies.

For systems that originally used the Phoenix BIOS, contact Micro Firmware (www.firmware.com or 800-767-5465). Micro Firmware typically supplies updated Phoenix flash BIOS code on disk for systems they support. See the Web site for the current list of supported systems and motherboards.

For systems that originally used the Award, AMI, MR BIOS, or Phoenix BIOS (including systems not supported by Micro Firmware), contact Unicore Software (www.unicore.com or 800-800-BIOS). Unicore might supply the update on disk or as a replacement MR BIOS chip. Contact these vendors for details and prices, which vary by system.

Precautions to Take Before Updating a BIOS

Use the following checklist to be safe, not sorry, when updating a BIOS.

First, back up your data. An "almost working" BIOS that doesn't quite work with your hard drive can blow away your data.

Back up your current BIOS code if you can. Some BIOS update loader programs offer this option, but others don't. As an alternative, some BIOS chips keep a mini-BIOS onboard that can be reactivated in the event that a botched update destroys the main BIOS. Some motherboards have a jumper that can be used to switch to the backup; check your system documentation. For others, check the Micro Firmware Web site for its Flash BIOS Recovery Disks page to find out whether your motherboard is listed. If the BIOS update isn't completed properly, you could have a dead system that will need a trip to the manufacturer for repair. See the next section, "How to Recover from a Failed BIOS Update Procedure," for a typical recovery procedure.

Record your hard drive configuration information, including the following:

- Cylinders

- Heads

- Sectors per Track

- Translation (Normal, LBA [greater than 504MB], Large, and so on)

If you are switching to a different brand of BIOS, you might need to re-enter this information.

Record other non-standard BIOS settings, such as hard disk transfer rate settings, built-in serial and parallel port settings, and so on. A worksheet you can use as a guide is found later in this chapter.

Read carefully and completely the information provided with the flash BIOS download or chip-type BIOS update kit. Check online or call the BIOS manufacturer if you have any questions before you ruin your BIOS.

Check to see whether your system has a *write-protect* setting jumper on the motherboard that must be adjusted to allow a BIOS update to take place. Some motherboards disable BIOS updates by default to protect your system's BIOS from unauthorized changes. Set your motherboard to allow the change before you install the flash BIOS update, and reset the protection after the update is complete.

How to Recover from a Failed BIOS Update Procedure

Most motherboards with soldered-in flash ROMs have a special BIOS Recovery procedure that can be performed. This hinges on a special unerasable part of the flash ROM that is reserved for this purpose.

In the unlikely event that a flash upgrade is interrupted catastroph-ically, the BIOS might be left in an unusable state. Recovering from this condition requires the following steps. A minimum of a power supply, a speaker, and a floppy drive configured as drive A: should be attached to the motherboard for this procedure to work:

1. Change the Flash Recovery jumper to the recovery mode position. Virtually all Intel motherboards and many third-party motherboards have a jumper or switch for BIOS recov-ery, which is normally labeled Recover/Normal.

2. Install the bootable BIOS upgrade disk you previously created to perform the flash upgrade into drive A: and reboot the system.

   Because of the small amount of code available in the non-erasable flash boot block area, no video prompts are available to direct the procedure. In other words, you will see nothing onscreen. In fact, it is not even necessary for a video card to be connected for this procedure to work. The procedure can be monitored by listening to the speaker and looking at the floppy drive LED. When the system beeps and the floppy drive LED is lit, the system is copying the BIOS recovery code into the flash device.

3. As soon as the drive LED goes off, the recovery should be complete. Power the system off.

4. Change the flash recovery jumper back to the default position for normal operation.

When you power the system back on, the new BIOS should be installed and functional. However, you might want to leave the BIOS upgrade floppy in drive A: and check to see that the proper BIOS version was installed.

> **Note**
>
> Note that this BIOS recovery procedure is often the fastest way to update a large number of machines, especially if you are performing other upgrades at the same time. This is how it is normally done in a system assembly or production environment.

Plug-and-Play BIOS

The role of the traditional BIOS was to manage the essential devices in the system: the hard drive, floppy drive, video, parallel and serial ports, and keyboard and system timer. Other devices were left to fight for the remaining IRQs and other hardware resources listed in Chapter 2, "System Components and Configuration." When Windows 95 was introduced, the role of the BIOS changed dramatically. To support Windows 95, the Plug-and-Play BIOS was introduced, changing how cards were installed and managed. Table 3.2 compares a Plug-and-Play (PnP) BIOS to a conventional BIOS.

Table 3.2   Plug-and-Play BIOS Versus Conventional BIOS

Task	Conventional BIOS	Plug-and Play BIOS
Hardware configuration	Motherboard-based devices and video only	All PnP devices as well as motherboard devices
Configuration type	Static (fixed settings)	Dynamic (settings can be altered as various devices are installed)
Configuration	Manual configuration	Manual, BIOS-assisted, or operating method system assisted
Operating system relationship to BIOS	Accepts all BIOS settings without alteration	Receives PnP device information from BIOS and can alter settings as required

> **Note**
>
> A complete list of PnP device IDs is found in the Technical
> Reference section of the CD included with *Upgrading and
> Repairing PCs, 12th Edition.*

PnP BIOS Configuration Options

While PnP BIOSes vary widely in their features, the following settings are typical. Use the list in Table 3.3 along with the tables that
follow to help you make configuration changes when necessary.

Resource Configuration

The Resource Configuration menu is used for configuring the memory and interrupt usage of non–Plug-and-Play (legacy) ISA bus-
based devices. Table 3.3 shows the functions and options found in
a typical modern BIOS.

Table 3.3	Typical Resource Configuration Menu[1]	
Feature	**Options**	**Description**
Memory Reservation	C800 CBFF Available (default) I Reserved CC00 CFFF Available (default) I Reserved D000 D3FF Available (default) I Reserved D400 D7FF Available (default) I Reserved D800 DBFF Available (default) I Reserved DC00 DFFF Available (default) I Reserved	Reserves specific upper memory blocks for use by legacy ISA devices.
IRQ Reservation	IRQ 3 Available (default) I Reserved IRQ 4 Available (default) I Reserved IRQ 5 Available (default) I Reserved IRQ 7 Available (default) I Reserved IRQ 10 Available (default) I Reserved IRQ 11 Available (default) I Reserved	Reserves specific IRQs for use by legacy ISA devices. An asterisk (*) displayed next to an IRQ indicates an IRQ conflict.

1. *Based on the Phoenix BIOS used by the Intel SE440BX2 motherboard. Used by permission of Intel Corporation.*

Note that these settings are only for legacy (non–Plug-and-Play) ISA
devices. For all Plug-and-Play ISA devices, as well as PCI devices
(which are Plug-and-Play by default), these resources are instead
configured by the operating system or by software that comes with
the cards.

Setting these resources here does not actually control the legacy ISA
device; that usually must be done by moving jumpers on the card.
By setting the resource as reserved here, you are telling the Plug-
and-Play operating system that the reserved resources are off-limits,
so it won't accidentally set a Plug-and-Play device to use the same
resource as a legacy ISA device. Reserving resources in this manner
is sometimes required because the Plug-and-Play software can't
detect all legacy ISA devices and therefore won't know which settings the device might be using.

In a system with no legacy devices, reserving any resources via this menu is not necessary.

Some boards have additional configuration options for the Plug-and-Play (PnP) BIOS features as well as the PCI bus. These features are largely chipset dependent, but some common examples are shown in Table 3.4.

Table 3.4 Typical PnP and PCI Options[1]	
DMA n Assigned to	When resources are controlled manually, assign each system DMA channel as one of the following types, depending on the type of device using the interrupt:
	• Legacy ISA devices compliant with the original PC AT bus specification, requiring a specific DMA channel
	• PCI/ISA PnP devices compliant with the Plug-and-Play standard, whether designed for PCI or ISA bus architecture
PCI IRQ Activated by	Leave the IRQ trigger set at Level unless the PCI device assigned to the interrupt specifies edge-triggered interrupts.
PCI IDE IRQ Map to	This field enables you to select PCI IDE IRQ mapping or PC AT (ISA) interrupts. If your system does not have one or two PCI IDE connectors on the system board, select values according to the type of IDE interface(s) installed in your system (PCI or ISA). Standard ISA interrupts for IDE channels are IRQ 14 for primary and IRQ 15 for secondary.
Primary/Secondary IDE INT#	Each PCI peripheral connection is capable of activating up to four interrupts: INT# A, INT# B, INT# C, and INT# D. By default, a PCI connection is assigned INT# A. Assigning INT# B has no meaning unless the peripheral device requires two interrupt services rather than one. Because the PCI IDE interface in the chipset has two channels, it requires two interrupt services. The primary and secondary IDE INT# fields default to values appropriate for two PCI IDE channels, with the primary PCI IDE channel having a lower interrupt than the secondary.
	Note that all single-function PCI cards normally use INT# A, and each of these must be assigned to a different and unique ISA interrupt request (IRQ).
Used Mem base addr	Select a base address for the memory area used by any peripheral that requires high memory.
Used Mem Length	Select a length for the memory area specified in the previous field. This field does not appear if no base address is specified.
Assign IRQ for USB	Select Enabled if your system has a USB controller and you have one or more USB devices connected. If you are not using your system's USB controller, select Disabled to free the IRQ resource.

1. *Based on the Phoenix BIOS used by the Intel SE440BX2 motherboard. Used by permission of Intel Corporation.*

When to Use the PnP BIOS Configuration Options

In an ideal situation involving PnP-aware operating systems—such as Windows 9x or 2000, a computer with a PnP BIOS, and a PnP device—the BIOS detects the PnP device and Windows configures it without user intervention. Table 3.5 lists the circumstances under which you might need to use PnP BIOS configuration options.

Table 3.5   Solving Configuration Problems with the PnP BIOS Configuration Options

Problem	Solution	Notes
Legacy (non-PnP) card needs particular IRQ or DMA setting already in use by PnP device.	Set DMA and IRQ used by legacy card to "ISA" option in BIOS.	This prevents PnP devices from using the resource; verify legacy card setting matches BIOS selections.
Windows 9x/Me/2000 is not detecting and configuring PnP devices not needed at boot time (such as modems, printers, and so on).	Set "Plug and Play Aware Operating System" option to "Yes" in BIOS.	
PCI video card is assigned an IRQ that you need for another device.	Set "Assign IRQ to VGA" option to "No" in BIOS.	This frees up the IRQ without ill effects in most cases; might not work if the video card is used for MPEG movie playback.
New PnP device can't be detected by system.	Set "PCI Slot x IRQ Priority" to desired (unused) IRQ; install card into designated PCI slot.	If setting the IRQ for the PCI slot doesn't work, remove all non-essential PnP cards, install new PnP card first, and then reinstall others.

Other BIOS Troubleshooting Tips

Use Table 3.6 to help solve some other typical system problems through BIOS configuration settings.

Table 3.6   Troubleshooting Common BIOS-Related System Problems

Problem	Solution	Notes
Can't access system because passwords for startup or setup access aren't known.	Passwords are stored in CMOS non-volatile RAM (NVRAM) and are configured through BIOS.	Remove battery on motherboard and wait for all CMOS settings to be lost or use MB jumper called "clear CMOS"; before clearing CMOS, view bootup configuration information and note hard drive and other configuration information, because all setup information must be re-entered after CMOS is cleared.

Table 3.6   Troubleshooting Common BIOS-Related System Problems Continued

Problem	Solution	Notes
System wastes time detecting hard drives at every bootup.	Disable automatic drive detection in BIOS; "lock in" settings for drives by using "detect drives" option in BIOS.	
System drops network or modem connection when system is idle.	Power management not set correctly for IRQs in use by modem or network card.	Determine which IRQs are used by devices and adjust power management for those devices; disable power management in BIOS.
Parallel or serial port conflicts.	Change configuration in BIOS.	See Chapters 6 and 7 for details.

For more about troubleshooting and adjusting BIOS configuration settings, see Chapter 5 of *Upgrading and Repairing PCs, 12th Edition*, published by Que.

Soft BIOS CPU Speed and Multiplier Settings

Conventional motherboards might require the user to configure CPU speed, FSB (motherboard or system bus) speed, and clock multipliers through a series of jumpers or switches or through BIOS configuration screens. One danger to BIOS configuration is that the user might create a configuration that won't allow the system to boot, and might require the CMOS configuration to be deleted to enable the user to try another option.

As an alternative, ABIT motherboards have pioneered BIOS-controlled configuration of CPU speeds, clock multipliers, FSB (motherboard/system bus) speeds, and other options using a feature called SoftMenu III that also enables hardware overrides.

SoftMenu III enables users to do the following:

- Adjust FSB speeds up to 200MHz
- Adjust core voltage
- Adjust AGP and PCI clock ratios

If the user creates an "impossible" combination of settings that won't permit the system to boot, a set of DIP switches on motherboards using SoftMenu III can override the BIOS configuration, enabling the system to boot.

Determining Which BIOS You Have

It's important to know which BIOS brand and version a computer has for two reasons.

First, in the event of a boot failure, BIOS error codes, which vary by brand and model, can be used to help you find the cause of the problem and lead you to a solution.

Second, knowing which BIOS brand and version you have can enable you to get help from the BIOS or system vendor for certain chipset configuration issues.

To determine which BIOS you have, use the following methods:

- Watch your system startup screen for information about the BIOS brand and version, such as "Award BIOS v4.51PG."

- Use a hardware test-and-reporting utility, such as Microsoft's venerable MSD.EXE, AMIDiag, CheckIt, or others.

Note that the best source for machine-specific information about error codes and other BIOS issues is your system manufacturer. Major vendors, such as IBM, Dell, Compaq, Gateway, Hewlett-Packard, and others, maintain excellent Web sites that list specific information for your system. However, if you are working with a white-box clone system made from generic components, BIOS-level information might be the best information you can get.

Determining the Motherboard Manufacturer for BIOS Upgrades

While knowing the BIOS brand and version is sufficient for troubleshooting a system that won't start, solving problems with issues such as year-2000 compliance, large hard disk support, and power management requires knowing exactly which motherboard you have and who produced it. Because motherboard manufacturers tailor BIOS code to the needs of each motherboard model, the motherboard or system vendor—not the BIOS vendor—is the source to turn to for BIOS upgrades and other BIOS configuration issues.

Identifying Motherboards with AMI BIOS

Motherboards using AMI BIOS versions built from 1991 to the present (AMI's High-Flex BIOS or WinBIOS) display a long string of numbers at the bottom of the first screen that is displayed when the system is powered on or restarted:

```
51-0411-001771-00111111-071595-82439HX-F
```

Interpret a number such as this one with the following numerical key (see Table 3.7):

AB - CCCC - DDDDDD - EFGHIJKL - mmddyy - MMMMMMM - N

Table 3.7	AB-CCCC-DDDDDD-EFGHIJKL-mmddyy-MMMMMMM-N
Position	**Description**
A	Processor Type:
	0 = 8086 or 8088
	2 = 286
	3 = 386
	4 = 486
	5 = Pentium
	6 = Pentium Pro/II
B	Size of BIOS:
	0 = 64KB BIOS
	1 = 128KB BIOS
CCCC	Major and minor BIOS version number
DDDDDD	Manufacturer license code reference number:
	0036xx = AMI 386 motherboard, xx = Series #
	0046xx = AMI 486 motherboard, xx = Series #
	0056xx = AMI Pentium motherboard, xx = Series #
	0066xx = AMI Pentium Pro motherboard, xx = Series #
	(for other numbers see the following note)
E	1 = Halt on POST Error
F	1 = Initialize CMOS every boot
G	1 = Block pins 22 and 23 of the keyboard controller
H	1 = Mouse support in BIOS/keyboard controller
I	1 = Wait for F1 key on POST errors
J	1 = Display floppy error during POST
K	1 = Display video error during POST
L	1 = Display keyboard error during POST
mmddyy	BIOS Date, mm/dd/yy
MMMMMMM	Chipset identifier or BIOS name
N	Keyboard controller version number

> **Note**
>
> Use the following resources to determine the manufacturer of non-AMI motherboards using the AMI BIOS:
>
> AMI has a listing of U.S. and non-U.S. motherboard manufacturers at the following address:
>
>   http://www.ami.com/amibios/support/identify.html
>
> AMI also offers a downloadable utility program called AMIMBID for use with Windows 9x/2000/NT and MS-DOS. Follow the AMI Motherboard Identification Utility link from the AMI Technical Support page, available as a link from the following address:
>
>   http://www.ami.com
>
> A more detailed listing, including complete identification of particular motherboard models, is available at Wim's BIOS page (www.ping.be/bios). This site also has links to motherboard manufacturers for BIOS upgrades.

Identifying Motherboards with Award BIOS

Motherboards with the Award Software BIOS also use a numerical code, although the structure is different from that for the AMI Hi-Flex BIOS.

The following is a typical Award BIOS ID:

    2A59IABDC-00

The sixth and seventh characters (bolded for emphasis) indicate the motherboard manufacturer, whereas the eighth character can be used for the model number or the motherboard family (various motherboards using the same chipset).

> **Note**
>
> For lookup tables of these codes, see the following Web sites:
>
> Award Software's official table for manufacturers only is available at www.phoenix.com/pcuser/bios-award-vendors.html.
>
> An expanded list, also containing chipset information (stored in the first five characters of the Award BIOS ID), is available at Wim's BIOS site (www.ping.be/bios/).

Identifying Motherboards with Phoenix or Microid Research BIOS

Unfortunately, neither Phoenix nor Microid Research (MR BIOS) use any type of a standardized motherboard ID number system.

For systems using a Phoenix BIOS, see whether your motherboard or system is listed on the Micro Firmware BIOS upgrades page. Links from this page for Intel and Micronics motherboards list the codes that show up onscreen during boot. Match these codes to your system and you might be able to use a Micro Firmware upgrade. Most MR BIOS (Microid Research BIOS) installations are done as upgrades rather than in original equipment. See the list of supported chipsets (identified by chipset brand and model, not motherboard vendor) and motherboards using Intel's Triton-series chipsets to see whether your system can use an MR BIOS, or contact Microid Research directly for system-specific information.

Accessing the BIOS Setup Programs

The BIOS is configured in one of several ways. Early computers, such as the IBM PC and PC/XT, used DIP switches on the motherboard to set a limited range of BIOS options, including memory size and the number of floppy disk drives. The IBM PC/AT introduced a disk-based configuration utility to cope with the many additional options on 286-based CPUs. Since the late 1980s, most computers have had their BIOS Setup programs incorporated into the BIOS chip itself. The Setup program is accessed on these systems by pressing a key or key combination early in the system startup procedure. Most recent computers display the correct keystroke(s) to use during the system startup. If not, use Table 3.8 to learn the keystrokes used to start common BIOS types.

Table 3.8 Common Keystrokes Used to Access the BIOS Setup Program		
BIOS	**Keystrokes**	**Notes**
Phoenix BIOS	Ctrl+Alt+Esc	
	Ctrl+Alt+F1	
	Ctrl+Alt+S	
	Ctrl+Alt+Enter	
	Ctrl+Alt+F11	
	Ctrl+Alt+Ins	
Award BIOS	Ctrl+Alt+Esc	
	Esc	
AMI BIOS	Del	

Table 3.8   Common Keystrokes Used to Access the BIOS Setup Program Continued

BIOS	Keystrokes	Notes
IBM BIOS	Ctrl+Alt+Ins*F1	*—Early notebook models; press when cursor is in upper-right corner of screen
Compaq BIOS	F10*	Keystroke actually loads Compaq Setup program from hard disk partition; press when cursor is in upper-right corner of screen

Note

See Chapter 5 of *Upgrading and Repairing PCs, 12th Edition* to see how a typical BIOS Setup program operates.

How the BIOS Reports Errors

The BIOS will use three methods for reporting errors: beep codes, error/status codes, and onscreen messages. Error/status codes must be read with a special interface board, whereas the others require no special equipment.

BIOS Beep Codes and Their Purposes

Virtually all systems make a polite "beep" noise when started, but most systems have a special series of beep codes that serve the following purposes.

Beeps alert you to serious system problems, many of which can prevent your system from even starting (a so-called *fatal error*) or from working to its full potential (a so-called *non-fatal error*).

Because most fatal and many non-fatal errors take place before the video subsystem is initialized (or might indicate the video isn't working), beeps can be used to determine the cause of the problem.

A system that can't start and is reporting a problem with beep codes will give the code once and then halt. To hear the code again, restart the computer.

Use the following tables of beep codes to determine why your system will not start. To solve the problem reported by the beep codes, repair or replace the device listed in the description. If your repair or replacement has solved the problem, the beep code will no longer sound when you restart the system.

For errors involving removable devices (socketed chips, memory, or video), an easy fix is to remove and replace the item because a device that's not securely in its socket will cause the test to fail.

> **Note**
>
> For an exhaustive list of BIOS codes, beep codes, and error messages, see the CD accompanying *Upgrading and Repairing PCs, 12th Edition.*

AMI BIOS Beep Codes

> **Note**
>
> AMI BIOS beep codes used by permission of American Megatrends, Inc.

Beeps	Error Message	Description
1	DRAM Refresh Failure	The memory refresh circuitry on the motherboard is faulty.
2	Parity Error	A parity error occurred in system memory.
3	Base 64KB (First Bank) Memory Failure	Memory failure in the first bank of memory.
4	System Timer Failure	Memory failure in the first bank of memory, or Timer 1 on the motherboard is not functioning.
5	Processor Error	The processor on the motherboard generated an error.
6	Keyboard Controller Gate A20 Failure	The keyboard controller might be bad. The BIOS cannot switch to protected mode.
7	Virtual Mode Processor Exception Interrupt Error	The processor generated an exception interrupt.
8	Display Memory Read/Write Error	The system video adapter is either missing or its memory is faulty.
9	ROM Checksum Error	ROM checksum value does not match the value encoded in BIOS.
10	CMOS Shutdown Register Read/Write Error	The shutdown register for CMOS RAM failed.
11	Cache Error/L2 Cache Bad	The L2 cache is faulty.
1 long, 3 short	Conventional/extended memory failure	The motherboard memory is faulty.
1 long, 8 short	Display/retrace test failed	The video card is faulty; try reseating or moving to a different slot.

Award BIOS Beep Codes

Currently only one beep code exists in the Award BIOS. A single long beep followed by two short beeps indicates that a video error has occurred and the BIOS cannot initialize the video screen to display any additional information.

Phoenix BIOS Beep Codes

The following beep codes are for the current version of Phoenix BIOS, version 4.0, release 6. Other versions will have somewhat different beeps and Port 80h codes. To view the Port 80h codes, you will need a POST diagnostics card with a two-digit LED readout, available from many sources for diagnostic tools. I recommend a PCI-based POST card because ISA slots are becoming obsolete.

> **Note**
>
> Phoenix BIOS beep codes used by permission of Phoenix Technologies, Ltd.

Beeps	Port 80h Code	Explanation
1-2-2-3	16h	BIOS ROM checksum
1-3-1-1	20h	Test DRAM refresh
1-3-1-3	22h	Test keyboard controller
1-3-3-1	28h	Autosize DRAM
1-3-3-2	29h	Initialize POST memory manager
1-3-3-3	2Ah	Clear 512KB base RAM
1-3-4-1	2Ch	RAM failure on address line xxxx
1-3-4-3	2Eh	RAM failure on data bits xxxx of low byte of memory bus
1-4-1-1	30h	RAM failure on data bits xxxx of high byte of memory bus
2-1-2-2	45h	POST device initialization
2-1-2-3	46h	Check ROM copyright notice
2-2-3-1	58h	Test for unexpected interrupts
2-2-4-1	5Ch	Test RAM between 512KB and 640KB
1-2	98h	Search for option ROMs; one long, two short beeps on checksum failure
1	B4h	One short beep before boot

IBM BIOS Beep and Alphanumeric Error Codes

After completing the power on self test (POST), an audio code indicates either a normal condition or that one of several errors has occurred.

> **Note**
>
> IBM BIOS and alphanumeric error codes used by permission of IBM.

Audio Code	Sound Graph	Description
1 short beep	•	Normal POST—system okay
2 short beeps	••	POST error—error code on display
No beep		Power supply, system board
Continuous beep	————	Power supply, system board
Repeating short beeps	••••••	Power supply, system board
1 long, 1 short beep	-•	System board
1 long, 2 short beeps	-••	Video adapter (MDA/CGA)
1 long, 3 short beeps	-•••	Video adapter (EGA/VGA)
3 long beeps	- - -	3270 keyboard card

Microid Research Beep Codes

The MR BIOS generates patterns of high and low beeps to signal an error condition.

The following beep codes are for the current and recent versions (3.x) of the MR BIOS.

Note

MR BIOS beep codes used by permission of Phoenix Technologies, Ltd.

Port 80h Code	Beep Codes	Error Messages
03h	LH-LLL	ROM-BIOS Checksum Failure
04h	LH-HLL	DMA Page Register Failure
05h	LH-LHL	Keyboard Controller Selftest Failure
08h	LH-HHL	Memory Refresh Circuitry Failure
09h	LH-LLH	Master (16-bit) DMA Controller Failure
09h	LH-HLH	Slave (8-bit) DMA Controller Failure
0Ah	LH-LLLL	Base 64KB Pattern Test Failure
0Ah	LH-HLLL	Base 64KB Parity Circuitry Failure
0Ah	LH-LHLL	Base 64KB Parity Error
0Ah	LH-HHLL	Base 64KB Data Bus Failure
0Ah	LH-LLHL	Base 64KB Address Bus Failure
0Ah	LH-HLHL	Base 64KB Block Access Read Failure
0Ah	LH-LHHL	Base 64KB Block Access Read/Write Failure
0Bh	LH-HHHL	Master 8259 (Port 21) Failure
0Bh	LH-LLLH	Slave 8259 (Port A1) Failure
0Ch	LH-HLLH	Master 8259 (Port 20) Interrupt Address Error

Port 80h Code	Beep Codes	Error Messages
0Ch	LH-LHLH	Slave 8259 (Port A0) Interrupt Address Error
0Ch	LH-HHLH	8259 (Port 20/A0) Interrupt Address Error
0Ch	LH-LLHH	Master 8259 (Port 20) Stuck Interrupt Error
0Ch	LH-HLHH	Slave 8259 (Port A0) Stuck Interrupt Error
0Ch	LH-LHHH	System Timer 8254 CH0/IRQ 0 Interrupt Failure
0Dh	LH-HHHH	8254 Channel 0 (System Timer) Failure
0Eh	LH-LLLH	8254 Channel 2 (Speaker) Failure
0Eh	LH-HLLH	8254 OUT2 (Speaker Detect) Failure
0Fh	LH-LHLH	CMOS RAM Read/Write Test Failure
0Fh	LH-HHLH	RTC Periodic Interrupt/IRQ 8 Failure
10h	LH-LLHLH	Video ROM Checksum Failure at Address XXXX, Mono Card Memory Error at Address XXXX, Mono Card Memory Address Line Error at Address XXXX, Color Graphics Card Memory Error at Address XXXX, Color Graphics Card Address Line Error at Address XXXX
11h	none	Real Time Clock (RTC) Battery is Discharged
11h	none	Battery Backed Memory (CMOS) is Corrupt
12h	LH-HLHLH	Keyboard Controller Failure
14h	LH-LHHLH	Memory Parity Error_18h_19h
14h	LH-HHHLH	I/O Channel Error_18h_19h
14h 18h 19h	none	RAM Pattern Test Failed at XXXX, Parity Circuit Failure in Bank XXXX, Data Bus Test Failed: Address XXXX, Address Line Test Failed at XXXX, Block Access Read Failure at Address XXXX, Block Access Read/Write Failure: Address XXXX, Banks Decode to Same Location: XXXX and YYYY
12h 15h	none	Keyboard Error—Stuck Key Keyboard Failure or no Keyboard Present
17h	LH-LLLHH	A20 Test Failure Due to 8042 Timeout
17h	LH-HLLHH	A20 Gate Stuck in Disabled State (A20=0)
17h	none	A20 Gate Stuck in Asserted State (A20 Follows CPU)
1Ah	LH-LHLHH	Real Time Clock (RTC) is Not Updating
1Ah	none	Real Time Clock (RTC) Settings are Invalid
1Eh	none	Disk CMOS Configuration is Invalid, Disk Controller Failure, Disk Drive A: Failure, Disk Drive B: Failure
1Fh	none	Fixed Disk CMOS Configuration is Invalid, Fixed Disk C:(80) Failure, Fixed Disk D:(81) Failure, Please Wait for Fixed Disk to Spin Up
20h	none	Fixed Disk, Disk, Serial Port, Parallel Port, Video, Memory, or Numeric Coprocessor Configuration Change
21h	none	System Key is in Locked Position—Turn Key to Unlocked Position
29h	none	Adapter ROM Checksum Failure at Address XXXX

Note for beep codes: L=low tone and H=high tone

Reading BIOS Error Codes

Because beep codes can indicate only some of the problems in a system at startup, most BIOSes also output a series of status codes during the boot procedure. These codes are sent to an I/O port address that can be read by specialized diagnostic cards, which you can purchase from many different vendors. These *POST cards* (so named from the power on self test) feature a two-digit LED panel that displays the status codes output by the BIOS. The simpler POST cards are hard-wired to pick up signals from the most commonly used I/O port address 80hex, but more expensive models can be adjusted with jumper blocks to use other addresses used by certain BIOSes (such as Compaq).

These cards are normally sold with manuals that list the error/status codes. While the cards are durable, the codes can become outdated. To get an updated list of codes, contact the system or BIOS vendor's Web site.

Most POST cards have been based on the ISA bus, but the latest models are now being made to fit into PCI slots because ISA is becoming obsolete. For diagnosing portable systems, and to avoid the need to open a system to insert a POST card, Ultra-X offers a MicroPOST display unit that attaches to the parallel port. Contact Ultra-X at www.uxd.com for more information.

Onscreen Error Messages

An onscreen error message is often the easiest of the error methods to understand, because you don't need to count beeps or open the system to install a POST card. However, because some systems use numeric error codes, and even "plain English" codes need interpretation, these messages can still be a challenge to interpret. Because the video circuits are tested after components such as the motherboard, CPU, and BIOS, an onscreen error message is usually indicative of a less-serious error than one that is reported with beep codes.

Interpreting Error Codes and Messages

Because beep codes, error/status codes, and onscreen messages vary a great deal by BIOS vendor (and sometimes BIOS model), you must know what BIOS a system has before you can choose the correct table. With major-brand systems (and some others), you'll typically find a list of error codes and messages in the system documentation. You can also contact the BIOS or system vendors' Web sites for this information, or check on the CD included with *Upgrading and Repairing PCs, 12th Edition.*

BIOS Configuration Worksheet

BIOS configuration options vary a great deal, and incorrect settings can cause a system to fail, lose data, or not work correctly with PnP-compatible operating systems, such as Windows 9x/2000/Me. The following worksheet can be used to record the most critical BIOS configuration information. Use it when you are unable to print out the actual configuration screens.

System ID_____**Brand & Model #** _____

Date Recorded_____**Operating System**_____

Hard Disk Partitions_____

Notes_____

_____

Standard CMOS/BIOS Configuration

(Configuration Option)	(Setting—circle or write down setting used)
Drive A	1.44MB
	2.88MB
	Other_____
	None
Drive B	1.44MB
	2.88MB
	Other_____
	None
1st IDE Drive	*Drive Type:*
	Hard Disk
	CD-ROM
	Other (specify)
	_____
	Hard disk Geometry
	*Cyl:*_____
	Sectors/Track: ____
	Heads: _____
	LBA Y/N:
2nd IDE Drive	*Drive Type:*
	Hard Disk
	CD-ROM
	Other (specify)
	_____
	Hard disk Geometry
	*Cyl:*_____

Standard CMOS/BIOS Configuration

	Sectors/Track: _____
	Heads: _____
	LBA Y/N:
3rd IDE Drive	*Drive Type:*
	Hard Disk
	CD-ROM
	Other (specify)
	_____
	Hard disk Geometry
	Cyl:_____
	Sectors/Track: _____
	Heads: _____
	LBA Y/N:
4th IDE Drive	*Drive Type:*
	Hard Disk
	CD-ROM
	Other (specify)
	_____
	Hard disk Geometry
	Cyl:_____
	Sectors/Track: _____
	Heads: _____
	LBA Y/N:

Other BIOS Configuration Screens

Boot Sequence	*1st drive: _____*
	2nd drive:_____
	3rd drive:_____
	4th drive:_____
Anti-Virus or Write-Protect Boot Sector	Enable / Disable
PS/2 Mouse	Enable / Disable
Password	Power On
	Password: _____
	Setup
	Password: _____
External Memory Cache (Level 2)	Enable / Disable
Internal Memory Cache (Level 1)	Enable / Disable

Shadow RAM / ROM Shadowing	*Specify Range(s) In Use:*
	_____
	_____
	_____
	_____
<u>*USB Ports*</u>	Enable / Disable
USB Legacy Support (keyboard & mouse)	Enable / Disable
Memory Timing Configuration	Auto / Manual
	If Manual, specify changes from system default below:
	_____
	_____
	_____
	_____
	_____
Power Management	Enable / Disable
	If Enabled, specify changes from system default below:
	_____
	_____
	_____
	_____
	_____
Plug and Play (PnP)	Enable / Disable
	If Enabled, specify changes from system default below:
	_____
	_____
	_____
	_____
	_____
LPT Port	*Mode Selected:*
	Standard EPP ECP Bi-Di
	Disabled
	EPP Version # _____
	IRQ: 7 5 _____
	DMA for ECP Mode: _____
	I/O Port Address:
	378H

LPT Port	*Mode Selected:*
	278H
	3BCH
	Disabled
Serial (COM) Port 1	*I/O Port Address:*
	3FH (COM1)
	2FH (COM2)
	3EH (COM3)
	2EH (COM4)
	Disabled
	Notes: _____
Serial (COM) Port 2	*I/O Port Address:*
	3FH (COM1)
	2FH (COM2)
	3EH (COM3)
	2EH (COM4)
	Disabled
	Notes: _____
IDE Hard Disk Interface #1	*Interface:*
	Enable / Disable
	32-bit Mode: Enable / Disable
	PIO Mode: 0 1 2 3 4
	UDMA Mode: 33MHz 66MHz 100MHz
	Block Mode: Enable / Disable
	# of Blocks: _____
IDE Hard Disk Interface #2	*Interface:*
	Enable / Disable
	32-bit Mode: Enable / Disable
	PIO Mode: 0 1 2 3 4
	UDMA Mode: 33MHz 66MHz 100MHz
	Block Mode: Enable / Disable

Chapter 4

SCSI and IDE Hard Drives and Optical Drives

Understanding Hard Disk Terminology

When installing IDE hard disks in particular, at least three parameters must be indicated in the BIOS Setup program to define a hard disk.

> ### Note
>
> Understanding how hard drives store data is an enormous topic. If you'd like to learn more, see Chapters 9 and 10 of *Upgrading and Repairing PCs, 12th Edition*, also published by Que.

Heads, Sectors per Track, and Cylinders

If this information is not accurately listed in the BIOS configuration, the full capacity of the drive will not be available unless special hard disk drivers or supplementary BIOS cards are used. Whenever possible, the computer's own ROM BIOS should fully support the drive's capacity.

For drives larger than 504MB (binary) or 528 million bytes, additional translation options are also required with MS-DOS and Windows to achieve full capacity.

Hard Drive Heads

A hard drive is comprised of one or more platters, normally made of aluminum but occasionally made of glass. These platters are covered with a thin rigid film of magnetized material. The magnetic structures of the platters are read or changed by read/write heads that move across the surface of the platters but are separated from it by a thin cushion of air. Virtually all platters are read from both sides.

Sectors per Track

The magnetic structures stored on the hard disk platters are organized into sectors of 512 data bytes each, plus additional areas in each sector for identifying the sector location on the hard disk. These sectors form concentric circles numbering from the outside of each platter to the hub area of the platter.

Cylinders

The third factor used to calculate the size of the hard disk is the number of cylinders on the hard disk. The identically positioned tracks on each side of every platter together make up a cylinder.

The BIOS calculates the size of the hard disk in MB—or more often today, GB—from the number of cylinders, the number of heads, and the number of sectors per track. Most BIOSs make this calculation in binary MB or GB (the same way as the hard disk preparation program FDISK does), but a few make the calculation in decimal MB or GB (see Chapter 1, "General Technical Reference," for the differences in these numbering methods). BIOSs that use decimal MB or GB calculations report the size of the drive the same way that drive manufacturers do. Either way, the same number of bytes will be available *if* the drive is fully and accurately handled by the ROM BIOS and operating system. Most recent and current drives print the cylinder, head, and sectors per track information (collectively called the drive's *geometry*) on a label on the top of the drive for easy reference during installation.

Note that all three elements of the drive geometry are actually logical, not physical, on IDE drives. This factor explains why the geometry can be translated (see the following), and why some IDE drives in older machines are working, despite being installed with "incorrect" geometries.

Use the worksheet at the end of Chapter 3, "BIOS Configurations and Upgrades," to record your hard drive geometry and other information for each system you manage.

IDE Hard Drive Identification

Integrated Drive Electronics (IDE), more properly called ATA drives (AT Attachment), are the overwhelming favorite for client PC installations. Although SCSI hard drives (see the following) offer benefits for network and high-performance workstation use, the combination of constantly-improving performance, rock bottom pricing per MB (under 1 cent and falling!), and enormous capacities (up to 75GB and climbing) will continue to make IDE/ATA drives the choice of most users. Figure 4.1 shows the typical IDE drive connectors.

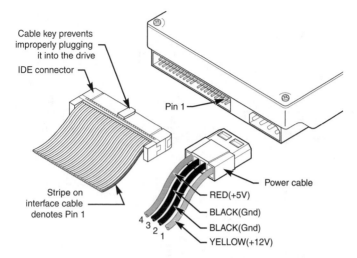

Figure 4.1   Typical ATA (IDE) hard drive connectors.

Master and Slave Drives

As Figure 4.2 demonstrates, virtually every IDE drive interface is designed to handle two drives with a single 40-pin interface cable.

Because the cable has no twist, unlike a typical 34-pin floppy interface cable, jumper blocks must be used on each hard drive to distinguish between the first (or *master*) drive on the cable and the second (or *slave*) drive on the cable.

Most IDE drives can be configured with four possible settings:

- Master (single-drive), also called Single
- Master (dual-drive)
- Slave (dual-drive)
- Cable Select

For virtually all systems, the Cable Select setting can be ignored because it must be used with a non-standard IDE cable. Thus, only three settings are really used, as seen in Table 4.1.

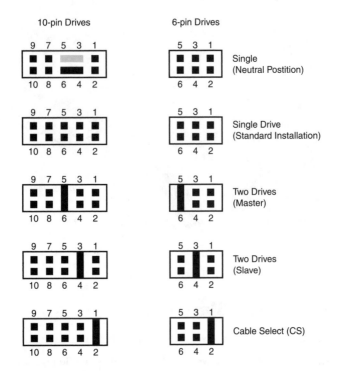

Figure 4.2   ATA (IDE) cable.

Table 4.1 Jumper Settings for Typical ATA IDE-Compatible Drives			
Jumper Name	**Single-Drive**	**Dual-Drive Master**	**Dual-Drive Slave**
Master (M/S)	On or off[1]	On	Off
Slave Present (SP)	Off	On	Off

1. Varies with drive; check user documentation.

Use Table 4.1 as a general guideline only. Follow your drive manufacturer's recommendations if they vary.

The jumpers on the hard drive might be located on the back of the drive (between the power and data connectors) or on the bottom of the drive. Typical hard disk jumpers are shown in Figure 4.3.

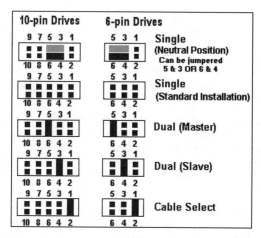

Figure 4.3   ATA (IDE) drive jumpers. Many drives now have eight, nine, or ten jumper pins to allow for special configurations required on some systems to break the 528-million-byte drive barrier (see the following sections).

Breaking the 504MB (528-Million-Byte) Drive Barrier

Because IDE was developed in the late 1980s, the combination of MS-DOS's limit of 1,024 cylinders, the standard BIOS's limit of 16 heads, and the IDE interface's limitation of 63 sectors per track limited the original size of IDE drives to 504MB (about 528 million bytes). This limit was merely theoretical until 1994, when IDE drives larger than this began to appear. A revised version of the IDE/ATA standard, ATA-2 (also called *enhanced IDE*) defined an enhanced BIOS to avoid these limits.

An enhanced BIOS circumvents the limits by using a different geometry when talking to the drive than when talking to the software. What happens in between is called *translation*. For example, if your drive has 2,000 cylinders and 16 heads, a translating BIOS will make programs think that the drive has 1,000 cylinders and 32 heads. The most common translation methods are listed in Table 4.2. These methods are also followed by newer versions of the ATA specification, such as ATA-3 and above.

Table 4.2 ATA-2 Translation Methods		
BIOS Mode	**Operating System to BIOS**	**BIOS to Drive Ports**
Standard CHS	Logical CHS Parameters	Logical CHS Parameters
Extended CHS	Translated CHS Parameters	Logical CHS Parameters
LBA	Translated CHS Parameters	LBA Parameters

A BIOS that supports only Standard CHS recognizes only a maximum of 1,024 cylinders, 16 heads, and 63 sectors per track for any IDE/ATA drive. Thus, if you install a 6.4GB IDE/ATA drive in a system with this type of BIOS, it will recognize only 504MB with MS-DOS and Windows. Non-DOS operating systems such as Novell NetWare, UNIX, and Linux don't require translation if they will be the only operating system on the disk partition.

On systems that provide translation, this BIOS mode is called *Normal* because the geometry isn't changed. Configuring a drive to use Normal mode is correct for operating systems such as UNIX, Linux, and Novell NetWare, but not for systems that use MS-DOS file structures, including MS-DOS itself, Windows 9x/NT/2000/Me, and OS/2.

The other two modes, Extended CHS and LBA (Logical Block Addressing), do translate the geometry. Extended CHS is also called *Large* mode and is recommended only for >504MB drives that cannot be operated in LBA mode. Most enhanced BIOSs don't offer Large mode, but all offer LBA mode. However, a few (such as older Acer BIOSs) might call it something different, such as DOS mode or >504MB mode.

Using LBA Mode

LBA mode can be enabled in two ways, depending on the BIOS. On most current BIOSs, using the automatic detection option in the BIOS or during system boot will detect the basic hard drive geometry and select LBA mode automatically. On some BIOSs, though, the automatic detection sets up the basic cylinder-head-sectors per track drive geometry but doesn't enable LBA mode unless you set it yourself. Depending on the BIOS release used by a given system, the LBA mode setting can be performed on the same BIOS configuration screen used for standard drive configuration, or it might be located on an Advanced CMOS configuration or Peripheral Setup screen.

A BIOS that performs LBA translation should enable you to use an IDE hard drive as large as 8.4GB with MS-DOS. If you find that you can use a 2.1GB hard disk, but not larger ones, the version of LBA mode supported by your BIOS is a very early version, and your BIOS should be updated. Support for drives larger than 8.4GB is discussed later in this chapter.

When LBA Mode Is Necessary—and When Not to Use It

Use Table 4.3 to determine when to use LBA mode.

Table 4.3	Using LBA Mode		
Drive Size	**Operating System**	**Use LBA Mode**	**Reason**
<=504MB	Any	No	Not necessary
>504MB	MS-DOS, Windows 9x/ NT/2000, OS/2	Yes	Drive will be limited to 504MB without LBA mode because of 1,024-cylinder limit
>504MB	Linux, UNIX, Novell NetWare	No	No 1,024-cylinder limit with these operating systems

Problems with LBA Support in the BIOS

Ideally, LBA mode would be automatically enabled in a clearly understood way on every system with an enhanced BIOS. And, it would also be easy to know when you did *not* need to use it. Unfortunately, this is often not the case.

Many 1994–1996 versions of the AMI text-based and graphical (WinBIOS) BIOSs listed the basic hard drive geometry on one screen and listed the LBA mode option on a different screen altogether. To make matters worse, the automatic drive setup options on many of these BIOSs didn't set the LBA mode for you; you had to find it and then set it. But perhaps the worst problem of all was for users who had carefully set the LBA mode and then ran into problems with other BIOS configurations. Most AMI BIOS versions offer a feature called *Automatic configuration* with either BIOS/Optimal defaults (high performance) or Power-On/Fail-Safe defaults (low performance). In AMI BIOSs in which the LBA mode was *not* listed on the same screen with the hard disk geometry, *any* automatic configuration would reset LBA mode to its default setting—off.

Because the location of the LBA setting can vary from system to system, always verify that LBA mode is still enabled if you make any changes to a BIOS configuration on systems that use LBA mode.

Dangers of Altering Translation Settings

Depending on the operating system and drive configuration, one of several unpleasant events takes place when LBA translation is turned off after a drive is configured using LBA. Table 4.4 summarizes these problems—some of which can be fatal to data!

Table 4.4   Problems Associated with Disabling LBA Mode

Drive Configuration	Operating System	Symptom	End Result
C: and D: partitions on single physical drive	MS-DOS	Can't access D: because part of it is beyond cylinder 1024.	Usually no harm to data, because drive is inaccessible until LBA mode is reset
C: or C:, D:, etc.	Windows 9x, Windows 2000, Windows NT, Windows Me	Can't boot drive because of incorrect geometry.	Usually no harm to data because drive is inaccessible until LBA mode is reset
C: only	MS-DOS	System boots and operates normally until data is written to a cylinder beyond 1024.	Drive wraps around to cylinder 0 (location of partition table and other vital disk structures) because LBA translation to access cylinders past 1024 is absent; drive overwrites beginning of disk, causing loss of all data

I used the last scenario in a computer troubleshooting class a few times, and it was quite a surprise to see a hard disk "eat" itself! However, it is never a good idea to "play" with LBA translation after it has been set in a system.

Detecting Lack of LBA Mode Support in Your System

To determine whether your system lacks LBA support or doesn't have LBA support enabled, do the following:

1. Install the hard drive set for Master, Slave, or Cable Select as appropriate.

2. Turn on the computer and detect the drive in the BIOS Setup program. Note the size of the drive reported.

3. Boot the computer from a floppy disk containing the operating system and FDISK.

4. Select the drive you want to view with option #5.

5. Use the #4 option—View Current Partitions—and check what capacity FDISK reports.

6. If FDISK reports the drive size as only 504MB and the drive is larger, LBA support is lacking or is not enabled.

7. Enable LBA mode and try steps 2–5 again. If FDISK reports the same or similar size to what the BIOS reports, your drive is being translated correctly by the BIOS if your hard disk is <=8.4.GB. If FDISK still reports a size significantly less than your hard disk's actual capacity, see Table 4.5 for solutions.

8. If your hard disk is >8.4GB *and* you are using Windows 9x/2000/Me/NT, the size that FDISK should report might be *greater* than what the BIOS displays. If FDISK reports only 8.4GB and the hard disk is larger, see Table 4.5 for solutions.

> **Note**
>
> Remember that hard drive manufacturers rate their hard disks in decimal MB or GB, and most BIOSs follow the FDISK standard for rating drives in binary MB or GB. See the MB, GB, and TB translation table (Table 1.2) in Chapter 1 for equivalents.

9. If you can't start the computer after installing the new hard drive, the BIOS is incapable of handling the drive's geometry. See Table 4.8 for solutions.

Using FDISK to Determine Compatibility Problems Between the Hard Disk and BIOS

A mismatch between the capacity that FDISK reports for a hard disk and what the BIOS reports for the hard disk indicates a problem with LBA translation or with support for hard disks above 8.4GB.

FDISK can also be used to determine when the dangerous "DOS wraparound" condition exists, in which a drive prepared with LBA translation has the LBA translation turned off.

I've included a mock-up of how the FDISK Display Partition Information screen appears. See the discussion of LBA mode earlier in this chapter for solutions. In Figure 4.7, FDISK indicates no problems, because the values for X (size of hard disk partition) and Y (total size of drive) are equal.

```
Display Partition Information      Current fixed
disk drive: 1
Label   Mbytes   System   Usage    C: 1
A       PRI DOS
```

```
Label      MBytes   System   Usage
Partition  Status   Type     Volume
W95US1U    1626     FAT16    100%
             X
```

```
    Total disk space is 1626 Mbytes (1 Mbyte =
1048576 bytes)
                        Y


    Press Esc to continue
```

X=Size of hard disk partition (drive has already been FDISKed)

Y=Total disk space (as seen by FDISK)

Use Table 4.5 to determine what the FDISK total disk space figure is telling you about your system.

Table 4.5	FDISK Disk Space Detected as a Guide to Disk Problems		
X Value[1]	**Y Value[2]**	**Drive Size**	**Underlying Cause**
>504MB	=504MB	>504MB Binary /FDISK (528MB Decimal)	Drive was prepared with LBA mode enabled, but LBA mode has been disabled in BIOS. See "Dangers of Altering Translation Settings" earlier in this chapter.
Not listed	=504MB	>504MB	LBA mode not enabled in BIOS or not present.
Not listed	8192MB	>8192MB (8.38 billion bytes)	BIOS supports LBA mode, but not Extended Int13h modes.

1. *The X value appears only when a drive has already been FDISKed.*

2. *The Y value appears on any drive being viewed through FDISK, whether the FDISK process has been completed or not.*

For more information about using FDISK, see the section "Using FDISK" later in this chapter.

Getting LBA and Extended Int13h Support for Your System

If your computer is incapable of detecting the full capacity of your hard disk or locks up after you install the hard drive, your BIOS is not compatible with your hard drive. Use Table 4.6 to determine the causes and solutions that will help you get full capacity from your new hard disk with maximum safety.

	Drive	Operating		
Symptom	**Size**	**System**	**Cause**	**Solution**
System locks up after installing new drive.	>2.1GB	Any	BIOS cannot handle 4,096 cylinders or more even with LBA enabled.	Upgrade BIOS (see Table 4.7).
	>32GB	Any	BIOS cannot handle capacity even with LBA enabled.	Upgrade BIOS (see Table 4.7).
Full capacity not available.	>504MB–8.4GB	MS-DOS, Windows 9x/NT/2000, OS/2	No LBA mode or inadequate LBA support in BIOS.	Upgrade BIOS (see Table 4.7).
	>8.4GB	Windows NT	Atapi.sys not correct version; BIOS lacks Extended Int13h support, required for large drives.	Update Atapi.sys (included in SP3 or above of NT 4.0) and upgrade BIOS if necessary (see Table 4.7).
	>8.4GB	Novell NetWare 4.11	Drivers are needed to support drive at full capacity.	Contact Novell for drivers; NetWare 5 will support >8.4GB drives; upgrade BIOS if necessary.
	>8.4GB	IBM OS/2 Warp	Patch needed to support drive at full capacity.	Contact IBM for patch file; upgrade BIOS if necessary.
	>8.4GB	Windows 9x Windows 2000 Windows Me	Windows 9x has Enhanced Int13h support for drive, but BIOS lacks support.	Upgrade BIOS (see Table 4.7).
	>8.4GB	MS-DOS	MS-DOS can't use IDE drives above 8.4GB.	Buy 8.4GB or below; update to Windows 9x; use SCSI drives; use big.

Table 4.6 Why IDE Drive Is Not Detected at Full Capacity

Determining Whether Your System Supports Extended Int13h

Drives that are 8.4GB or larger require Extended Int13h support in the BIOS to be accessible at full capacity. This size represents a second barrier to drive capacity for MS-DOS, and one that cannot be overcome without changing to a different type of drive (SCSI) or making the move to Windows 9x/2000/Me.

Even if you have updated versions of operating systems that support IDE capacities beyond 8.4GB, your BIOS must also offer this support. Table 4.7 describes the differences between how LBA and Extended Int13h drive support work.

Table 4.7	LBA Mode Versus Extended Int13h	
Mode	**Setting**	**BIOS Drive Capacity Listing**
LBA	Must be set in BIOS by user or automatically by drive-type detection.	Indicates full capacity of drive; might or might not indicate translation in BIOS.
Extended Int13h	Automatically enabled when LBA mode is enabled on systems that support Extended Int13h functions.	BIOS configuration might or might not indicate full capacity of drive.

This support is not "visible" in the BIOS; there is no Enhanced Int13h option to enable as there is with LBA mode.

Also, in some cases, the geometry reported by drives of varying sizes doesn't change either. On a system that supports Extended Int13h but doesn't display the full drive capacity in the BIOS configuration, an 8.4GB hard disk will report a geometry to the BIOS of 16 heads, 16,383 cylinders, and 63 sectors per track, and a 20.4GB hard disk reports the same geometry! Support of hard disks beyond 8.4GB on some systems breaks the usual rule about the BIOS configuration matching the drive's capacity.

As with the previously mentioned LBA mode issues, use FDISK to determine whether your system supports your greater-than-8.4GB IDE hard drive at full capacity.

Drive Capacity Issues in Microsoft Windows 95 and 98

Table 4.8 lists the capacity limitations and issues for Windows 95 and 98.

Table 4.8	Drive Capacity Issues for Windows 95 and 98	
Windows Version	**Drive Capacity Limitation**	**Fix**
Windows 95 (all releases)	32GB	None; upgrade to Windows 98, NT, 2000, or Me before installing larger hard drive. See Microsoft online document Q246818 for details.

Table 4.8	**Drive Capacity Issues for Windows 95 and 98 Continued**	
Windows Version	**Drive Capacity Limitation**	**Fix**
Windows 98 (all releases)	32GB and up	Graphical version of ScanDisk lists errors for all sectors beyond 32GB on some systems using Phoenix BIOS with BitShift IDE drive translation. See Microsoft online document Q243450 for download (Microsoft Knowledgebase). Use command-line ScanDisk as a workaround.
Windows 98 (all releases)	64GB and up	Drive works at full capacity, but FDISK reports capacity as 64GB lower than actual; see Microsoft online document Q263044 for patch download instructions.
Windows 98 (all releases)	64GB and up	FORMAT run from command line reports capacity as 64GB lower than actual, but FORMAT works correctly; use FORMAT option within Windows Explorer as a workaround. See Microsoft online document Q263045.

Sources for BIOS Upgrades and Alternatives for Large IDE Hard Disk Support

If your BIOS doesn't support the full capacity of your hard disk, use Table 4.9 to choose your best solution.

Table 4.9	**Sources for BIOS and Alternative Support for Large Hard Drives**		
Solution	**Benefits**	**Cost**	**Concerns**
Upgrade BIOS.	Best all-around solution to hard disk and other support issues.	Free if BIOS is Flash type and is supported by motherboard or system maker. If BIOS is no longer supported by MB or manufacturer, purchase upgrade.	Be sure to correctly identify your system or motherboard before installing the upgrade; test afterward (see Chapter 3 for details). See Chapter 3 for sources and system details.

Table 4.9   Sources for BIOS and Alternative Support for Large Hard Drives Continued

Solution	Benefits	Cost	Concerns
Purchase BIOS upgrade card.	May be less expensive than purchasing BIOS replacement or new motherboard; fast, easy install.	$35–$75; can be combined with Y2K date-rollover support or UDMA 33/66 features.	Make sure card is designed for full capacity of your hard disk; many early versions had 2.1GB or 8.4GB limits; requires open ISA or PCI slot.
Use BIOS replacement feature in hard disk installation software supplied with drive.	You probably received a copy of it with your drive.	Download it from your hard disk vendor if your drive didn't come with a copy.	Worst choice for large hard disk support because software drivers and non-standard disk structures can be altered and destroyed very easily.

After you decide on a strategy for handling the full capacity of your hard disk, don't change it! Don't use a BIOS replacement option in a program such as Disk Manager or EZ-Drive and then decide to install a BIOS upgrade (flash, chip, or card). The BIOS support won't be capable of working with your drive because it's already being translated by the software. Make your choice before you finish your drive installation.

Standard and Alternative Jumper Settings

If you decide to use the BIOS replacement software shipped with the hard drive instead of downloading or purchasing a BIOS upgrade, you might need to use alternative jumper settings on your hard disk. An example of these settings as used by some Western Digital drives with capacities at 32GB or above is shown in Figure 4.4. Many other drive makers use similar approaches to deal with this problem, as well as with the previous capacity limitation of 2.5GB seen with older systems. Note that two jumper blocks are used; the normal master and slave jumper block plus a second jumper block to reduce the reported capacity of the drive.

The Normal configurations (top) are used for IDE drives installed in systems whose BIOSs can handle drives with capacities over 32GB.

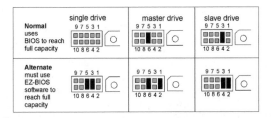

Figure 4.4   Normal (top) and Alternative (bottom) jumpers for Western Digital 32GB or larger IDE hard disks with 10-pin jumper blocks.

The Alternate configurations (bottom)are used to limit the drive's reported capacity to less than 32GB. This configuration is required if installing a drive with more than 32GB of capacity causes the system to lock up because of BIOS incompatibilities. This condition affects many systems with BIOS dates before 6/1/1999. While jumpering details vary from brand to brand, two jumper blocks are used in almost all cases.

A drive configured this way requires the use of EZ-Drive, MAXBlast, or other drive-manufacturer–supplied disk utility programs to access the full capacity of the drive. In some cases, the system might need to be shut down at the end of a session rather than warm-booted. Check with the drive manufacturer for details on using this configuration with Windows NT/2000 or with Linux, UNIX, or Novell NetWare.

Improving Hard Disk Speed

Although the ATA-2/EIDE standard is best known for establishing LBA mode as a means of allowing larger hard drives to be used on the IDE interface, a second major benefit of ATA-2/EIDE was improving data transfer rates, as shown in Table 4.10.

Table 4.10	PIO Modes and Transfer Rates		
PIO Mode	**Cycle Time (ns)**	**Transfer Rate (MB/Sec)**	**Specification**
0	600	3.33	ATA
1	383	5.22	ATA
2	240	8.33	ATA
3	180	11.11	ATA-2, EIDE, fast-ATA
4	120	16.67	ATA-2, EIDE, fast-ATA

PIO modes 0–2 could be achieved with the original 16-bit mother-board or expansion slot-based IDE/ATA host adapters, but PIO modes 3 and above require a local-bus connection—either VL-Bus, PCI card, or (most often) a PCI motherboard connection.

The first ATA-2/EIDE hard drives introduced in 1994 were capable of PIO 3 transfer rates, but newer drives run at PIO 4 transfer rates or above. Most recent BIOSs detect the correct PIO mode as well as the basic drive geometry and set it for you. On BIOSs that offer a PIO mode setting that you must make manually, consult the drive vendor for the correct mode. Setting the PIO mode too high will cause data corruption.

Ultra DMA

The newest hard drives and motherboards support an even faster method of data transfer called Ultra DMA, or UDMA for short. See Table 4.11 for common Ultra DMA modes.

Table 4.11	Common Ultra DMA Modes	
UDMA Mode	**Transfer Rate (MB/Sec)**	**Specification**
2	33.33	ATA-4, Ultra-ATA/33
4	66.67	ATA-5, Ultra-ATA/66
5	100.00	Ultra-ATA/100

With both PIO and UDMA modes, the transfer rates listed are maximum (burst) transfer rates; sustained rates are much slower. Nevertheless, you will want to run your hard disk at the highest PIO or UDMA mode it's capable of.

UDMA/66 and UDMA/100 Issues

Most of the greater-than-10GB hard drives now on the market are designed to support UDMA/66 (also called Ultra ATA-66) *if* certain requirements are met; many larger drives also support the even faster UDMA/1000 standard introduced in the summer of 2000. Table 4.12 lists the requirements for UDMA/66 and UDMA/100 compliance.

Table 4.12	Ultra DMA/66 and UDMA/100 Requirements	
Item	**Features**	**Notes**
Drive	Drive must have firmware for desired mode.	Some drives automatically sense compliance; others require you to run a configuration program to enable the mode; consult drive vendor.
Motherboard chipset	Must have UDMA/66 or UDMA/100 support.	Check system or MB vendor for compliance; for highest performance, you should also install an UDMA device driver for operating system (see Table 4.13).

Table 4.12	Ultra DMA/66 and UDMA/100 Requirements Continued	
Item	**Features**	**Notes**
		If motherboard can't run drive at full speed, you can add a UDMA/66 or UDMA/100 PCI-based IDE interface card from sources such as SIIG (www.siig.com) or Promise Technologies (www.promise.com).
Cable	Cable must be 80-wire cable (40 data wires separated by 40 ground wires).	Connect blue end of UDMA/66 and UDMA/100 data cable to mother-board to ensure proper operation.

Any system that cannot run the drive at UDMA/66 or UDMA/100 can use the drive at the system's maximum speed (UDMA/33, PIO 4, and so on).

See Figure 4.5 for a comparison of a standard IDE 40-wire cable with an 80-wire cable required for UDMA/66 and UDMA/100 operation.

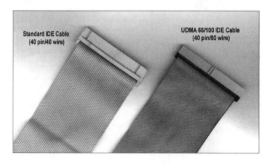

Figure 4.5 A standard 40-wire IDE cable (left) compared to an 80-wire UDMA/66-100 IDE cable (right). Both cables use the same 40-pin connector. The standard cable's 40 wires give the cable a pronounced ridged appearance when compared to the smaller and finer wires in the 80-wire cable.

Bus-Mastering Chipsets for IDE

Most late-model Pentium-class and higher motherboards can support bus-mastering drivers for their IDE interfaces. The benefits of bus-mastering include faster IDE data transfer for CD-ROM, CD-R/CD-RW, and hard drives, and lower CPU utilization rates (the percentage of total time the CPU spends handling a particular task). Table 4.13 lists the major chipsets providing bus-mastering features and where to get the driver. Be sure you install the correct driver for your chipset.

Even if you enable UDMA/33 or faster UDMA modes in your system BIOS, you must install the bus-mastering driver for your hardware and operating system to get the maximum benefit out of your UDMA-compatible drives.

Table 4.13   Bus-Mastering Chipsets by Vendor and Operating System

Vendor	Chipsets	Driver Source by Operating System
Intel	430FX 430HX 430VX 440FX 430TX 440LX 440BX 440EX 440GX 440ZX 440ZX-66 450NX	(Same driver for all Intel chipsets at left) Windows 95 original and OSR1 (95a): Download BM-IDE driver from the Intel Web site. Windows 95B, 95C (OSR 2.x), Windows 98: Included on Windows CD-ROM.
Intel	810 810E 820 840	Download Ultra ATA Storage Driver (version 5.x or above) from Intel Web site. Works with Windows 98, 98SE, Windows 2000, and Windows NT 4.0. All but Windows 2000 require use of Chipset Software Installation Utility; download from Intel Web site.
VIA Apollo	KX133 Pro 133A Pro Plus Pro PM-601 MPV4 MVP3 VP3 VP2 VPX VP1	For Windows 95 (any version) and NT 3.51 and higher: Download the drivers from the VIA Web site. For Windows 98, 2000, Me: Included on CD-ROM.
SiS	611 85c496 5513**, 5581/5582, 5591, 5571*** 5597/5598, 5600 IDE Driver* SiS530/5595 & SiS620/5595 IDE Driver	Download the drivers from the SiS Web site. *(For SiS chipsets 5511/5512/5513, 5596/ 5513, 5571, 5581/5582, 5598/5597, 5591/ 5595, 600/5595) **(Separate driver available for use with Windows 2000) ***(Separate driver available for use with Windows 98)
ETEQ	Various motherboard models	See www.soyo.com.tw to look up models and drivers; download there or from related FTP site.

Table 4.13 Bus-Mastering Chipsets by Vendor and Operating System Continued		
Vendor	**Chipsets**	**Driver Source by Operating System**
PCChips	Various motherboard models	See www.pcchips.com to look up IDE drivers by model and operating system (Windows 95, 98, and Windows NT 4.0).
Ali (Acer Labs) (see note) Aladdin V Aladdin Pro2 Linux www.acerlabs.com	Aladdin III Aladdin IV Windows 95/98/NT	Windows 95/NT

All Intel chipsets that contain a PIIXn device (PIIX, PIIX3, PIIX4, PIIX4E, and so on) are bus-mastering chipsets.

Although PCChips chipset names are similar to certain Intel Pentium chipsets (Triton series TX, HX, and VX), the drivers listed are strictly for PCChips chipsets, not Intel's.

ALi (Acer Labs) recommends checking with motherboard manufacturers' Web sites first for drivers because drivers might be customized for a particular vendor's products.

Benefits of Manual Drive Typing

Even though virtually every BIOS used since the mid-1990s supports automatic drive detection (also called *drive typing*) at startup, a couple of benefits to performing this task within the BIOS configuration screen do exist:

- In the event that you need to move the drive to another system, you'll know the drive geometry and translation scheme (such as LBA) that was used to access the drive. If the drive is moved to another computer, the identical drive geometry (cylinder, head, sectors per track) and translation scheme must be used in the other computer; otherwise, the data on the drive will not be accessible and can be lost. Because many systems with autoconfiguration don't display these settings during the startup process, performing the drive-typing operation yourself might be the only way to get this information.

- If you want to remove a drive that is already in use and the BIOS displays the drive geometry, write it down! Because the IDE interface enables a drive to work with *any* defined geometry that doesn't exceed the drive's capacity, the current BIOS configuration for any given drive might *not* be what the manufacturer recommends (and what would be detected by the BIOS, using the IDE identify drive command). I ran a 203MB Conner drive successfully for years with an incorrect BIOS setting that provided 202MB, because technical information about drives in the early days of IDE wasn't always easy to get. Drives working with the "wrong" geometry should *not* be "corrected" because this would require a complete backup of the drive and resetting the geometry in the BIOS, FDISK, FORMAT, and restore. Just label the drive with the actual head, cylinder, and sectors per track it uses now.

Troubleshooting IDE Installation

In addition to the BIOS capacity and PIO/UDMA mode configuration issues, you might run into other problems during an IDE drive installation. Use Table 4.14 to determine problems, causes, and solutions.

Table 4.14   Other IDE Drive Installation Problems and Solutions

Problem	Causes	Solution
Drive is not recognized by BIOS, but system will boot from floppy (drive is spinning).	Drive cabling installed incorrectly.	Make sure pin 1 on IDE interface and IDE drive are connected to pin 1 (colored edge) of IDE cable; some cables are keyed with a plugged hole at pin 20 or with a "bump" over the middle of the cable that corresponds with a cutout in the plastic skirt that surrounds the cable. On non-skirted motherboard IDE connectors, make sure pins are connected to both rows of the cable, without any offsets.
System display remains blank after power on. No boot or other activity.	Drive cabling reversed; pin 1 is connected to pin 39 at either drive or interface connector.	Many systems cannot initialize the video card until the IDE hard drive is successfully initialized. Use of keyed cables will help to eliminate this problem (see previous tip).
Drive not recognized by BIOS, but system will boot from floppy (drive is not spinning).	Drive power cable is not connected or defective.	If a Y-splitter or power extender is in use, check it for damage or remove it and plug drive directly to power supply; make sure Molex power connector is tightly inserted into drive; use a Digital Multimeter (DMM) to check power leads; drive might be defective if power checks out okay.
One or both IDE drives on a single cable are not recognized by system (drives are spinning).	Drives might be jumpered incorrectly: both as master or both as slave.	Jumper boot drive as master, second drive.

Table 4.14 Other IDE Drive Installation Problems and Solutions Continued		
Problem	**Causes**	**Solution**
One or both IDE drives on a single cable are not recognized by system (drives are spinning and are jumpered correctly).	Drives might not be 100% compliant with ATA standards (very likely when trying to mix various brands of IDE drives, especially older ones).	Reverse master and slave jumpering; move second drive to other IDE connector and jumper both drives accordingly.

SCSI

The small computer system interface (SCSI) is a very flexible and high-performance drive and device interface. In addition to supporting hard drives, it also can support non-bootable optical and tape storage, scanners, and many other device types.

SCSI Types and Data Transfer Rates

While many types of SCSI exist, different SCSI types can be mixed on the same host adapter. For best results, you should buy a host adapter capable of running your fastest devices at their top speeds *and* one that enables various types of devices to run without slowing each other down. Use Table 4.15 to learn common SCSI types and their characteristics.

Table 4.15 SCSI Data-Transfer Rates						
Bus Width	**Standard SCSI**	**Fast SCSI**[1]	**Fast-20 (Ultra)**[2]	**Fast-40 (Ultra2)**[2]	**Fast-80 (Ultra3)**[2]	**Cable Type**
8-bit (narrow)	5MB/sec	10MB/sec	20MB/sec	40MB/sec	80MB/sec	A (50-pin)
16-bit (wide)	10MB/sec	20MB/sec	40MB/sec	80MB/sec	160MB/sec[3]	P (68-pin)

1. *SCSI-2*

2. *SCSI-3*

3. *Ultra2Wide*

> **Note**
>
> The A cable is the standard 50-pin SCSI cable, whereas the P
> cable is a 68-pin cable designed for 16-bit. Maximum cable
> length is 6 meters (about 20 feet) for standard speed SCSI, and
> only 3 meters (about 10 feet) for Fast/Fast-20/Fast-40 (Ultra)
> SCSI. Ultra2Wide allows cable lengths up to 12 meters (about
> 40 feet!).

Single-Ended Versus Differential SCSI

SCSI is not only a flexible interface, it's also a multi-platform interface. Traditionally, PCs have used single-ended SCSI, whereas other
platforms use differential SCSI. Because these two types of SCSI are
not interchangeable, you should never mix them on a host adapter
designed for single-ended SCSI. Use the markings in Figure 4.6 to
distinguish between these.

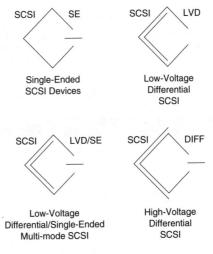

Figure 4.6   Single-ended and differential SCSI universal symbols.

Low-Voltage Differential Devices

Ultra2Wide SCSI devices, which run at 80MB/sec maximum transfer
rates, use a modified version of differential SCSI called low-voltage
differential (LVD). Workstation-oriented cards, such as Adaptec's
AHA-2940U2W, enable the use of LVD Ultra2Wide devices and

standard single-ended SCSI devices on the same card. Cards with this feature use two buses—one for LVD and one for standard SCSI devices.

> **Note**
>
> If you do need to use single-ended and differential SCSI devices on the same cable, adapters are available that will safely handle the connection. Paralan Corporation (4655 Ruffner St., San Diego, CA 92111, Tel.: (858) 560-7266; Fax: (858) 560-8929, www.paralan.com) offers the SD10B and SD16B adapters.

Recognizing SCSI Interface Cables and Connectors

Because SCSI is actually a family of standards, each with its own cable and connector, matching cables and connectors to the appropriate SCSI "family member" is important. Use the following figures to determine this information.

8-Bit SCSI Centronics 50-Pin Connector

Older, narrow (8-bit) SCSI adapters and external devices use a full-size Centronics type connector that normally has wire latches on each side to secure the cable connector. Figure 4.7 shows what the low-density, 50-pin SCSI connector looks like.

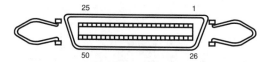

Figure 4.7   Low-density, 50-pin SCSI connector.

SCSI-2 High-Density Connector

The SCSI-2 revision added a high-density, 50-position, D-shell connector option for the A-cable connectors. This connector now is called Alternative 1. Figure 4.8 shows the 50-pin high-density SCSI connector.

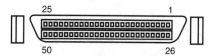

Figure 4.8   High-density, 50-pin SCSI connector.

The Alternative 2 Centronics latch-style connector remains unchanged from SCSI-1.

SCSI-3 68-Pin P Cable

A new 68-conductor P cable was developed as part of the SCSI-3 specification. Shielded and unshielded high-density D-shell connectors are specified for both the A and P cable. The shielded high-density connectors use a squeeze-to-release latch rather than the wire latch used on the Centronics-style connectors. Active termination for single-ended buses is specified, providing a high level of signal integrity. Figure 4.9 shows the 68-pin high density SCSI connector.

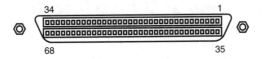

Figure 4.9   High-density, 68-pin SCSI connector.

RAID Array, Hot Swappable 80-Pin Connector

Drive arrays normally use special SCSI drives with what is called an 80-pin Alternative-4 connector, which is capable of wide SCSI and also includes power signals. Drives with the 80-pin connector are normally *hot swappable*—they can be removed and installed with the power on—in drive arrays. The 80-pin Alt-4 connector is shown in Figure 4.10.

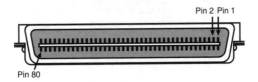

Figure 4.10   80-pin Alt-4 SCSI connector.

Apple and some other non-standard implementations from other vendors (such as Iomega SCSI Zip drives) used a 25-pin cable and connector for SCSI devices.

They did this by eliminating most of the grounds from the cable, which unfortunately resulted in a noisy, error-prone connection. I don't recommend using 25-pin cables and connectors; you should avoid them if possible. The connector used in these cases was a standard female DB-25 connector, which looks exactly like a PC parallel port (printer) connector. Unfortunately, it is possible to

damage equipment by plugging printers into DB-25 SCSI connectors or by plugging SCSI devices into DB-25 printer connectors. So,
if you use this type of SCSI connection, be sure it is marked well,
because it's impossible to tell DB-25 SCSI from DB-25 parallel
printer connectors by looking at them. The DB-25 connector is
shown in Figure 4.11.

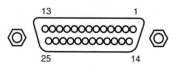

Figure 4.11   DB-25 SCSI connector.

Again, I recommend you avoid making SCSI connections using this
type of cable or connector. If you must use this type of device, add
it to the end of the daisy-chain. The 25-wire connector can prevent
important signals from reaching devices designed to use 50-pin
connectors, causing them to not be initialized and not function.

SCSI Drive and Device Configuration

SCSI drives (and other devices) are not too difficult to configure,
but they are more complicated than IDE drives. The SCSI standard
controls the way the drives must be set up. You need to set two
items when you configure a SCSI drive or device:

- SCSI ID setting (0–7 or 0–15)

- Terminating resistors

The number of SCSI IDs available on a host adapter depends on its
design: 0–7 on SCSI adapters with an 8-bit bus; 0–15 on SCSI
adapters with a 16-bit bus; two groups of 0–15 on a 16-bit bus with
a dual-processor host bus adapter.

SCSI Device ID

Up to 7 SCSI devices (plus the adapter, for a total of 8) can be used
on a single narrow SCSI bus (8-bit) or up to 15 devices (plus the
adapter, for a total of 16) on a wide (16-bit) SCSI bus. Now, dual-
processor, 16-bit host adapters are available that can operate up to
30 devices plus the host adapter. In every case, each device must
have a unique SCSI ID address. The host adapter takes one address,
so the rest are free for up to 7 SCSI peripherals (or more as defined
by the host adapter). Most SCSI host adapters are factory-set to ID 7

or 15, which is the highest priority ID. All other devices must have unique IDs that do not conflict with one another. Some host adapters boot only from a hard disk set to a specific ID. Older Adaptec host adapters required the boot hard disk to be ID 0; newer ones can boot from any ID. A SCSI device containing multiple drives (such as a CD-ROM tower or changer) will have a single ID, but each physical drive or logical drive will also be known by a logical unit number (LUN). For example, a 5-CD changer is SCSI ID #3. Each "virtual drive" or disc position within SCSI ID #3 has a LUN of 0–4. So the last "drive" has drive letter J and is also identified by Windows as SCSI ID#3, LUN 4.

Setting the SCSI ID

The methods for setting the SCSI ID vary with the device. For internal drives, the settings are made with jumper blocks. Use Table 4.16 to set the jumpers. Note that the column to the left is the lowest numbered ID jumper, which may be identified as A0 or SCSI ID0, depending on the drive vendor.

Table 4.16	SCSI ID Jumper Settings				
SCSI ID#	ID A0	Jumper A1	Settings A2	A3	(WD and Quantum Markings)
	ID0	ID1	ID2	ID3	(Seagate Markings)
00	0	0	0	0	
01	1	0	0	0	
02	0	1	0	0	
03	1	1	0	0	
04	0	0	1	0	
05	1	0	1	0	
06	0	1	1	0	
07	1	1	1	0	
08	0	0	0	1	
09	1	0	0	1	
10	0	1	0	1	
11	1	1	0	1	
12	0	0	1	1	
13	1	0	1	1	
14	0	1	1	1	
15	1	1	1	1	

1 = Jumper On, 0 = Jumper Off

SCAM—Automatic ID Setting

Some SCSI hard drives and host adapters support SCAM (SCSI Configure AutoMagically), which automatically assigns the drive a unique SCSI ID number. To use SCAM, both the host adapter and drive must support SCAM, and SCAM must be enabled (usually by a jumper on the drive).

SCSI ID Setting for External Devices

SCSI drives and devices can be used both internally and externally, often with the same interface card. For external devices, one of the following methods will apply for each device in the SCSI daisy-chain. Use Table 4.14 as a general reference. Typically, the ID setting control is at the back of the device, near the SCSI interface cable. Depending on the device, the device ID can be set by a rotary dial, a push-button control, or a sliding switch. Not all SCSI ID numbers are available with every device; many low-cost devices allow a choice of only two or three numbers. Regardless of the setting method, each internal and external device on a single SCSI daisy-chain of devices must have a unique ID! If you use Adaptec SCSI interface cards, use the SCSI Interrogator program before you add a new SCSI device to determine which device IDs you have remaining. If you are adding a new SCSI device with limited ID choices (such as the Iomega Zip 100 SCSI drive), you might need to move an existing device to another ID to make room for the new device.

For high-performance SCSI cards that offer multiple buses, you should be able to reuse device numbers 0–7 for each separate bus on the card. If you have problems with duplicate ID numbers on various buses, the device drivers for either the device or the interface card might not be up-to-date. Contact the device and card maker for assistance.

SCSI Termination

SCSI termination is simple. Termination is required at both ends of the bus; there are no exceptions. If the host adapter is at one end of the bus, it must have termination enabled. On the other hand, if the host adapter is in the middle of the bus—and if both internal and external bus links are present—the host adapter must have its termination disabled, and the devices at each end of the bus must have terminators installed. Unfortunately, the majority of problems that I see with SCSI installations are the result of improper termination.

Terminators can be external or internal (set with a jumper block or with switches or sliders). Some devices also terminate themselves automatically.

The pass-through models are required when a device is at the end of the bus and only one SCSI connector is available.

SCSI Configuration Troubleshooting

When you are installing a chain of devices on a single SCSI bus, the installation can get complicated very quickly. Here are some tips for getting your setup to function quickly and efficiently:

- **Start by adding one device at a time**—Rather than plugging numerous peripherals into a single SCSI card and then trying to configure them at the same time, start by installing the host adapter and a single hard disk. Then, you can continue installing devices one at a time, checking to make sure that everything works before moving on.

- **Keep good documentation**—When you add a SCSI peripheral, write down the SCSI ID address and any other switch and jumper settings, such as SCSI Parity, Terminator Power, and Delayed or Remote Start. For the host adapter, record the BIOS addresses, IRQ, DMA channel, and I/O Port addresses used by the adapter, and any other jumper or configuration settings (such as termination) that might be important to know later.

- **Use proper termination**—Each end of the bus must be terminated, preferably with active or Forced Perfect (FPT) terminators. If you are using any Fast SCSI-2 device, you must use active terminators rather than the cheaper, passive types. Even with standard (slow) SCSI devices, active termination is highly recommended. If you have only internal or external devices on the bus, the host adapter and last device on the chain should be terminated. If you have external and internal devices on the chain, you generally will terminate the first and last of these devices but not the SCSI host adapter (which is in the middle of the bus).

- **Use high-quality shielded SCSI cables**—Make sure that your cable connectors match your devices. Use high-quality shielded cables and observe the SCSI bus-length limitations. Use cables designed for SCSI use and, if possible, stick to the same brand of cable throughout a single SCSI bus. Various brands of cables have different impedance values, which sometimes causes problems, especially in long or high-speed SCSI implementations.

- **Have the correct driver for your SCSI host adapter and for each device**—SCSI, unlike IDE, is not controlled by your computer's motherboard BIOS, but by software drivers. A SCSI device cannot be used unless the appropriate software drivers are installed for it. As with any other software-driven peripheral, these drivers are often updated periodically. Check for improved drivers and install them as needed.

Following these tips will help minimize problems and leave you with a trouble-free SCSI installation.

Use Table 4.17 to help you record SCSI information. Table 4.18 shows a form I use to record data about my system. You can attach this information to the System Template referred to in Chapter 2, "System Components and Configuration."

Table 4.17	SCSI Device Data Sheet			
Interface Card	**IRQ**	**DMA**	**I/O Port Address**	**Slot Type**
Interface card Notes and details				
Device information				
Include SCSI interface card and all devices below				
Device ID Y/N	**Device Name**	**Internal or External**	**Cable/ Connector Type**	**Terminated?**
0				
1				
2				
3				
4				
5				
6				
7				
8				
9				
10				
11				
12				
13				
14				
15				

Table 4.18   Completed SCSI Device Data Sheet

Interface Card	IRQ	DMA	I/O Port Address	Slot Type
Adaptec AHA-1535	10	5	0130h–0133h	ISA
Interface Card Notes and Details	Bus-mastering card with internal and external cable connectors; allows pass-through so that both connectors can be used at once			

Device Information

Include SCSI interface card and all devices

Device ID Y/N	Device Name	Internal or External	Cable/ Connector Type	Terminated?
0				
1				
2	Epson Expression 636 flatbed scanner with transparency adapter	External	50-pin Centronics	No
3	Polaroid SprintScan 35Plus slide and filmstrip scanner	External	50-pin Centronics and DB-25 25-pin	Yes
4	Philips CDD2600 CD-Recorder (CD-R)	Internal	50-pin ribbon cable	Yes
5				
6	Iomega Zip 100 Zip drive	External	DB-25 25-pin	No
7	Adaptec AHA-1535 SCSI host adapter card	Internal	50-pin ribbon (internal)	
			50-pin high-density (external)	No
8–15	(No devices)			

Note that both ends of the daisy-chain are terminated and that the actual end of the internal daisy-chain is *not* the AHA-1535 SCSI host adapter, but the Philips CDD2600 drive. Also note that some SCSI devices support different types of cables.

Use the worksheet shown in Figure 4.12 to help you plan your SCSI cabling and physical layout. Start with the host adapter card. Figure 4.13 shows a completed worksheet.

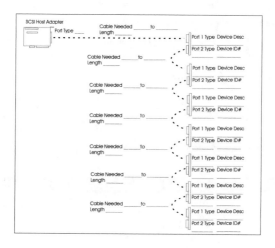

Figure 4.12   SCSI Cabling Worksheet (blank). See Figure 4.13 for a completed example. Use data recorded on the SCSI Device Data Sheet shown in Table 4.18.

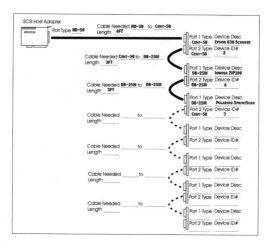

Figure 4.13   SCSI Cabling Worksheet (completed). This uses data from the completed SCSI Device Data Sheet from Table 4.18.

Hard Disk Preparation

The formatting process for a hard disk drive subsystem has three major steps:

1. Low-level formatting

2. Partitioning

3. High-level formatting

Table 4.19 outlines the steps for preparing a drive for use after installation.

Table 4.19 Comparing the Steps in the Formatting Process		
Process Step	**When Necessary**	**How Performed**
Low-level formatting (LLF)	IDE and SCSI hard drives are low-level formatted at the factory; reformat only to correct errors.	
	With SCSI only, to configure drive for use with a specified host adapter and its driver software. This is usually required for Windows 3.x/MS-DOS systems, but not for Windows 9x systems.	Use factory-supplied LLF or diagnostic utilities; use Ontrack Disk Manager (generic or OEM version); use MicroScope version 7 software for IDE. For SCSI, use the host adapter's BIOS or software routines (such as Adaptec's EZ-SCSI) if necessary.
Partitioning	Always required for both SCSI and IDE hard drives; indicates which portion of the drive will be used for each operating system and how the drive letters will be defined.	Use operating system utility (FDISK or equivalent) if BIOS provides full support for drive capacity; EZ-Drive, Disk Manager, and similar products can be used for both FDISK and FORMAT options.
		With SCSI drives under Windows 3.x/MS-DOS, host-adapter–specific partitioning and formatting routines are normally used.
High-level formatting	Always required for all drive letters defined by FDISK or partitioning utility.	Use operating system utility (FORMAT or equivalent); EZ-Drive, Disk Manager, and similar products can be used for both FDISK and FORMAT options.
		With SCSI drives under Windows 3.x/MS-DOS, host-adapter–specific partitioning and formatting routines are normally used.

Using FDISK

FDISK is the partitioning utility used with MS-DOS, Windows 95, and above and has equivalents in all other operating systems. In most cases with SCSI and all cases with IDE drives, it's the first software program you run after you physically install a hard disk and properly detect it in the BIOS.

FDISK is used to set aside disk space (or an entire physical drive) for use by an operating system, and to specify how many and what size the logical drives will be within that space. By default, the MS-DOS and Windows 9x versions of FDISK prepares a single physical drive as a single drive letter (up to the limits listed), but FDISK can also be used to create multiple drives. By not preparing all of a hard disk's capacity with FDISK, you can use the remaining room on the hard disk for another operating system.

Drive-Letter Size Limits

We've already considered the physical drive size limits caused by BIOS limitations and how to overcome them. Those limits define the maximum size a *physical* hard drive can be. However, depending on the version of Windows in use (and with any version of MS-DOS), it might be necessary to subdivide a hard drive through the use of FDISK to allow its full capacity to be used through the creation of multiple logical drive letters.

The original release of Windows 95 and all versions of MS-DOS from DOS 3.3x support FAT16, which allows no more than 65,536 files per drive and a single drive letter no more than 2.1GB in size. Thus, a 6GB hard disk prepared with MS-DOS or the original Windows 95 must have at a minimum three drive letters and could have more (see Figure 4.14). The primary disk partition (C: on a single drive system) can be bootable and contains only a single drive letter. An extended partition, which cannot be bootable, contains the remainder of the drive letters (called *logical DOS drives* in most versions of FDISK).

Large Hard Disk Support

If you use the Windows 95B or above (Win95 OSR 2.x), Windows 98, or Windows Me versions of FDISK with a hard drive greater than 512MB, FDISK offers to enable large hard disk support.

Choosing to enable large hard disk support provides several benefits:

- You can use a large hard disk (greater than 2.1GB) as a single drive letter; in fact, your drive can be as large as 2TB and still be identified by a single drive letter. This is because of the FAT-32 file system, which allows for many more files per drive than FAT-16.

- Because of the more efficient storage methods of FAT-32, your files will use less hard disk space. FAT-32 is not supported by Windows NT 4.0 or earlier, but is supported by Windows 2000.

- Note that a FAT-32 drive cannot be directly accessed by older versions (pre-OSR 2.x) of Windows 95, Windows 3.1x/MS-DOS, or any other operating system. If you occasionally need to run older applications that cannot run under Windows 95B or Windows 98 and you want to store those applications on a hard drive, be sure you create a hard drive letter that uses FAT-16. This way you can boot your older operating system and still access your program files. You can, of course, access data on a FAT-32 drive over a network with any computer using a compatible network protocol.

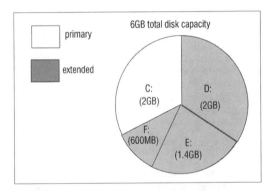

Figure 4.14   Adding a hard drive above 2.1GB in size to an MS-DOS or original Windows 95 computer forces the user to create multiple drive letters to use the entire drive capacity. The logical DOS drives are referenced like any other drive, although they are portions of a single physical hard disk.

Benefits of Hard Disk Partitioning

Even though it might seem like a lot of trouble to partition a single physical hard disk into multiple drive letters, especially with FAT-32, several good reasons exist for both FAT-16 and FAT-32 users to partition their hard disks:

- **Multiple partitions can be used to separate the operating system, application programs, and data for easier backup and greater security**—This method for dividing a hard disk into C: (Windows and drivers), D: (applications), and E: (data) is recommended by PowerQuest (makers of the popular PartitionMagic disk utility), and I've followed their advice for some time. Some time ago, I lost both C: and D: drives to a completely unexpected disk crash, but my data, on E:, stayed safe!

- **For FAT-16 operating systems in particular (MS-DOS, Windows 95/95a, and others using FAT-16), partitioning the drive results in significantly less disk space wasted**—Because files are actually stored in clusters (or allocation units) that are multiples of the 512-byte disk sector, a small file must occupy an entire cluster. As Table 4.20 indicates, the bigger the drive, the greater the space wasted.

Table 4.20   FAT-16 Cluster Sizes

Drive Size (Defined by FDISK) Binary MB/GB	Drive Size (Defined by Drive Maker) Decimal MB/GB	Cluster Size in Binary KB	Cluster Size in Bytes
0–127MB[1]	0–133MB[1]	2KB	2,048
128–255MB	134–267MB	4KB	4,096
256–511MB	268–537MB	8KB	8,192
512MB–1023MB	538MB–1073MB	16KB	16,384
1024MB (1GB)– 2048MB (2GB)	1074MB–2113MB	32KB	32,768

1. *If you create a partition under 15MB (binary) in size, the operating system actually uses the old FAT-12 file system, which results in a cluster size of 8KB!*

FAT-32 Versus FAT-16 Cluster Sizes

FAT-32 is far more efficient than FAT-16 and is used by virtually every recent system with a pre-installed copy of Windows 95 OSR 2.x (95B/95C),Windows 98, or Windows Me. If you are installing an additional hard disk on a system that uses these operating systems, use Table 4.21 to determine the relative efficiencies of FAT-16 versus FAT-32 because you can choose either FAT type for the entire new drive or any partitions on it. This chart uses binary (FDISK/BIOS) sizes only.

Table 4.21   FAT-16 Versus FAT-32

Cluster Size	FAT-16 Partition Size	FAT-32 Partition Size
4KB	128MB—255MB	260MB—8GB
8KB	256MB—511MB	8GB—16GB
16KB	512MB—1024MB	16GB—32GB
32KB	1025MB—2048MB	32GB—2TB

Converting FAT-16 Partition to FAT-32

If your existing hard disk uses FAT-16, you can convert any partition on it to FAT-32 *if* one of the following is true:

- You have Windows 95B or above (OSR 2.x) *and* PowerQuest's PartitionMagic v3.x or newer. PartitionMagic has a FAT-16–to–FAT-32 converter, which can also reverse the process (FAT-32 to FAT-16).

- You have Windows 98. Windows 98 comes with its own FAT-16–to–FAT-32 converter, and it can also use PartitionMagic version 4.x or newer.

NTFS Considerations and Default Cluster Sizes

New Technology File System (NTFS) is the high-performance file system that can be used on Windows NT and Windows 2000 systems. It has much more efficient storage by default than FAT-16, but it can't be directly accessed by other versions of Windows or MS-DOS. NTFS in Windows 2000 also supports encryption and the merging of several physical drives into a single logical folder.

Use the following guidelines when considering the use of NTFS:

- Windows 2000 can install a drive of any size recognized by the BIOS as a single NTFS volume up to the limits of the BIOS.

- Windows NT 4.0 must partition a drive of over 4GB into at least two drive letters because its boot drive cannot exceed 4GB.

- Windows 2000 can be used in a dual-boot environment with Windows 98, but if it is installed on the same hard drive partition as Windows 98, NTFS cannot be used.

- NTFS drives require special disk utility programs for defragmentation and disk maintenance because their internal structure is different from FAT-16 and FAT-32 drives.

The default cluster sizes for NTFS in Windows 3.51 and above (including Windows NT 4.0 and Windows 2000) are listed in Table 4.22.

Table 4.22 Default NTFS Cluster Sizes	
Drive Size	**NTFS Cluster Size**
512MB or less	512 bytes
513MB–1024MB(1GB)	1024 bytes (1KB)
1025MB–2048MB(2GB)	2048 bytes (2KB)
2049MB and larger	4096 bytes (4KB)

Note that NTFS drives can be larger than FAT-16 drives and are even more efficient than FAT-32 drives.

The default cluster sizes for FAT-16 drives under Windows NT 4.0 and Windows 2000 are the same as for Windows 9x and MS-DOS. In addition, three more large drive sizes are supported by Windows NT 4.0 only (see Table 4.23).

Table 4.23   Additional FAT-16 Cluster Sizes Supported by Windows NT 4.0

Drive Capacity	Size of FAT (Using FAT-16)
2048–4096MB (2–4GB)	64KB
4096–8192MB (4–8GB)	128KB
8192–16384MB (8–16GB)	256KB

How FDISK and the Operating System Create and Allocate Drive Letters

Two types of partitions can be created with the FDISK in Windows 9x/Me/2000/NT and MS-DOS: *primary* and *extended*. The primary partition can be bootable and can occupy all, part, or none of a hard disk's capacity. If you have only one hard disk in a system and it's bootable, at least a portion of that drive's partition is primary.

An extended partition is similar to a "pocket" that holds one or more logical DOS drives inside it. Table 4.24 shows how FDISK identifies these various disk structures as they might be found in a typical 13GB hard disk divided into three drives—C:, D:, and E:.

Table 4.24   FDISK Primary, Extended, and Logical DOS Drives Compared (13GB Hard Disk)

Partition Type	Size	Contained Within	Bootable?	% of Total Disk Space	% of Partition
Primary	4GB	n/a	Yes	32.5%	
Drive C:	4GB	Primary	Yes	32.5%	100% of primary
Extended	9GB	n/a	No	67.5%	
Logical DOS drive D: partition	4GB	Extended	No	32.5%	44.4% of extended
Logical DOS drive E: partition	5GB	Extended	No	35.0%	55.6% of extended

With FDISK, the partitions shown earlier must be created in the following order:

1. Create the primary partition to occupy less than 100% of disk space at the size you choose up to any limits imposed by your operating system.

2. Create an extended partition to use the *remainder* of disk space unused by the primary partition.

3. Create one or more logical DOS drives to occupy the extended partition.

4. Before leaving FDISK, make the primary partition (C:) active to enable it to boot.

Assigning Drive Letters with FDISK

You can use FDISK in many ways, depending on the number of hard drives you have in your system and the number of drive letters you want to create.

With a single drive, creating a primary partition (C:) and an extended partition with two logical DOS drives within it will result in the following drives, as you saw earlier:

Partition Type	*Contains Drive Letter(s)*
Primary	C:
Extended	D: and E:

A second drive added to this system should have drive letters that follow the E: drive.

However, you must understand how drive letters are allocated by the system to know how to use FDISK correctly in this situation. Table 4.25 shows how FDISK assigns drive letters by drive and partition type.

Table 4.25	Drive Letter Allocations by Drive and Partition Type		
Drive	**Partition**	**Order**	**First Drive Letter**
1st	Primary	1st	C:
2nd	Primary	2nd	D:
1st	Extended	3rd	E:
2nd	Extended	4th	F: or higher

How does this affect you when you add another hard drive? If you prepare the second hard drive with a primary partition and your first hard drive has an extended partition on it, the second hard drive will take the primary partition's D: drive letter. This moves all the drive letters in the first hard drive's extended partition up at least one drive letter.

This example lists a drive with C:, D:, and E: as the drive letters (D: and E: were in the extended partition). Table 4.26 indicates what happens if a second drive is added with a primary partition on it.

Table 4.26   Drive Letter Changes Caused by Addition of Second Drive with Primary Partition

Drive	Partition Type	Order	Original Drive Letter(s) (First Drive Only)	New Drive Letter(s) After Adding Second Drive
1st	Primary	1st	C:	C:
2nd	Primary	2nd	—	D:
1st	Extended	3rd	D:, E:	E:, F:

This principle extends to third and fourth physical drives as well: The primary partitions on each drive get their drive letters first, followed by logical DOS drives in the extended partitions.

How can you avoid the problem of changing drive letters? If you're installing an additional hard drive (not a replacement), remember that it can't be a bootable drive. If it can't be bootable, there's no reason to make it a primary partition. FDISK will enable you to create an extended partition using 100% of the space on any drive.

Table 4.27 shows the same example used in Table 4.25 with the second drive installed as an extended partition.

Table 4.27   Drive Letter Allocations After the Addition of a Second Drive with an Extended Partition Only

Drive	Partition Type	Order	Original Drive Letter(s) (First Drive Only)	New Drive Letter(s) After Adding Second Drive
1st	Primary	1st	C:	C:
1st	Extended	2nd	D:, E:	D:, E:
2nd	Extended	3rd	—	F:

This operating system behavior also explains why some of the first computers with IDE-based (ATAPI) Iomega Zip drives identified the Zip drive as D:, with a single 2.5GB or larger hard disk identified as C: and E:—the Zip drive was treated as the second hard drive with a primary partition.

High-Level (DOS) Format

The final step in the installation of a hard disk drive is the high-level format. Similar to the partitioning process, the high-level format is specific to the file system you've chosen to use on the drive. On Windows 9x/Me/NT/2000 and DOS systems, the primary function of the high-level format is to create a FAT and directory system on the disk so the operating system can manage files. You must run FDISK before formatting a drive. Each drive letter created by FDISK must be formatted before it can be used for data storage. This process might be automated with setup programs for some operating systems, such as Windows 9x retail versions. In the following notes, I provide the steps for a manual drive preparation in which you'll install a full operating system copy later.

Usually, you perform the high-level format with the FORMAT.COM program or the formatting utility in Windows 9x/Me Explorer. FORMAT.COM uses the following syntax:

```
FORMAT C: /S /V      (at a: prompt)
```

This high-level command formats drive C:, writes the hidden operating system files in the first part of the partition (/S), and prompts for the entry of a volume label (/V) to be stored on the disk at the completion of the process.

The FAT high-level format program performs the following functions and procedures:

1. Scans the disk (read only) for tracks and sectors marked as bad during the LLF and notes these tracks as being unreadable.

2. Returns the drive heads to the first cylinder of the partition and at that cylinder (Head 1, Sector 1), it writes a DOS volume boot sector.

3. Writes a FAT at Head 1, Sector 2. Immediately after this FAT, it writes a second copy of the FAT. These FATs essentially are blank except for bad-cluster marks noting areas of the disk that were found to be unreadable during the marked-defect scan.

4. Writes a blank root directory.

5. If the /S parameter is specified, copies the system files, IO.SYS and MSDOS.SYS (or IBMBIO.COM and IBMDOS.COM, depending on which DOS you run) and COMMAND.COM to the disk (in that order).

6. If the /V parameter is specified, prompts the user for a volume label, which is written as the fourth file entry in the root directory.

Now, the operating system can use the disk for storing and retrieving files, and the disk is a bootable disk.

> **Note**
>
> Because the high-level format doesn't overwrite data areas beyond the root directory of the hard disk, using programs such as Norton Utilities to unformat the hard disk that contains data from previous operations is possible—provided no programs or data has been copied to the drive after high-level formatting. Unformatting can be performed because the data from the drive's previous use is still present.

If you create an extended partition, the logical DOS drive letters located in the extended partition need a simpler FORMAT command because system files aren't necessary—for example, FORMAT D:/V for drive D: and FORMAT E:/V for drive E:, and so on.

Replacing an Existing Drive

Previous sections discuss installing a single hard drive or adding a new hard drive to a system. Although formatting and partitioning a new hard disk can be challenging, replacing an existing drive and moving your programs and files to it can be much more challenging.

Drive Migration for MS-DOS Users

When MS-DOS 6.x was dominant, many users used the following straightforward method to transfer the contents of their old hard drive to their new hard drive:

1. The user creates a bootable disk containing FDISK, FORMAT, and XCOPY.

2. The new hard drive is prepared with a primary partition (and possibly an extended partition, depending on the user's desires).

3. The new hard drive is formatted with system files, although the operating system identifies it as D:.

4. The XCOPY command is used to transfer all non-hidden files from C:\ (the old hard drive) to D:\, as in the following:

   ```
   XCOPY C:\ D:\/S/E
   ```

   The XCOPY command also is used as necessary to transfer files from any remaining drive letters on the old hard drive to the corresponding drive letters on the new drive.

Because the only hidden files such a system would have were probably the operating system boot files (already installed) and the Windows 3.1 permanent swap file (which could be re-created after restarting Windows), this "free" data transfer routine worked well for many people.

After the original drive was removed from the system, the new drive would be jumpered as master and assigned C:. You would need to run FDISK from a floppy and set the primary partition on the new C: drive as Active. Then, exit FDISK and the drive would boot.

Drive Migration for Windows 9x/Me Users

Windows 9x and Me have complicated the once simple act of data transfer to a new system by their frequent use of hidden files and folders (such as \Windows\Inf, where Windows hardware drivers are stored). The extensive use of hidden files was a major reason for a greatly enhanced version of XCOPY, known as XCOPY32, to be included in Windows 9x and Me.

Note

XCOPY32 is automatically used in place of XCOPY when XCOPY is started within a DOS session under Windows. XCOPY32, as the name implies, must be run within Windows.

XCOPY32 for Windows 9x Data Transfer

Compared to the classic XCOPY, XCOPY32 can copy hidden files; preserve file attributes such as system, hidden, read-only, and archive; automatically create folders; and is compatible with long filenames. Thus, using it to duplicate an existing drive is possible, but with these cautions:

- The XCOPY32 command is much more complex.

- Errors might occur during the copy process because of Windows' use of temporary files during normal operation, but XCOPY32 can be forced to continue.

This command line calls XCOPY32 and transfers all files and folders with their original attributes intact from the original drive (C:) to the new drive (D:). *This command must be run from an MS-DOS session under Windows 9x or Me:*

```
xcopy32 c:\. d:\/s/c/h/e/r/k
```

The command switches are explained here:

- /**S**—Copies folders beneath the starting folder.

- /**C**—Continues to copy after errors. (The Windows swap file can't be copied due to being in use.)

- /**H**—Copies hidden and system files.

- /**E**—Copies folders, even if empty.

- /**R**—Overwrites read-only files.

- /**K**—Preserves file attributes.

Repeat the command with appropriate drive-letter changes for any additional drive letters on your old drive.

After the original drive is removed from the system, the new drive needs to be jumpered as master (or single); the operating system will assign it C:. You also must run FDISK from a floppy and set the primary partition on the new C: drive as Active. Then, exit FDISK, and the drive will boot.

This process can take a long time because of the overhead of running an MS-DOS session beneath Windows.

If your hard disk comes with a disk preparation utility, such as EZ-Drive, Data Lifeguard Tools, MAXBlast, Disk Manager, Disc Wizard, or others, it might include a fast data transfer utility you can use in place of this procedure. I also recommend the PowerQuest utility DriveCopy, which uses a special method called SmartSector copying to copy hundreds of megabytes of data from the old drive to the new drive in just a few minutes.

Note

If your hard drive was original equipment in your computer, or if you purchased a replacement from bulk stock, you might not have received the appropriate installation disk for your drive. Check the drive maker's Web site for a downloadable version.

Hard Disk Drive Troubleshooting and Repair

Hard disk problems fall into two categories: hard and soft. *Hard* problems are triggered by mechanical problems that cause the drive to emit strange grinding or knocking noises (or no noise at all!), whereas *soft* problems are read and write errors that occur in a drive that sounds normal. Before deciding a hard disk is defective, test it on another known-working system. If the problem goes away on another system, the drive is not the problem (see Table 4.28).

> **Note**
>
> Before using this table, verify that your drive's BIOS configuration is correct. If your system's LBA or other drive translation settings are disabled and your drive needs them, it will appear to hang.

Table 4.28   Hard and Soft Problems and Solutions

Symptom	Cause	Solution
Drive makes banging noise on initial power up; can't boot without restarting the computer a couple of times; usually found on very old (under 100MB) RLL or MFM hard disks only; these drives use two (20-pin and 34-pin) data and signal cables.	*Stiction* (Static friction) is causing the heads to stick to the media because of an aging mechanism and lubrication problems internally.	If drive hangs, try tapping gently on one corner to free the heads or mount the drive upside down. Back up data and replace drive as soon as possible.
Drive makes scratching or "boinging" noise internally; won't boot.	Severe head damage, probably caused by impact (fall or drop).	Replace drive.
Drive spins normally but can't be recognized.	If cable and jumpering okay, probably failed logic board.	Replace logic board or replace drive.
Drive has repetitive errors detected by SCANDISK or other disk testing utility.	If system rebooted or was turned off without proper shutdown, these are temporary files that weren't closed. This does not indicate a hardware problem.	Remind user to shut down computer normally.
	If normal shutdown procedure followed, might indicate marginal disk surface.	If normal shutdown procedure was followed, get manufacturer utility to detect and remap sectors and retest drive frequently. If drive doesn't improve, replace as soon as possible.

If replacing the logic assembly does not solve the problem, contact the manufacturer or a specialized repair shop that has clean-room facilities for hard disk repair.

Optical Drive Interface Types

Most internal CD-ROM, CD-R, and CD-RW drives are ATAPI-based (ATAPI uses the standard IDE interface). Some high-performance drives in either internal or external form factors are SCSI-based. Physical installation and cabling is the same as for any other IDE (ATAPI) or SCSI device, as seen earlier in this chapter.

Some external drives use parallel-port or USB port connectors. See Chapter 7, "Parallel Ports, Printers, Scanners, and Drives," and Chapter 8, "USB and IEEE-1394 Ports and Devices," for troubleshooting and configuration tips for drives using these interface types.

MS-DOS Command-Line Access to CD-ROM Drives for Reloading Windows

CD-ROM drives are normally controlled in Windows 9x and Me by 32-bit drivers, but these drivers *will not work* if the operating system becomes corrupted or if Windows will only work in Safe mode. In those cases, having access to the CD-ROM drive becomes critical to enable you to reload the operating system.

In Windows 98 and Me, the Emergency Disk you can create during initial installation or later contains drivers that work for most IDE/ATAPI and SCSI-based CD-ROM drives. In addition, the disk will try each driver until it finds one that works.

In Windows 95, the Emergency Disk does *not* contain drivers for the CD-ROM. Follow these general guidelines to create a working boot disk with CD-ROM support. This same process will work for MS-DOS/Windows 3.1 users.

The following instructions are for IDE (ATAPI) CD-ROM drives. SCSI-based, CD-ROM drives will also require SCSI device drivers for the host adapter and devices attached:

1. Create the Windows 95 Emergency Disk (it's bootable) from the Control Panel's Add/Remove Programs icon—Windows Setup tab. This process destroys all previous contents on the disk.

2. Copy the following files to your bootable disk in the A: drive:

    - **MYCDROM.SYS**—Use the actual driver name for your CD-ROM drive and copy it from the file's actual location. If you don't have an MS-DOS driver, you can download one from the drive's manufacturer, or download an ATAPI driver called AOATAPI.SYS available from several Web sites.

- **MSCDEX.EXE**—Copy from C:\WINDOWS\
  COMMAND or your CD-ROM drive's folder; the same
  file for any CD-ROM drive.

Next, you'll need to create a CONFIG.SYS file that will load the CD-
ROM device driver and an AUTOEXEC.BAT that will load the
MSCDEX.EXE CD-ROM extensions for MS-DOS program. Use a text
editor, such as the Windows Notepad.

Contents of CONFIG.SYS:

- DEVICE=*MYCDROM.SYS* /D:mscd001
- Lastdrive=M

Contents of AUTOEXEC.BAT:

- MSCDEX.EXE /d:mscd001 /m:10 /L:M

Note

Note that the /d: switch refers to the same device name, which
could be Charlie or Kumquat or anything that matches! A mismatch will cause the loading process to fail.

Check your computer's BIOS setup and verify that the floppy drive
is the first bootable device. Then, restart the computer with this
floppy in drive A: and you should see the CD-ROM driver initialize.
Next, MSCDEX should assign the CD-ROM the drive letter listed
after the /L: option (M:).

If you don't have a suitable Windows 95 disk with CD-ROM support, a popular workaround is to use a Windows 98 or Windows
Me startup disk because they both contain the CD-ROM drivers
you need to access your CD for reinstallation of files or the entire
operating system.

Troubleshooting Optical Drives
Failure Reading a CD

If your CD-ROM drive fails to read a CD, try the following solutions:

- Check for scratches on the CD's data surface.
- Check the drive for dust and dirt; use a cleaning CD.

- Make sure the drive shows up as a working device in System Properties.

- Try a CD that you know works.

- Restart the computer (the magic cure-all).

- Remove the drive from the Device Manager in Windows 9x, allow the system to redetect the drive, and reinstall drivers (if PnP-based system).

Failure Reading CD-R and CD-RW Disks in a CD-ROM or DVD Drive

If your CD-ROM or DVD drive fails to read CD-R and CD-RW disks, try the following solutions:

- Check compatibility; some very old 1x CD-ROM drives can't read CD-R media. Replace the drive with a newer, faster, cheaper model.

- Many early-model DVD drives can't read CD-R and CD-RW media; check compatibility.

- CD-ROM drive must be multi-read compatible to read CD-RW because of lower reflectivity of media; replace drive.

- If some CD-Rs but not others can be read, check media color combination to see whether some color combinations work better than others; change brand of media.

- Packet-written CD-Rs (from Adaptec DirectCD and backup programs) can't be read on MS-DOS/Windows 3.1 CD-ROM drives because of limitations of the operating system.

IDE/ATAPI CD-ROM Drive Runs Slowly

If your IDE/ATAPI CD-ROM drive performs poorly, check the following items:

- Check the cache size in the Performance tab of the System Properties Control Panel. Select the quad-speed setting (largest cache size).

- Check to see whether the CD-ROM drive is set as the slave to your hard disk; move the CD-ROM to the secondary controller if possible.

- Your PIO or UDMA mode might not be set correctly for your drive in the BIOS; check the drive specs and use autodetect in BIOS for best results.

- Check to see that you are using bus-mastering drivers on compatible systems; install the appropriate drivers for the motherboard's chipset and operating system in use.

- Check to see whether you are using the CD-ROM interface on your sound card instead of an IDE connection on the motherboard. Move the drive connection to the IDE interface on the motherboard and disable the sound card IDE, if possible, to free up IRQ and I/O port address ranges.

- Open the System Properties Control Panel and select the Performance tab to see whether the system is using MS-DOS Compatibility mode for the CD-ROM drive. If all the IDE drives are running in this mode, see www.microsoft.com and query on "MS-DOS Compatibility Mode" for a troubleshooter. If only the CD-ROM drive is in this mode, see whether you're using CD-ROM drivers in CONFIG.SYS and AUTOEXEC.BAT. Remove the lines containing references to the CD-ROM drivers (don't actually delete the lines—REM them), reboot the system, and verify that your CD-ROM drive still works and that it's running in 32-bit mode. Some older drives require at least the CONFIG.SYS driver to operate.

Trouble Using Bootable CDs

Bootable CDs are terrific vehicles for installing a standard software image on a series of computers, or as a "bulletproof" method of running antivirus software, but they can be tricky to use.

If you are having problems using a bootable CD, try these possible solutions:

- Check the contents of bootable floppy disk from which you copied the boot image during the creation of the bootable CD. To access entire contents of a CD-R, a bootable disk must contain CD-ROM drivers, AUTOEXEC.BAT, and CONFIG.SYS. Test the bootable disk by starting the system with it and seeing whether you can access the CD-ROM drive afterward.

- Use ISO 9660 format. Don't use the Joliet format because it is for long-filename CDs and can't boot.

- Check your system's BIOS for boot compliance and boot order; CD-ROM should be listed first.

- Check the drive for boot compliance.

- SCSI CD-ROMs need a SCSI card with BIOS and bootable capability, as well as special motherboard BIOS settings.

- You must use your mastering software's Bootable CD option to create the bootable CD-ROM from the files on the bootable floppy. The bootable disk's AUTOEXEC.BAT, CONFIG.SYS, and basic boot files are stored on a bootable CD as files called BOOTIMG.BIN and BOOTCAT.BIN by the mastering software's Bootable CD mastering option.

Chapter 5

Floppy, Removable, Tape, and Flash Memory Storage

Floppy Drives

A 3 1/2-inch 1.44MB floppy drive, the most common type of floppy drive in use today, isn't very expensive to replace. However, when it stops working, you might *not* need to replace it right away, if you have the "inside story." Figure 5.1 shows an exploded view of a typical 3 1/2-inch 1.44MB floppy drive.

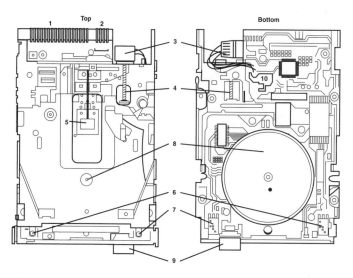

Figure 5.1 A typical 3 1/2-inch floppy disk drive.

1. 34-pin data cable connector

2. 4-pin power connector

3. Head-actuator motor

4. Worm gear to drive actuator motor

5. Read-write head (one of two)

6. Write-protect sensor

7. Media sensor (720KB or 1.44MB)

8. Spindle (left) and drive motor (right)

9. Disk ejector button

10. Logic board

Where Floppy Drives Fail—and Simple Fixes

I spent several years on the road carrying around disassembled PCs for use in computer-troubleshooting classes. Typically, I had more floppy-drive failures than about anything else, due to the combination of inexperienced students, rough handling by airline baggage carousels, and the simple fact that a floppy drive is designed to be used within the confines of a computer case. I learned how to fix drives the hard way—when the only spare I had wasn't working, either.

The Drive Cover

The drive cover acts as a dust cover, which is obviously a good idea for a drive that uses exposed, relatively soft flexible magnetic media. However, a damaged or bent drive cover can bind the disk ejector, preventing it from moving. The drive cover can easily be removed and bent back into shape.

The Stepper Motor

The stepper motor moves the head actuator across the surface of the floppy disk media, reading or writing data (see Figure 5.2).

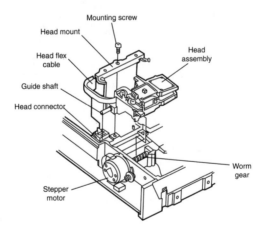

Figure 5.2   An expanded view of a stepper motor and head actuator.

On a 3 1/2-inch drive, the stepper motor is often a worm-gear arrangement rather than the band drive that was used on the older 5 1/4-inch drives. The worm gear is very compact, but can be jammed by shock. To free it up, carefully unscrew the stepper motor from the rear of the drive frame and move the head actuator back and forth gently until the worm gear moves freely again. Reassemble the drive and test it outside the case by running the data and power cable to it before you secure it into its normal position.

Interface Circuit Boards

A drive's *interface circuit board* (also called *logic board*) can be damaged by shock, static electricity, or a power surge. Usually, it can easily be removed from the bottom of the drive and replaced by a spare circuit board from an identical drive with a bad read/write head or stepper motor. Keep such failures around for spare parts.

Read/Write Heads

Because of the contact between the heads and disk, a buildup of the magnetic material from the disk eventually forms on the heads. The buildup should periodically be cleaned off the heads as part of a preventive-maintenance or normal service program.

The best method for cleaning the heads involves the use of a commercial wet-method disk head cleaner and a program that spins the cleaning disk and moves the heads around the cleaning media. MicroSystems Development (www.msd.com) offers the TestDrive floppy drive testing program, which contains such a cleaning utility. Depending on the drive use and the amount of contaminants (smoke, dust, soot) in the air, you should clean the read/write heads on a floppy drive only about once every six months to a year.

Do *not* use standard 3 1/2-inch floppy head cleaners with LS-120 SuperDisk floppy drives; although these drives can read and write to standard disks as well as the 120MB SuperDisk media, a conventional cleaner will damage their special read/write heads. Check www.superdisk.com for a SuperDisk-compatible cleaning kit.

Floppy Drive Hardware Resources

Whether they are built in or not, all primary floppy controllers use a standard set of system resources:

- IRQ 6 (Interrupt Request)

- DMA 2 (Direct Memory Address)

- I/O ports 3F0-3F5, 3F7 (Input/Output)

These system resources are standardized and generally not changeable. This normally does not present a problem because no other devices will try to use these resources (which would result in a conflict).

Don't Use a Floppy Drive While Running a Tape Backup

About the only circumstance that would cause a hardware conflict is the use of a floppy drive while a tape backup is running. While most high-capacity tape backup drives today no longer use the floppy interface, they still often use DMA 2 for fast data transfers. Because DMA transfers are not checked by the CPU or any other part of the system, simultaneous use of DMA 2 by a tape backup and a floppy drive can easily result in data loss on either or both media types.

Disk Drive Power and Data Connectors

Two sizes are used for disk drive power connectors. Figure 5.3 shows the original "Molex" power connector used on 5 1/4-inch floppy drives. Most 3 1/2-inch floppy drives and tape backups use a smaller connector, but either size normally has the same 4-wire pinout shown in the figure.

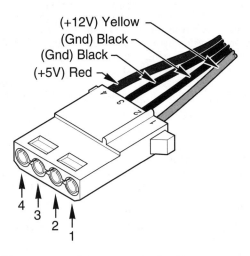

Figure 5.3   A disk drive female power supply cable connector.

Some 3 1/2-inch tape drives come with an extension cable with only two wires: a ground wire (black) and a +5v wire (red), because their motors use the same +5v power as the logic board does.

Figure 5.4 shows a typical 5-connector floppy data cable. Typically, the 5 1/4-inch edge connectors are seldom used today, unless a 3 1/2-inch drive has a pin-to-edge connector adapter attached.

Table 5.1 compares floppy and hard disk ribbon cables.

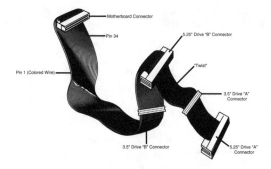

Figure 5.4   Standard five-connector floppy interface cable.

Table 5.1	**Comparing Ribbon Cables—Floppy Versus Hard Disk**			
Interface Type	**Floppy**	**ST-506 ESDI**	**IDE**	**SCSI**
Cable Width	34-pin	34-pin	40-pin or 80-strand	50-pin or 68-pin
Notes	Almost all have twist between A: drive connectors and B: drive connectors; twist toward pin 1 (colored edge of cable)	Can be straight or twisted; twist away from pin 1; obsolete and seldom seen today; used with 20-pin ribbon cable	80-strand cable has 40 pins; designed for use with UDMA/66 motherboards and drives	

Table 5.2 lists the parameters for current and obsolete disk drives used on PCs. If you are preparing a drive with FORMAT that is smaller than the drive's capacity, you will need to set the FORMAT parameters manually.

A damaged media descriptor byte will prevent programs from properly accessing the disk; however, this problem can be fixed with Norton Utilities.

Table 5.2	**Floppy Disk Logical Formatted Parameters**							
	Current Formats					**Obsolete Formats**		
Disk Size (inches)	3 1/2	3 1/2	3 1/2	5 1/4	5 1/4	5 1/4	5 1/4	51/4
Disk Capacity (KB)	2,880	1,440	720	1,200	360	320	180	160
Media Descriptor Byte	F0h	F0h	F9h	F9h	FDh	FFh	FCh	Feh
Sides (Heads)	2	2	2	2	2	2	1	1

Table 5.2   Floppy Disk Logical Formatted Parameters Continued

	Current Formats					Obsolete Formats		
Tracks per Side	80	80	80	80	40	40	40	40
Sectors per Track	36	18	9	15	9	8	9	8
Bytes per Sector	512	512	512	512	512	512	512	512
Sectors per Cluster	2	1	2	1	2	2	1	1
FAT Length (Sectors)	9	9	3	7	2	1	2	1
Number of FATs	2	2	2	2	2	2	2	2
Root Dir. Length (Sectors)	15	14	7	14	7	7	4	4
Maximum Root Entries	240	224	112	224	112	112	64	64
Total Sectors per Disk	5,760	2,880	1,440	2,400	720	640	360	320
Total Available Sectors	5,726	2,847	1,426	2,371	708	630	351	313
Total Available Clusters	2,863	2,847	713	2,371	354	315	351	313

Floppy Drive Troubleshooting

Table 5.3   Floppy Drive Troubleshooting Tips

Problem	Cause	Solution
Dead drive—the drive does not spin and the LED never comes on.	Bad power supply or power cable.	Measure the power at the cable with a voltmeter; ensure that 12v and 5v are available to the drive.
	Drive or controller not properly configured in BIOS setup.	Check BIOS setup for proper drive type and ensure the controller is enabled if built in to the motherboard; if an add-on card contains a floppy controller and the motherboard also has one, disable one or the other.
	Bad data cable.	Replace the cable and retest.
	Defective drive.	Replace the drive and retest.
	Defective controller.	Replace the controller and retest. If the controller is built into the motherboard, disable it via the BIOS setup, install a card-based controller, and retest, or replace the entire motherboard and retest.

Table 5.3   Floppy Drive Troubleshooting Tips Continued

Problem	Cause	Solution
Drive LED remains on continuously.	Data cable is on backward at either the drive or controller connection.	Reinstall the cable properly and retest.
	The data cable could be offset on the connector by one or more pins.	Reinstall the cable properly and retest; replace cable if this doesn't work.
Phantom directories—you have exchanged disks in the drive, but the system still believes the previous disk is inserted, and even shows directories of the previous disk.	Defective cable.	Replace the cable and retest.
	Improper drive configuration.	Older drives must have their DC jumper (for Drive Changeline support) enabled.
	Defective drive or interface.	Replace the drive and retest.

Note

Windows users: Windows does *not* automatically refresh the display with File Manager, Explorer, and so on by default. Use the F5 key or click Refresh to re-read the disk.

Common Floppy Drive Error Messages—Causes and Solutions

Table 5.4   Handling Floppy Drive Error Messages

Error Message	Cause	Solution
Invalid Media or Track Zero Bad, Disk Unusable	You are formatting the disk and the disk media type does not match the format parameters.	Make sure you are using the right type of disk for your drive and formatting the disk to its correct capacity.
	Defective or damaged disk.	Replace the disk and retest.
	Dirty read/write heads.	Clean drive, allow heads to dry, and retest.
CRC Error or Disk Error 23	The data read from the disk does not match the data that was originally written. (CRC stands for Cyclic Redundancy Check.)	Replace the disk and retest. Clean the drive heads, allow them to dry, and retest. Use Norton Utilities or SpinRite to recover data from disk.

Table 5.4   Handling Floppy Drive Error Messages Continued

Error Message	Cause	Solution
General Failure Reading Drive A, Abort, Retry, Fail, or Disk Error 31	The disk is not formatted or has been formatted for a different operating system (Macintosh, for example).	Reformat the disk and retest.
	Damaged areas on the disk medium.	Replace the disk and retest. Use Norton Utilities or SpinRite to recover data from disk.
	Disk not seated properly in drive.	Remove and reinsert in drive. Try holding disk in place with your hand. If you can read the data, copy it to a reliable disk.
Access Denied	You are trying to write to a write-protected disk or file.	Move the write-protect switch to allow writing on the disk, or remove the read-only file attribute from the file(s). File attributes can be changed by the ATTRIB command or through the file properties in Windows.
Insufficient Disk Space or Disk Full	The disk is filled, or the root directory is filled.	Check to see if sufficient free space is available on the disk for your intended operation. Use folders on the disk to store files, or change to a new disk.
Bytes in Bad Sectors (greater than 0)	Displayed after FORMAT, CHKDSK, or SCANDISK if allocation units (clusters) have been marked bad.	Operating system will not use bad sectors, but this is a sign of a marginal disk; reformat or discard and use a new disk with no bad sectors.
Disk Type or Drive Type Incompatible or Bad	You are attempting to DISKCOPY between two incompatible drive disk types.	Disks can be copied only between drives using the same disk density and size. Use COPY or XCOPY unless you are trying to create an exact copy.

Removable Storage Drives

For backup or alternative main storage, many users today are de-emphasizing floppy disks in favor of alternative storage media. Table 5.5 describes the varying types of storage media, and Table 5.6 provides an overview of storage types. Of the drives listed, only the LS120/SuperDisk, Sony HiFD, and Caleb it drives are also read/write compatible with standard 3 1/2-inch floppy media.

Drives that use SCSI or IDE (ATAPI) interfaces are installed the same way as other SCSI or IDE devices. Refer to Chapter 4, "SCSI and IDE Hard Drives and Optical Drives," for details.

Table 5.5 Quick Reference to Removable Magnetic and Flash Storage Devices (In Order by Capacity)

Media Type	Media Brands	Mfrs	Capacity	Interface Type	Best Use
Flash memory	SmartMedia, ATA Data Flash, Compact Flash, Memory Stick	Various	2MB–512MB, depending on brand and model	Proprietary, PC Card or floppy via adapters, PC Card Type II	Digital camera "film," storage for PDAs, portable devices
Flexible magnetic disk	Clik!, Zip, LS-120 SuperDisk, Sony HiFD, Caleb it	Various	40MB–250MB, depending on brand and model	Parallel, IDE, SCSI, USB, PC Card (PCMCIA)	Data and program backups and storage for direct access
Hard disk	MicroDrive	IBM	170MB and 340MB	CF+ Type II, PC Card via adapter	Digital camera "film," program and data storage for notebook computers
Hard disk	DataPak	Kingston	520MB and 1GB	PC Card Type III	Digital camera "film," program and data storage for notebook computers
High-performance, flexible magnetic disk	Jaz	Iomega	1GB and 2GB	SCSI	Program storage, data and program backups
High-performance, hard disk cartridge	Orb	Castlewood	2.2GB	IDE, SCSI, USB, parallel	Program storage, data and program backups
.315" magnetic tape cartridge	Travan and Travan NS	Various	Up to 10GB[1], depending on brand & model	IDE, SCSI, parallel, USB	Data and program backups, full drive backup
ADR magnetic tape cartridge	ADR 30GB and 50GB	OnStream	15GB[1] and 25GB[1]	IDE, SCSI, parallel, USB	Data and program backups, full drive backup; works in progress storage and playback
DAT, Exabyte 8MM, AIT magnetic tape	Various	Various	Up to 50GB[1]	SCSI	Data and program backups, full drive backup

1. Uncompressed capacity: Tape drives are usually rated at 2:1 compression; multiply uncompressed capacity by actual compression ratio obtained to determine your nominal working capacity.

Table 5.6 Removable Drive Specifications (In Order by Capacity)

Drive Type Mfr.	Disk/Cartridge Capacity/Type	Average Seek Time	Data Transfer Rate
Iomega Clik Parallel	40MB Clik	not listed	620KB/sec
Iomega Zip Parallel[1]	100MB Zip	29ms	1.4MB/sec
Iomega Zip IDE/ATAPI	100MB Zip	29ms	1.4Mb/sec
Iomega Zip SCSI[1]	100MB Zip	29ms	1.4MB/sec
Iomega Zip USB	100MB Zip	29ms	1.2MB/sec
Iomega Zip 250 SCSI[2]	250MB Zip	29ms	2.4MB/sec
Iomega Zip 250 Parallel[2]	250MB Zip	29ms	0.8MB/sec
Iomega Zip 250 ATAPI/IDE[2]	250MB Zip	29ms	2.4MB/sec
Imation LS-120 IDE Internal[3]	120MB SuperDisk	60ms	1.1MB/sec
Imation LS-120 Parallel[4]	120MB SuperDisk	60ms	750KB/sec
Imation LS-120 USB[5]	120MB SuperDisk	60ms	700KB/sec
Imation LS-120 PCMCIA	120MB SuperDisk	70ms	440KB/sec
Caleb it (UHD144)[6]	144MB UHD144	30ms	770KB/sec sustained
Parallel, PC Card burst USB, IDE/ATAPI			1.16MB/sec
Sony HiFD[7] Parallel	200MB HiFD	49ms	600KB/sec
Sony HiFD USB	200MB HiFD	49ms	700KB/sec
Sony HiFD[8] 1.2MB/	200MB HiFD	49ms	900KB-sec write
IDE/ATAPI			3.6MB/sec read
Iomega Jaz (SCSI)[9]	2GB Jaz	12ms	7.35MB/sec
Castlewood ORB IDE	2.2GB ORB	12ms	12.2MB/sec
Castlewood ORB SCSI	2.2GB ORB	12ms	12.2MB/sec
Castlewood ORB Parallel	2.2GB ORB	12ms	2MB/sec

1. *While Iomega rates Zip 100 parallel and SCSI versions as having the same transfer rate, SCSI versions are as much as 8x faster in actual use.*

2. *Zip 250 drives can also read/write Zip 100 media.*

3. *New version; original version maximum transfer rate was 660KB/second. All LS-120 SuperDisk models can read/write standard 1.44MB/720KB 3.5" floppy media.*

4. *New version; original version maximum transfer rate was 290KB/second.*

5. *New version; original version maximum transfer rate was 400KB/second.*

6. *All Caleb it (UHD144) models can read/write standard 1.44MB/720KB 3.5" floppy media.*

7. *Parallel and USB versions of Sony HiFD sold by Sony; all HiFD models can read/write standard 1.44MB/720KB 3.5" floppy media.*

8. *Sold by IBM in its Options by IBM line; can read/write standard 1.44MB/720KB 3.5" floppy media.*

9. *Jaz 2GB drive can also read/write Jaz 1GB cartridges.*

Sources for "Orphan" Drive Media, Repairs, Drivers, and Support

Several removable-media drives have become "orphans" over the last few years. While the best long-term recommendation you can make is to copy all readable data off an orphan drive and transfer it to industry-standard storage devices, you might need to buy replacement drives, media, repairs, or parts to enable your clients to complete the move to new storage devices. Use Table 5.7 to help you locate these sources.

Table 5.7 Sources for "Orphan" Drive Parts, Service, and Media			
Drive	**Status**	**Parts or Repairs**	**Media Drivers**
Avatar Shark 250	Mfr out of business.	Weymouth Technologies (508)735-3513 www.weymouthtech.com	www.windrivers.com/ company.htm ("Dead Boards" section)
Iomega Alpha 8 inch, Beta 5.25 inch, 21MB floptical, LaserSafe	Obsolete products not supported by Iomega.	Comet Enterprises, Inc. (801)444-3600 www.gocomet.com	Follow links from www.gocomet.com (some are at Iomega's Web site, others on Comet Enterprises' Web site)
All SyQuest products (SparQ, EZ-Flyer, others)	SYQT, Inc. purchased product and parts inventory from Iomega after Iomega bought Syquest's intellectual property in 1999.	Parts, repairs, drives, media, and drivers are available from the SYQT, Inc. Web site: www.syqt.com.	

Emergency Access to Iomega Zip Drive Files in Case of Disaster

Most removable-media drives are optimized for use with Windows 9x/NT/2000/Me. But in the event that the operating system fails, you want to be able to access your files, even if you must boot the machine to a command prompt.

The Iomega Zip drive is the most popular removable-media drive, and files stored on the PC version can be accessed from an MS-DOS prompt using its real-mode Guest.exe driver, even if the drive was originally used with Windows 9x/NT/2000/Me. All long filenames and folder names will be displayed using their short (8+3 character) MS-DOS alias names.

Because the Iomega parallel-port Zip drive can be used on virtually any system, I recommend that organizations using Zip media have a parallel-port version, even though it's slower than other versions.

Table 5.8 indicates what is needed to access the parallel-port Zip drive. You can get the files needed from the IomegaWARE CD-ROM supplied with recent versions of the Zip drive, or from www.iomega.com. Copy the files in Table 5.8 to a bootable floppy disk.

Table 5.8	Accessing Parallel Port Zip Drives	
Drive	**Interface**	**File**
Iomega Zip 100, Zip 250	Parallel Set port to EPP (best choice) or bidirectional modes, not ECP	Guest.exe, guest.ini, Aspippm1.sys, Aspippm2.sys, Nibble.ilm, Nibble2.ilm, Guesthlp.txt, Manual.exe

Parallel-port versions of the SyQuest SparQ and EzFlyer 230 drives are also available from SYQT (formerly SyQuest). SYQT's Web site (www.syqt.com) also has drivers available for Windows 95; Windows 98/98SE; Windows NT; and Windows 2000 for SparQ, EzFlyer 230, and other models.

Troubleshooting Removable Media Drives

Table 5.9	Troubleshooting Removable Media Drives	
Drive/Interface	**Problem**	**Solution**
Any parallel-port model	Can't detect drive with install program.	Check for IRQ conflicts; IRQ for parallel port must not be used by sound cards or other devices; verify that install disk has correct drivers.
Any SCSI interface model	Drive not available.	Check SCSI IDs; each SCSI device must have a unique ID number; check termination; verify correct drivers installed; ASPI drivers must be installed for both SCSI interface and each device on interface.
Iomega Zip— any interface	Drive makes "clicking" sound; can't access files.	Drive might have "click of death" problem; physically examine media for damage; use Iomega Diagnostics to check media; download Trouble in Paradise (TIP) from Gibson Research (www.grc.com) for more thorough testing.
Any drive, any interface	Drive letter interferes with network, CD-ROM, and so on.	Under Windows 9x/NT/2000, check drive properties and select an available drive letter not used by CD-ROM or network.

Types of Flash Memory Devices

Several different types of flash memory devices are in common use today, and knowing which ones your digital camera is designed to use is important. The major types include the following:

- CompactFlash

- SmartMedia

- ATA PC Cards (PCMCIA)

- Memory Stick

SmartMedia and CompactFlash cards are available from many manufacturers, but Memory Sticks are available only from the originator, Sony, as of this writing.

ATA PC Cards can use flash memory or an actual hard disk. They can be read directly by the Type II or Type III PC Card (PCMCIA) slots found on most notebook computers.

CompactFlash, SmartMedia, and Sony Memory Stick flash memory devices require the use of a card reader to interface with notebook or desktop computers. Card readers can plug in to any of the following:

- Parallel port

- USB port

- PC Card Type II slot

Most devices that use flash memory storage can be connected via serial ports for downloading of images or other data, but this is much slower and is not recommended for heavy-duty use.

Tape Backup Drives and Media
Common Tape Backup Standards

Several tape backup standards exist for individual client PC and small server tape backup drives:

- **QIC, QIC-Wide, and Travan**—Three branches of a large and diverse family of low-cost "entry-level" tape backup drives, which can handle data up to 20GB@2:1 compression

- **DAT (Digital Audio Tape)**—A newer technology than QIC and its offshoots, using Digital Data Storage technology to store data up to 40GB@2:1 compression

- **OnStream's ADR (Advanced Digital Recording)**—The newest technology aimed at desktop and small network backup needs, featuring capacity up to 50GB@2:1 compression

Other tape backup standards, such as DLT (Digital Linear Tape) and 8mm are used primarily with larger network file servers and are beyond the scope of this book.

Travan Tape Drives and Media

Imation created the Travan family of tape drives to provide a standardized development from the crazy-quilt of QIC and QIC-Wide MC (minicartridge) tape drives that stemmed from the original QIC-40 and QIC-80 drives and their DC-2120 cartridges. Note that Travan-1 through Travan NS-8 retain read-only compatibility with the QIC-80 cartridge.

Table 5.10   Travan Family Cartridges and Capacities

Travan Cartridge (previous name)	Capacity/2:1 Compression	Read/Write Compatible with	Read Compatible with
Travan-1 (TR-1)	400MB/800MB	QIC-80, QW5122	QIC-40
Travan-3 (TR-3)	1.6GB/3.2GB	TR-2, QIC-3020, QIC-3010, QW-3020XLW, QW-3010XLW	QIC-80, QW-5122, TR-1
Travan 8GB (Travan 4/TR-4)	4GB/8GB	QIC-3095	QIC-3020, QIC-3010, QIC-80, QW-5122, TR-3, TR-1
Travan NS-8[1] QIC-80	4GB/8GB		QIC-3020, QIC-3010,
Travan NS-20	10GB/20GB		Travan 8GB, QIC-3095

1. *This cartridge is replacing the Travan 8GB (TR-4); a single cartridge can be used on either NS8 or TR-4 drives.*

Future developments might include an NS-36 model.

> **Note**
>
> Backward compatibility can vary with each drive; consult the manufacturer before purchasing any drive to verify backward-compatibility issues.

Proprietary Versions of Travan Technology

Ironically, since Travan technology was designed to bring an end to the QIC MC/QIC-Wide tape "wars", some drives exist that use proprietary versions of the Travan standard. Non-standard sizes include

- 5GB Tecmar/Iomega DittoMax
- 5GB HP/Colorado
- 6.6GB AIWA Bolt
- 7GB Tecmar/Iomega DittoMax
- 10GB Tecmar DittoMax
- 14GB HP/Colorado

The drive manufacturer is the principal supplier of media for some of these drives, whereas others are also supported with third-party media. Consult the drive manufacturers' Web sites for details.

For more information about older QIC and QIC-Wide tape drives and cartridges, see *Upgrading and Repairing PCs, 12th Edition*, Chapter 12.

Getting Extra Capacity with Verbatim QIC-EX Tape Media

Many older model, small-capacity tape backups are still in use on older workstations and small networks. The rapid increase in hard disk capacity is causing many problems in creating tape backups that are as safe as possible. The "1 backup = 1 tape" rule is harder to live by when Travan 3 (3.2MB compressed capacity) or smaller tape drives are used with 4GB or larger hard drives.

If you use any of the tape standards shown in Table 5.11, you can use the listed Verbatim QIC-Extra cartridges as replacements. Note that the same QIC-Extra series cartridge can be interchanged between a particular QIC, QIC-Wide, and Travan drive type. This is because QIC-EX tapes are the same width as normal QIC cartridges, but are much longer. Because some tape backup drives can't handle the extra capacity with their own backup software, some models of QIC-EX cartridges come with replacement backup software that will use the full capacity.

Table 5.11 QIC-EX Tape Media

Original Tape	Capacity/ Compressed 2:1	Verbatim QIC-Extra	Capacity/ Compressed 2:1
QIC-80[1] normal length (DC-2120)	125MB/250MB	DC2120EX	400MB/800MB
QIC-80 longer length (DC-2120XL)	170MB/340MB	DC2120EX	400MB/800MB
QW5122	210MB/420MB	DC2120EX	400MB/800MB
Travan 1 (TR-1)	400MB/800MB	DC2120EX	400MB/800MB
Travan 1 (TR-1)	400MB/800MB	TR-1EX	500MB/1.0GB
QIC-3020[2]	680MB/1.36GB	MC3020EX	1.6GB/3.2GB
QW-3020	850MB/1.7GB	MC3020EX	1.6GB/3.2GB
Travan 3 (TR-3)	1.6GB/3.2GB	MC3020EX	1.6GB/3.2GB
QIC-3020[2]	680MB/1.36GB	TR-3EX	2.2GB/4.4GB
Travan 3 (TR-3)	1.6GB/3.2GB	TR-3EX	2.2GB/4.4GB

1. Also known as "Ximat"

2. Also known as "Taumat"

General guidelines only are shown in the previous table. Check with the drive and backup software vendor to verify compatibility and maximum capacity with your drive. A more detailed cross-reference listing of many popular drive models is available online at www.ceservice.com/crossrefverbatim.htm.

OnStream ADR Tape Drives and Media

OnStream ADR drives offer both standard drive-backup features and the capability to treat the cartridge as a drive letter for faster access to data. Since their introduction in 1998, these have become very popular for new installations. Unlike Travan drives, though, they do not work with any media other than their own ADR cartridges.

Table 5.12 OnStream ADR Family Specifications

Drive Model	Interface	Performance	Retail	Media Used
DI30	IDE ATAPI	1–2MB/sec	$299	ADR 30GB
DP30	Parallel	.7–1.4MB/sec	$399	ADR 30GB
USB30	USB	.85–1.7MB/sec	$399	ADR 30GB
SC30	SCSI internal	2–4MB/sec	$499	ADR 30GB
SC30	SCSI external	2–4MB/sec	$599	ADR 30GB
FW30	IEEE-1394 (FireWire)	2–4MB/sec	$599	ADR 30GB
SC50	SCSI internal	2–4MB/sec	$699	ADR 50GB or 30GB
ADR50 Int	LVD SCSI internal	4–8MB/sec	$799	ADR 50GB or 30GB
ADR50 Ext	LVD SCSI external	4–8MB/sec	$949	ADR 50GB or 30GB

Choosing the Best High-Performance Backup Technology

Beyond Travan and ADR, several other high-performance backup technologies exist. All these technologies are available in various SCSI interface versions and can be purchased as internal or external drives. However, these drives are much more expensive than Travan or OnStream ADR drives. Additionally, they are more likely to be used as network tape backups than as individual PC backups, although current 20GB or larger EIDE hard drives are large enough to justify use of these drives for backup.

Unlike the confusing backward-compatibility picture for QIC-family drives, the more advanced drives in each family are backward compatible with smaller drives.

Table 5.13 summarizes the performance and other characteristics of these tape technologies and compares them to Travan 8GB, 20GB, and OnStream ADR. The prices of the tape drives vary tremendously depending on which version of SCSI is selected, whether the drive is internal or external, and whether a single-tape or tape library drive is selected. The approximate price range listed is for internal and external, single-cartridge tape drives.

The following standards are listed in order by native capacity. All drive interfaces are SCSI except as noted.

Table 5.13	High-Performance Tape Backup Standards Compared			
Drive Type	**Capacity/2:1 Compressed**	**Backup Speed (Native/ Compressed)**	**Drive Price Range**	**Media Cost**
DAT DDS-2	4GB/8GB	.5–1.1MB/sec	$500–$800	$9–$13
Travan 8GB and NS8	4GB/8GB	.6–1.2MB/sec	$200–$380	$32–$38
Exabyte 8mm (Eliant 820)	7GB/14GB	1–2MB/sec	$1200	$10
Travan 20GB and NS20	10GB/20GB	1–2MB/sec	$340–$470	$35–$42
DAT DDS-3	12GB/24GB	1.1–2.2MB/sec	$700–$1000	$18–$23
Exabyte 8mm (Mammoth-LT)	14GB/28GB	2–4MB/sec	$1200–$1500	$40
ADR 30GB	15GB/30GB	1–2MB/sec IDE 2–4MB/sec SCSI	$299–$599	$40
DAT DDS-4	20GB/40GB	2–4.8MB/sec	$1000–$1500	$35–$40
Exabyte 8mm (Mammoth)	20GB/40GB	3–6MB/sec	$2200–$3000	$65–$70
AIT-1	25GB/50GB or 35GB/70GB	3–6MB/sec	$1500–$2000	$75–$100

Table 5.13   High-Performance Tape Backup Standards Compared Continued

Drive Type	Capacity/2:1 Compressed	Backup Speed (Native/ Compressed)	Drive Price Range	Media Cost
ADR 50GB	25GB/50GB	2–4MB/sec SCSI;4–8MB/sec LVD SCSI	$699–$949	$60
AIT-2	50GB/100GB	6–12MB/sec	$3000–$3200	$110–$120
DLT 2000	15GB/30GB	1.2–2.5MB/sec	$1200–$1300	$30–$50
DLT 4000	20GB/40GB	1.5–3MB/sec	$1300–$1850	$60–$75
DLT 7000	35GB/70GB	5–10MB/sec	$4300–$4700	$70–$90

Successful Tape Backup and Restore Procedures

A backup tape might be the only thing separating you from a complete loss of data. To ensure that every backup can be restored, follow the guidelines shown in Tables 5.14 and 5.15 when you create a backup or restore one.

Table 5.14   Tape Backup Tips

Tip	Benefit	Notes
Perform the confidence test during tape backup software installation.	Tests DMA channels in computer for safe data transfer; sets default transfer rate for backup.	Keep a spare blank tape at all times to enable you to perform this test whenever new hardware is installed or before running a new backup for safety.
Select the correct backup type.	"Full" backup backs up contents of system, but operating system must be restored first before restoring backup. "Disaster Recovery" backup creates special boot disks and enables entire system recovery straight from tape to an empty hard drive. Other backup types are designed primarily for data backup.	Make a disaster recovery backup and test your ability to restore your backup to an empty hard drive. Use other backup types for periodic backups.
Choose speed and safety.	Maximum data compression uses the least amount of tape and is often about as fast as other backup types. Use Compare after to ensure readability.	

Table 5.14 Tape Backup Tips Continued		
Tip	**Benefit**	**Notes**
Don't use multiple tapes for a single backup.	Tape backups are typically rated with 2:1 compression assumed; this ratio is seldom achieved. Using multiple tapes for a single backup can cause loss of data if first tape is lost, because it contains tape catalog. Back up a large drive with a small tape drive by backing up sections.	Use actual compression ratio reported during your initial full backup to determine your nominal tape size. If your tape drive is a Travan 3 or smaller, get extra capacity per tape by using Verbatim QIC-EX series tapes (see Table 5.15).
Avoid multitasking during the tape backup.	Let the tape backup run without interruptions, due to DMA transfers. Turn off screensaver and power management. Turn off your monitor.	Don't use floppy drives because floppy DMA 2 is often used during backups.

Table 5.15 Tape Restore Tips	
Tip	**Benefit**
Restore full backups to an empty drive if possible.	Avoids overwriting drive with junk data if your backup has failed.
If your full backup is not a disaster recovery type, install the smallest possible operating system image first.	You'll wait less time before you can install your backup software and restore your backup.
Run the confidence test again before you start the restore process.	Verifies that DMA transfers will be successful; this requires a blank tape or one that can be overwritten, so keep one handy.

Tape Drive Troubleshooting

Tape drives can be troublesome to install and operate. Any type of removable media is more susceptible to problems or damage, and tape is no exception. This section lists some common problems and resolutions. After each problem or symptom is a list of troubleshooting steps.

Can't Detect the Drive

For parallel-port drives, use the tape backup as the only device on the drive and check the IEEE-1284 (EPP or ECP) mode required by the drive against the parallel port configuration.

For USB drives, be sure you're using Windows 98 or higher *and* that the USB port is enabled in the BIOS; many systems originally shipped with Windows 95 have this port disabled.

For IDE drives, ensure that the master/slave jumpers on both drives are set properly.

For SCSI drives, check termination and Device ID #s.

For external drives of any type, be sure the drive is turned on a few seconds before starting the system. If not, you might be able to use the Windows 9x/2000/Me Device Manager to "Refresh" the list of devices, but if this doesn't work, you'll need to restart the computer.

Backup or Restore Operation Failure

If your tape drive suffers a backup or restore operation failure, follow these steps:

1. Make sure you are using the correct type of tape cartridge.

2. Remove and replace the cartridge.

3. Restart the system.

4. Retension the tape.

5. Try a new tape.

6. Clean the tape heads.

7. Make sure all cables are securely connected.

8. Rerun the confidence test that checks data transfer speed with a blank tape (this test overwrites any data already on the tape).

Bad Block or Other Tape Media Errors

To troubleshoot bad block or other types of media errors, follow these steps:

1. Retension the tape.

2. Clean the heads.

3. Try a new tape.

4. Restart the system.

5. Try initializing the tape.

6. Perform a Secure Erase on the tape (previous data will no longer be retrievable from the tape).

Note that most minicartridge tapes are preformatted and cannot be reformatted by your drive. Do not attempt to bulk erase preformatted tapes because this will render the tapes unusable.

System Lockup or System Freezing When Running a Tape Backup

If your system locks up or freezes while running a tape backup, follow these steps:

1. Ensure that your system meets at least the minimum requirements for both the tape drive and backup software.

2. Check for driver or resource (IRQ, DMA, or I/O port address) conflicts with your tape drive controller card or interface; using the floppy drive while making a floppy or parallel-port tape backup is a major cause of DMA conflicts.

3. Set the CD-ROM to master and the tape drive to slave if both are using the same IDE port.

4. Check the BIOS boot sequence; be sure it is not set to ATAPI (tape/CD-ROM) devices if the tape drive is configured as a master device or as a slave with no master.

5. Make sure the hard drive has sufficient free space; most backup programs temporarily use hard drive space as a buffer for data transfer.

6. Hard drive problems can cause the backup software to lock up. Check your hard disk for errors with SCANDISK or a comparable utility.

7. Check for viruses.

8. Check for previous tape drive installations; ensure that any drivers from previous installations are removed.

9. Temporarily disable the current VGA driver and test with the standard 640×480×16 VGA driver supplied by Microsoft. If the problem does not recur, contact your graphics board manufacturer for an updated video driver.

10. Files in some third-party Recycle Bins can cause backup software to lock up. Empty the Recycle Bin before attempting a backup.

11. Disable antivirus programs and Advanced Power Management.

12. Try the tape drive on another computer system and different operating system, or try swapping the drive, card, and cable with known good, working equipment.

Other Tape Drive Problems

Other issues that might cause problems in general with tape back-ups include

- Corrupted data or ID information on the tape.

- Incorrect BIOS (CMOS) settings.

- Networking problems (outdated network drivers and so on).

- The tape was made by another tape drive. If the other drive can still read the tape, this might indicate a head alignment problem or incompatible environment.

Tape Retensioning

Retensioning a tape is the process of fast forwarding and then rewinding the tape to ensure even tension exists on the tape and rollers throughout the entire tape travel. Retensioning is recommended as a preventive maintenance operation when using a new tape or after an existing tape has been exposed to temperature changes or shock (for example, dropping the tape). Retensioning also restores the proper tension to the media and removes unwanted tight spots that can develop.

Some general rules for retensioning include the following:

- Retension any tapes that have not been used for over a month or two.

- Retension tapes if you have errors reading them.

- Retension any tapes that have been dropped.

- In some cases, it might be necessary to perform the retension operation several times to achieve the proper effect. Most tape drive or backup software includes a Retension feature as a menu selection

Chapter 6

Serial Ports and Modems

Understanding Serial Ports

The asynchronous serial interface was designed as a system-to-system communications port. *Asynchronous* means that no synchronization or clocking signal is present, so characters can be sent with any arbitrary time spacing.

Each character that is sent over a serial connection is framed by a standard start-and-stop signal. A single 0 bit, called the *start* bit, precedes each character to tell the receiving system that the next eight bits constitute a byte of data. One or two stop bits follow the character to signal that the character has been sent. At the receiving end of the communication, characters are recognized by the start-and-stop signals instead of by the timing of their arrival.

Serial refers to data that is sent over a single wire, with each bit lining up in a series as the bits are sent. This type of communication is used over the phone system because this system provides one wire for data in each direction. Compared to parallel ports, serial ports are very slow, but their signals can be transmitted a greater distance. The other wires in the serial port are used to control the flow of data to or from the port.

Serial ports are also referred to as *COM* ports because they are used to communicate between devices.

Physically, serial ports come in two forms, although through adapters or specially-wired cable, they have no problems communicating with each other. The following figures show the standard 9-pin (see Figure 6.1) and 25-pin (see Figure 6.2) serial ports. The 25-pin serial port has pins sticking out, as opposed to the 25-pin parallel port, which has holes for pins.

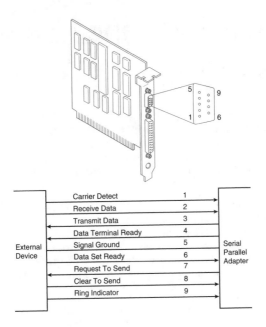

Figure 6.1 AT-style, 9-pin serial port connector specifications.

Pinouts for Serial Ports

Tables 6.1, 6.2, and 6.3 show the pinouts of the 9-pin (AT-style), 25-pin, and 9-pin-to-25-pin serial connectors.

Table 6.1 9-Pin (AT) Serial Port Connector

Pin	Signal	Description	I/O
1	CD	Carrier detect	In
2	RD	Receive data	In
3	TD	Transmit data	Out
4	DTR	Data terminal ready	Out
5	SG	Signal ground	—
6	DSR	Data set ready	In
7	RTS	Request to send	Out
8	CTS	Clear to send	In
9	RI	Ring indicator	In

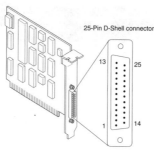

25-Pin D-Shell connector

Description	Pin	
NC	1	
Transmitted Data	2	
Received Data	3	
Request to Send	4	
Clear to Send	5	
Data Set Ready	6	
Signal Ground	7	
Received Line Signal Detector	8	
+ Transmit Current Loop Data	9	
NC	10	
- Transmit Current Loop Data	11	
NC	12	
NC	13	
NC	14	
NC	15	
NC	16	
NC	17	
+ Receive Current Loop Data	18	
NC	19	
Data Terminal Ready	20	
NC	21	
Ring Indicator	22	
NC	23	
NC	24	
- Receive Current Loop Return	25	

External Device — Asynchronous Communications Adapter (RS-232C)

Figure 6.2 Standard 25-pin serial-port connector specifications.

Table 6.2   25-Pin (PC, XT, and PS/2) Serial Port Connector

Pin	Signal	Description	I/O
1	—	Chassis ground	—
2	TD	Transmit data	Out
3	RD	Receive data	In
4	RTS	Request to send	Out
5	CTS	Clear to send	In
6	DSR	Data set ready	In
7	SG	Signal ground	—

Table 6.2   25-Pin (PC, XT, and PS/2) Serial Port Connector Continued

Pin	Signal	Description	I/O
8	CD	Carrier detect	In
9	—	+Transmit current loop return	Out
11	—	-Transmit current loop data	Out
18	—	+Receive current loop data	In
20	DTR	Data terminal ready	Out
22	RI	Ring indicator	In
25	—	-Receive current loop return	In

Table 6.3   9-Pin-to-25-Pin Serial Cable Adapter Connections

9-Pin		25-Pin	Signal
1	8	CD	Carrier detect
2	3	RD	Receive data
3	2	TD	Transmit data
4	20	DTR	Data terminal ready
5	7	SG	Signal ground
6	6	DSR	Data set ready
7	4	RTS	Request to send
8	5	CTS	Clear to send
9	22	RI	Ring indicator

> **Note**
>
> Macintosh systems use a similar serial interface, defined as RS-422. Most external modems in use today can interface with either RS-232 or RS-422, but it is safest to make sure that the external modem you get for your PC is designed for a PC, not a Macintosh.

Current Loop Serial Devices and 25-Pin Serial Ports

Whereas normal RS-232 serial devices can be connected to either a 9-pin or a 25-pin serial port, and 9-pin devices can be adapted to a 25-pin port, another type of serial device known as a *current loop* device will work with 25-pin ports only.

By comparing Figures 6.1 and 6.2, you can see that the current-loop pins (9, 11, 18, and 25) have no corresponding pins in the 9-pin serial port. Thus, if you need to connect current-loop devices to your computer (primarily devices for data acquisition), you must use a 25-pin serial port, not a 9-pin port. Adapters cannot be used because the current-loop pins are not present in the 9-pin port.

UARTs

The heart of any serial port is the Universal Asynchronous Receiver/Transmitter (UART) chip. This chip completely controls the process of breaking the native parallel data within the PC into serial format and later converting serial data back into the parallel format.

A few modem models lack a true UART and use the resources of the computer and operating system for communications in place of a UART. These so-called *Winmodems* are less expensive than ordinary modems, but are slower and not compatible with non-Windows operating systems, such as Linux.

UART Types

UART chips have been improved many times over the years, and it's important to know which UART your serial port(s) uses, especially under the following circumstances:

- You want to attach a modem to the serial port.

- You plan to transfer data between machines via the serial port.

- You want to ensure reliable multitasking while using Windows with your modem.

Table 6.4 summarizes the characteristics of the major UART chips (and equivalents) found in PCs. For more information about UARTs, see Chapter 18 of *Upgrading and Repairing PCs, 12th Edition*, from Que.

Table 6.4	Overview of UART Chip Types			
UART Type	Maximum Speed	Buffer	Typical System	Notes
8250	Up to 9600bps	No	8088	Original UART; replaced by 8250B
8250A	Up to 9600bps	No	8088	Not recommended because incompatible with 8250
8250B	Up to 9600bps	No	8088/286	Debugged version of 8250
16450	Up to 19200	No	386/486bps (19.2Kbps)	Minimum UART for OS/2

Table 6.4   Overview of UART Chip Types Continued

UART Type	Maximum Speed	Buffer	Typical System	Notes
16550A -> D	Up to 115000bps (115Kbps)	16-byte FIFO	386/486 Pentium	First chip suit able for multi-tasking; can be used as pin-compatible replacement for socketed 16450
16650	Up to 230000bps (230Kbps)	32-byte	Specialized I/O cards, ISDN terminal	Faster throughput than 16650 series adapters
16750	Up to 460000bps (460Kbps)	64-byte	Specialized I/O cards, ISDN terminal	Faster throughput than 16650, 16650 series adapters
16950	Up to 921600bps (921.6Kbps)	128-byte	Specialized I/O cards, ISDN terminal	Faster throughput than 16550, 16650, 16750 adapters

Note

The previous specifications reflect maximum speeds available with standard I/O card designs; some vendors use a clock-multiplication feature that can double the effective speed of some UARTs in some I/O card applications.

Identifying Your System UART

The minimum desirable UART chip is the 16550A series or above, but older systems and inexpensive multi-I/O cards might use the bufferless 8250 or 16450 series UARTs instead. Two major methods can be used to determine which UARTs you have in a system.

MS-DOS Method (also for Windows NT)

Use a diagnostic program such as Microsoft MSD, CheckIt, AMIDiag, or others to examine the serial ports. These programs also list the IRQ and I/O port addresses in use for each serial port. Because ports are virtualized under Windows, the reports from a DOS-based utility will not be accurate unless you boot straight to a DOS prompt and run the diagnostic from there.

OS/2 Method

Use the MODE COMx command from the OS/2 prompt to view serial port information. Look for an entry called Buffer in the list of serial port characteristics. If Buffer is set to Auto, the chip is a true 16650A or better. However, if Buffer is set to N/A, it's an older 16450 chip.

Windows 9x/2000/Me Method

Open the Start menu, and then choose Settings, Control Panel. Next, double-click Modems and then click the Diagnostics tab. The Diagnostics tab shows a list of all COM ports in the system, even if they don't have a modem attached to them. Select the port you want to check in the list and click More Info. Windows 95 or 98 communicates with the port to determine the UART type, and that information is listed in the Port Information portion of the More Info box. If a modem is attached, additional information about the modem is displayed.

High-Speed Serial Ports (ESP and Super ESP)

Some modem manufacturers have gone a step further in improving serial data transfer by introducing Enhanced Serial Ports (ESP) or Super High-Speed Serial Ports. These ports enable a 28.8Kbps or faster modem to communicate with the computer at data rates up to 921.6Kbps. The extra speed on these ports is generated by increasing the buffer size. These ports are usually based on a 16550, 16650, or 16750 UART, and some even include more buffer memory on the card.

Lava Computer Mfg. and Byte Runner Technologies are two of the vendors that offer a complete line of high-speed serial port cards; some models also include parallel ports.

Upgrading the UART Chip

Use Table 6.5 to determine where any UART chip might be located and what you would need to do to replace it.

Table 6.5 Upgrading UARTs		
Device Type	**UART Location**	**Upgrade Method**
Internal modem	Modem chipset	Replace modem
Multi-I/O card with 8250	Socketed or soldered chips	Replace card; 16550 not pin-compatible
Multi-I/O card with 16450	Socketed or soldered chips	Remove 16450 if socketed; replace card if soldered

Table 6.5 Upgrading UARTs Continued		
Device Type	**UART Location**	**Upgrade Method**
Multi-I/O card with Super I/O	Equivalent to normal UART inside a highly integrated surface-mounted chip	Replace card
Motherboard-with based I/O	Socketed MB chip	Remove and replace 16450 16550AF if socketed; disable serial I/O and install new multi I/O card with 16550AF or better UART
Newer systems— UART equivalent inside Super I/O	See the section "UARTs" earlier in this chapter	Disable serial I/O and install new multi I/O card as above

Serial Port Configuration

Each time a character is received by a serial port, it has to get the attention of the computer by raising an *interrupt request line* (*IRQ*). 8-bit ISA bus systems have 8 of these lines, and systems with a 16-bit ISA bus have 16 lines. The 8259 interrupt controller chip usually handles these requests for attention. In a standard configuration, COM 1 uses IRQ 4, and COM 2 uses IRQ 3.

When a serial port is installed in a system, it must be configured to use specific I/O addresses (called *ports*) and *interrupts*. The best plan is to follow the existing standards for how these devices should be set up. For configuring serial ports in either Windows or Linux, use the addresses and interrupts indicated in Table 6.6.

Table 6.6 Standard Serial I/O Port Addresses and Interrupts			
COM x	**I/O Ports**	**IRQ**	**Equivalent to Linux[2]**
COM 1	3F8–3FFh	IRQ 4	ttys0
COM 2	2F8–2FFh	IRQ 3	ttys1
COM 3	3E8–3EFh	IRQ 4[1]	ttys2
COM 4	2E8–2EFh	IRQ 3[1]	ttys3

1. *Although many serial ports can be set up to share IRQ 3 and 4 with COM 1 and COM 2, it is not recommended. The best recommendation is setting COM 3 to IRQ 10 and COM 4 to IRQ 11 (if available). If ports above COM 3 are required, it is recommended that you purchase a special multiport serial board.*

2. *Linux users must use distributions based on kernel 2.2 or better to enable IRQ sharing. With older distributions, use the setserial command (found in the Linux startup) to assign different IRQs to devices using ttys2 (COM3) and ttys3 (COM4); this also requires you to configure the cards to use those IRQs. For more information about setserial and serial ports under Linux, refer to the Linux Serial How-To at www.linuxdoc.org/HOWTO/Serial-HOWTO.html.*

Avoiding Conflicts with Serial Ports

Use Table 6.7 to understand possible conflicts with serial ports and avoid them.

Table 6.7	Troubleshooting Serial Port Conflicts	
Problem	**Reason**	**Solution**
DOS-based program can't find COM 3 or 4 on modem or other device	DOS and PC BIOS support COM 1 and 2 only	Disable COM 2 and set new device to use COM 2; use Windows program instead
Device using COM 3 or 4 conflicts with COM 1 and 2	Shared IRQs don't work for ISA devices	Relocate IRQ for device to a different port. If device is external, connect to multiport board. (Windows 95/98/NT/2000 can handle up to 128 serial ports!) (see earlier)

Note

For modem troubleshooting, see the section "Modems" later in this chapter.

Troubleshooting I/O Ports in Windows 9x and Me

Windows 9x and Me can tell you whether your ports are functioning. First, you need to verify that the required communications files are present to support the serial ports in your system:

1. Verify the file sizes and dates of both COMM.DRV (16-bit serial driver) and SERIAL.VXD (32-bit serial driver) in the SYSTEM directory, compared to the original versions of these files from the Windows CD-ROM. They should be the same date or *later*, not older.

2. Confirm that the following lines are present in SYSTEM.INI:

```
[boot]
comm.drv=comm.drv
[386enh]
device=*vcd
```

The SERIAL.VXD driver is not loaded in SYSTEM.INI; instead, it is loaded through the Registry.

If both drivers are present and accounted for, you can determine whether a particular serial port's I/O address and IRQ settings are properly defined by following these steps (which also work with Windows 2000):

1. Right-click the My Computer icon and select Properties. Or, you can open Control Panel and left-click the System icon twice.

   Then, click the Device Manager tab, Ports entry, and select a specific port (such as COM 1).

2. Click the Properties button and then click the Resources tab to display the current resource settings (IRQ, I/O) for that port.

3. Check the Conflicting Devices List to see whether the port is using resources that conflict with other devices. If the port is in conflict with other devices, click the Change Setting button and then select a configuration that does not cause resource conflicts. You might need to experiment with these settings until you find the right one.

4. If the resource settings cannot be changed, they most likely must be changed via the BIOS Setup. Shut down and restart the system, enter the BIOS setup, and change the port configurations there.

In addition to the COM 1/COM 3 and COM 2/COM 4 IRQ conflicts noted earlier, some video adapters have an automatic address conflict with COM 4's I/O port address (not IRQ).

You can also use the Modems Diagnostic tab (discussed earlier in this chapter) to test a serial port, whether or not a modem is actually present.

Advanced Diagnostics Using Loopback Testing

One of the most useful types of diagnostic test is the *loopback test*, which can be used to ensure the correct function of the serial port and any attached cables. Loopback tests are basically internal (digital) or external (analog). You can run internal tests by unplugging any cables from the port and executing the test via a diagnostics program.

The external loopback test is more effective. This test requires that a special loopback connector or wrap plug be attached to the port in question. When the test is run, the port is used to send data out to the loopback plug, which routes the data back into the port's receive pins so that the port is transmitting and receiving at the same time. A *loopback* or *wrap plug* is nothing more than a cable that is doubled back on itself.

Following is a list of the wiring necessary to construct your own loopback or wrap plugs. Check with the vendor of your testing software to determine which loopback plug design you need to use, or purchase pre-built ones from the vendor.

Loopback Plug Pinouts—Serial Ports

- Standard IBM type 25-Pin Serial (Female DB25S) Loopback Connector (Wrap Plug). Connect the following pins:

  1 to 7

  2 to 3

  4 to 5 to 8

  6 to 11 to 20 to 22

  15 to 17 to 23

  18 to 25

- Norton Utilities (Symantec) 25-Pin Serial (Female DB25S) Loopback Connector (Wrap Plug). Connect the following pins:

  2 to 3

  4 to 5

  6 to 8 to 20 to 22

- Standard IBM type 9-Pin Serial (Female DB9S) Loopback Connector (Wrap Plug). Connect the following pins:

  1 to 7 to 8

  2 to 3

  4 to 6 to 9

- Norton Utilities (Symantec) 9-Pin Serial (Female DB9S) Loopback Connector (Wrap Plug). Connect the following pins:

  2 to 3

  7 to 8

  1 to 4 to 6 to 9

To make these loopback plugs, you need a connector shell with the required pins installed. Then, you must wire wrap or solder wires, interconnecting the appropriate pins inside the connector shell as specified in the preceding list (see Figure 6.3).

One advantage of using loopback connectors is that you can plug them into the ends of a cable that is included in the test. This can verify that both the cable and the port are working properly.

Male and Female, 25-pin
Parallel loopback connectors

9-pin Serial
loopback connectors

Figure 6.3 Typical wrap plugs including 25-pin, 9-pin serial, and 25-pin parallel versions.

Modems

Modems provide a vital communications link between millions of small- to medium-sized businesses and homes and the Internet, electronic banking, and other services. The following information will help you get the most out of your modem.

Modems and Serial Ports

External modems connect to existing serial ports and don't contain a UART chip. Most internal modems contain their own serial port and do contain a UART chip.

Any external modem that will be used at speeds of 28Kbps or above must be connected to a 16550A-type UART or better to run at top speeds. For best results with external ISDN terminal adapters, use serial ports equipped with 16750 or 16950 UARTs because they support maximum speeds in excess of 460Kbps.

Modem Modulation Standards

Modems are frequently identified by their protocols. Use Table 6.8 to determine the speed and other characteristics of a particular protocol. Most modems support multiple protocols.

Table 6.8 Modem Modulation Standards and Transmission Rates		
Protocol	**Maximum Transmission Rate (bps)**	**Duplex Mode**
Bell 103	300bps	Full
CCITT V.21	300bps	Full
Bell 212A	1200bps	Full
ITU V.22	1200bps	Half
ITU V.22bis	2400bps	Full
ITU V.23	1,200/75bps	Pseudo-Full
ITU V.29	9,600bps	Half
ITU V.32	9,600bps	Full

Table 6.8 Modem Modulation Standards and Transmission Rates Continued		
Protocol	**Maximum Transmission Rate (bps)**	**Duplex Mode**
ITU V.32bis	14,400bps (14.4Kbps)	Full
ITU V.32fast	28,800bps (28.8Kbps)	Full
ITU V.34	28,800bps (28.8Kbps)	Full
ITU V.34bis	33,600bps (33.6Kbps)	Full
ITU V.90	56,000bps (56Kbps)[1]	Full

1. While the ITU V.90 (successor to the proprietary 56Kflex and X2 standards) allows for this speed of transmission, the U.S. FCC (Federal Communications Commission) allows only 53,000bps (53Kbps) at this time.

56Kbps Standards

Virtually every modem sold today corresponds to one or more of the so-called *56Kbps* standards for faster downloading from an Internet service provider (ISP). Uploading to a remote computer must run at the slower V.34bis speeds.

Table 6.9 lists the original and final 56Kbps standards.

Table 6.9 56Kbps Modem Standards		
Standard	**Modem Chipsets Supported** *(Major Brand Example)*	**Notes**
x2	Texas Instruments *US Robotics*	First 56Kbps standard in use; not compatible with K56flex.
K56flex	Rockwell *Hayes, Zoom*	Second 56Kbps standard in use; not compatible with x2.
V.90	All 56Kbps modems with updated firmware	Official ITU standard has replaced previous proprietary standards listed previously.
V.92	New ITU standard	Will allow higher upload speed (to 44Kbps), quicker access, and call-waiting compatibility. Look for products in late 2000 or early 2001. Might require new chipsets.

Because 56Kbps was originally a proprietary standard that was chipset dependent, many early adopters have had problems getting high-speed access as more and more ISPs have switched their x2- or K56flex-specific modem pools to V.90. Table 6.10 provides guidelines for upgrading your non-V.90 modem to the V.90 standard.

Table 6.10   Upgrade Options to V.90

Original Modem Model	Firmware in Modem	Upgrade Method
x2 or K56flex	Flash-upgradable	Check manufacturer's Web site for download to upgrade firmware.
x2 or K56flex	Not upgradable	Check manufacturer's Web site for details about a physical modem swap; might cost money.
V.34bis or earlier	Any	A firmware download or physical modem swap will be involved; will cost money.
Hayes, Practical Peripherals, and Cardinal Technologies (all defunct)	Any	Contact Modem Express at 612-553-2075 or on the Web at www.hayes.com for upgrades and drivers (costs and availability will vary by brand and model). Hayes-brand modems produced after June 11, 1999 are products of Zoom Telephonics, and are supported by Zoom's Hayes division. Check www.hayesmicro.com for details.

Upgrading from x2 or K56flex to V.90 with Flash Upgrades

The flash upgrades to V.90 work like a BIOS upgrade for a PC: You download the appropriate software from the modem vendor, run the flash software, wait a few minutes, and your modem is ready to dial in to V.90-based ISPs at top speeds. One major problem is what happens *inside* the modem to the existing firmware:

- **X2 Modems to V.90**—x2 and V.90 firmware can coexist in modem.

- **K56flex to V.90**—Most K56flex modems don't have room for both sets of firmware, so the V.90 firmware *replaces* the K56flex. The lack of a fallback standard has caused problems for some users of V.90 modems that were upgraded from K56flex models. Table 6.11 will help you find a solution if your V.90 connections aren't reliable.

Table 6.11   Troubleshooting the V.90 (ex-K56flex) Modems

Problem	Solution	Method
Can't get reliable connection with V.90.	Download and install the latest firmware revisions from the vendor's Web site, even if you have a brand new modem.	If you're having problems making the connection, dial in with your modem on a 33.6Kbps line, or pretend that your modem is an older model by installing it as a 33.6Kbps model from the same vendor.

Table 6.11 Troubleshooting the V.90 (ex-K56flex) Modems Continued		
Problem	**Solution**	**Method**
Your ISP supports both V.90 and K56flex, and you'd like a choice.	If your modem is a so-called "Dualmode" modem, install both K56flex and V.90 firmware.	The modem needs to have a 2MB ROM chip to have sufficient room for both firmware types.
	If your modem won't permit both firmware types, download both V.90 and K56flex firmware, try both, and see which one works better.	
You're not sure the latest firmware upgrade was really an improvement.	If your vendor has several versions of firmware available for download, try some of the earlier versions, as well as the latest version. An earlier version might actually work better for you.	
Your modem is a non-U.S./Canada model.	Download the country-specific upgrade for your modem.	Check the Web site for your country; contact tech support if your country isn't listed.
The firmware upgrade was installed, and the modem only works at 33.6Kbps or less.	Make sure you are using a V.90 dial-up number.	
	Make sure you downloaded updated INF files or other drivers for your operating system.	

Note

The problems with moving from K56flex to V.90 do not apply to users who have updated their V.34/V.34bis modems directly to the V.90 standard, whether by a downloadable firmware update or physical modem or chip swap. Even if your V.34/V.34bis modem was made by a company that later made K56flex modems, you don't need to worry about this unless you updated to K56flex before going to V.90. Then, the troubleshooting advice given earlier applies to you as well.

External Versus Internal Modems

Both external and internal modems are available for desktop systems. Table 6.12 helps you determine which type is better suited to your needs.

Table 6.12	External Versus Internal Modems	
Features	**External**	**Internal**
Built-in 16550 UART or higher	No (uses computer's serial port UART or can use USB).	Yes (if 14.4Kbps or faster).
Price comparison	Higher.	Lower.
Extras to buy	RS-232 Modem Interface cable or USB cable.	Nothing.
Ease of moving to another computer	Easy—unplug the cables and go! (USB modems require a functioning USB port on the other computer and Windows 98, 2000, or Me.[1])	Difficult—must open case and remove card, open other PC's case and insert card.
Power supply	Plugs into wall (brick type).	None—powered by host PC.
Reset if modem hangs	Turn modem off, and then on again.	Restart computer.
Monitoring operation	Easy—External signal lights.	Difficult—unless your communication software simulates the signal lights.
Interface type	Almost always via the RS-232 port although, USB modems are now on the market. Parallel-port modems were made a few years ago, but never proved.	Traditionally ISA, but many models now available in PCI, which should work better in new machines, allow mapping of COM 3 and 4 away from COM 1 and 2 to avoid IRQ sharing, and will be usable in machines of the future that will lack ISA slots.
	Popular	Portable computers use PC Card modems in either dedicated or combo card types.

1. *Although late versions of Windows 95 OSR 2.x have USB support, many USB devices actually require Windows 98 or better. Use Windows 98, 2000, or Me to achieve more reliable support for USB devices.*

Modem Troubleshooting

Table 6.13 will help you troubleshoot modem problems and get you back online.

Table 6.13	Modem Troubleshooting (All Types)	
Modem Type	**Problem**	**Solution**
Any	Modem fails to dial.	Check line and phone jacks on modem. Line jack—modem to telco service.
		Phone jack—modem to telephone receiver.
		If you've reversed these cables, you'll get no dial tone.
		Check the cable for cuts or breaks. If the cable looks bad, replace it.
		Make sure your modem has been properly configured by your OS. With Windows 9x, use the Modems icon in Control Panel to view and test your modem configuration. From the General tab, click the Diagnostics tab, click your modem on the serial port it's installed on, and then click More Info. This sends test signals to your modem. A properly working modem responds with information about the port and the modem.
External	Modem fails to dial.	Make sure the RS-232 modem cable is running from the modem to a working serial port on your computer and that it is switched on. Signal lights on the front of the modem can be used to determine if the modem is on and if it is responding to dialing commands. Make sure a USB modem is plugged tightly into a USB port. If it is connected to an external hub, verify that the hub is connected to your system.
PCMCIA/PCCard	Modem fails to dial.	Make sure it is fully plugged into the PCMCIA/PC Card slot. With Windows 9x/Me, you should see a small PCMCIA/PC card icon on the toolbar. Double-click it to view the cards that are currently connected. If your modem is properly attached, it should be visible. Otherwise, remove it, reinsert it into the PCMCIA/PC card slot, and see if the computer detects it.
		Check dongle used to attach modem PCMCIA/PC card modems to jack; carry a spare. If your dongle doesn't have a connector to a standard phone line, use a line coupler to attach the short dongle cable to a longer standard RJ-11 cable for easier use. Carry at least a 10 RJ-11 phone cable with you for easier use in hotel rooms.

Table 6.13   Modem Troubleshooting (All Types) Continued

Modem Type	Problem	Solution
Any	Couldn't Open Port error message.	Modem might be in use already, or IRQ I/O port–address conflict. Use Device Manager to check settings, and reinstall drivers.
	System can't dial from wall jack.	Never use a wall jack unless it is clearly marked as a "data jack" or you check with the staff. A digital phone system's jack looks identical to the safe analog jack your modem is made for, but its higher voltage will fry your phone. You can get phone-line voltage testers from sources such as `http://warrior.com`. If your hotel telephone has a data jack built-in, use it. Some hotels now offer built-in Ethernet in some rooms, so carry your NIC with you as well for faster Web access.
Internal	System locks up when trying to boot up or dial modem.	Modem trying to share a non-sharable IRQ with another port, probably a mouse. Move a serial mouse that uses the same IRQ as the modem to a different COM port with a different IRQ (from COM 1/IRQ 4 to COM 2/IRQ 3), or use a PS/2 mouse (IRQ 12). If your Pentium-class system lacks a visible PS/2 port, check with your system vendor for the (optional) header cable you need.
		Disable your system's COM 2; set the modem to COM 2 using IRQ 3.
External	Computer can't detect modem.	Check cable type. Must be RS-232 modem (not null modem or straight-through) cable (see the following pinouts).
		Check power switch and supply.
		COM port might not be working.
		Check BIOS and enable COM port; test port with CheckIt, Windows 9x/2000/ME Modem diagnostics, others; use loopback plug with CheckIt, AMIDiag, Norton, and so on for most thorough check.
		Check for IRQ conflicts.
USB	Computer can't detect modem.	Check USB ports; enable if necessary. Check USB cables and hubs.

Using Your Modem Sound to Diagnose Your V.90 Modem Connection

If you listen to your modem when it makes a connection, you may have realized that various types of modems make a distinctive connection sound, and that different connection speeds also make distinctive sounds.

The three types of 56Kbps modems (K56flex, X2, and V.90) have distinctly different "handshakes" of tones, buzzes, and warbles as they negotiate speeds with the ISP's modem. Learning what your modem sounds like when it makes a 56Kbps connection and when it settles for a V.34-speed connection can help you determine when you should hang up and try to connect at a faster speed.

The "56K=v.unreliable" Web site's troubleshooting section has a number of sound samples of various modems you can play back with Real Audio:

```
http://www.808hi.com/56k/trouble3.htm
```

Compare these sound samples to your own modem; make sure you adjust the speaker volume for your modem so you can hear it during the call.

Regardless of the modem, two handshake sounds indicate that your modem tried to connect at its 56Kbps mode, but failed and had to settle for the v.34 speed of 33.6Kbps or less.

Support for "Brand X" Modems

Many computer users today didn't install their modems, or even purchase them as a separate unit. Their modems came "bundled" inside the computer, and often have a bare-bones manual that makes no mention of the modem's origin or where to get help. Getting V.90 firmware, drivers, or even jumper settings for OEM modems like this can be difficult.

One of the best Web sites for getting help when you don't know where to start is www.windrivers.com, which features a modem identification page with the following features:

- FCC ID: Enter the FCC ID number attached to the modem to determine who made it

- Lookup by chipset manufacturer

- Modem throughput tests

- Links to major modem manufacturers

Pinouts for External Modem Cable (9-Pin at PC)

For most external modems, you need an RS-232 modem cable, which will have a 9-pin connector on one end and a 25-pin connector on the other end. Because RS-232 is a flexible standard encompassing many different pinouts, be sure the cable is constructed according to the following diagram:

1. PC (with 9-pin COM port - male)
   Modem (25-pin port - female)

3	TX data	2
2	RX data	3
7	RTS	4
8	CTS	5
6	DSR	6
5	SIG GND	7
1	CXR	8
4	DTR	20
9	RI	22

2. If you purchase an RS-232 modem cable pre-built at a store, you'll have a cable that works with your PC and your modem. However, you can use the preceding chart to build your own cable or, by using a cable tester, determine whether an existing RS-232 cable in your office is actually made for modems or some other device.

Win98SE, Windows 2000, Windows Me, and ICS

Windows 98 Second Edition, Windows 2000 Professional, and the new Windows Millennium Edition (Windows Me) all feature a built-in gateway program called *ICS (Internet Connection Sharing)*, which allows users to share a single dial-up, ISDN, cable modem, or xDSL connection. Win98SE, Windows Millennium Edition, and Windows 2000 Professional can be purchased as an upgrade to older versions of Windows, and users of the original version of Windows 98 can purchase a CD-ROM from Microsoft that will upgrade the original version to the Second Edition.

Because ICS is a gateway and clients use TCP/IP networking to use the gateway, only the gateway computer needs to use Win98SE,

Windows 2000, or Windows Me. Any computer using TCP/IP with the option to set up a gateway can be used as a client, including computers using older versions of Windows 9x and other operating systems.

Requirements for ICS

ICS requires a NIC (Network Interface Card) to be installed in the host computer and a network connection to each guest computer to share the host's Internet connection.

If the Internet connection is made through a NIC (as is the case with xDSL or two-way cable modem connections), two NICs are required: one for the Internet connection and one for sharing the connection.

ICS will not work with one-way cable modems or with DirecPC because these devices use a separate connection for downloading and uploading.

Overview of the Configuration Process

The configuration process has two parts:

* Installing ICS on the gateway computer

* Configuring the clients to use the ICS gateway to reach the Internet

Configuring ICS on the Gateway Computer with Windows 98SE or Windows Me

If ICS was not installed when Windows was installed, install it by choosing Start, Settings, Add/Remove Programs, Windows Setup. Select ICS from the Internet Tools category (Win98 Second Edition) or from the Communications category (WinMe).

Note
Windows Me will start the Home Networking Wizard as soon as you install ICS; the Home Networking Wizard performs the same tasks as ICS in the same sequence as discussed in the following list.

Next, specify whether you are using a dial-up connection (modem or ISDN) or a high-speed connection (LAN, including cable modem or DSL).

If you select dial-up, choose the dial-up connection (which must be set up already) you'll be sharing, followed by the NIC (Network

Interface Card) that connects you with the client PC's that will share the connection.

Windows will create a client configuration floppy and will prompt you to reboot the computer.

When you view the Network Configuration in the Control Panel after rebooting, you should see the following:

- Three "adapters" (your actual NIC, the Dial-Up adapter, and a new one called Internet Connection Sharing)

- Three Internet Connection Sharing protocol entries, listing the previously mentioned adapters

- Three TCP/IP protocol entries, listing the previously mentioned adapters

The TCP/IP protocol entry for "Home" must point to the NIC that connects the clients to the host PC; the TCP/IP protocol entry called "Shared" must point to Dial-Up Networking; and the remaining TCP/IP protocol entry must point to Internet Connection Sharing.

Also, check the TCP/IP configuration for "Home" (the NIC) and verify the IP address; it should be 192.168.0.1. This IP address must be provided to the computers that will share the Internet connection.

If the settings aren't correct, remove ICS and start over.

Start an Internet connection on the gateway (host) computer before continuing.

Configuring ICS on the Client Computers with a Windows 9x/Me Host

Although the ICS configuration process on the gateway (host) computer created a disk that can be used for setting up the ICS connection on client computers, most non-Microsoft sources advocate using manual configuration instead. The following steps are required:

- Install the TCP/IP protocol on each client.

- Set the Gateway option in the TCP/IP properties for each client's NIC to the IP address of the gateway (ICS) computer: 192.168.0.1 is the usual value (see above). Click Add to insert this value after you enter it.

- Use a Web browser on each guest to verify the connection is working; Internet Explorer should not have any dial-up settings configured for it, and should have no LAN settings enabled. The ICS client for Windows 98 disk selects Use a Proxy Server here, which is not correct. Netscape Navigator/Communicator should be set to Direct Connection to the Internet.

- Some versions of Netscape Navigator might not work unless you create a Dial-Up Networking "adapter" on the guest and set its gateway as previously discussed.

Reboot before you test the connection.

Setting Up ICS with a Windows 2000 Host Computer

Windows 2000 has built-in Internet connection sharing features. Log in as administrator before starting the following procedure. As with ICS for Windows 9x/Me, a LAN connection to the Internet must be shared by way of a second LAN card.

To share a connection, follow these steps:

1. Open the Network and Dial-Up Connections icon in the Control Panel.

2. Right-click the connection you want to share and select Properties.

3. Select the Internet Connection Sharing tab and enable sharing on your computer.

4. If this is a modem connection, you can select the Enable On-Demand Dialing check box on the same tab as Internet Connection sharing. Enabling this feature launches the connection whenever other computers connected to this host computer need Internet access.

To connect to a shared connection on a Windows 2000 host, follow these steps:

1. Make sure you are running Windows 9x, Windows NT, or Windows 2000 Professional on your client.

2. Verify that the NIC that connects your client to the host is set to the following:

   - Obtain an IP address automatically

   - Use DHCP for WINS resolution

   - Connect to a DNS server automatically

(These settings require changes to the default settings for your NIC's TCP/IP properties.)

3. Adjust the Internet Explorer settings to the following:

   • Never Dial a connection

   • Use a LAN connection

   • Automatically detect settings

   • Don't use automatic configuration script

   • Don't use a proxy server

Note

Useful Web sites that cover this process in more detail include

http://www.timhiggins.com/ppd/icsinstall.htm
http://www.duxcw.com/digest/Howto/network/win98se/

The following Microsoft Web page answers common questions about Win98SE:

http://support.microsoft.com/support/windows/faq/
win98se/w98seics.asp

If you want the additional benefits of a proxy server, check out products such as WinProxy (www.winproxy.com), WinGate (www.wingate.deerfield.com), and Sybergen SyGate (www.sybergen.com). Many home-oriented networks and modems are bundled with these or similar products, so if you're in the market for a new modem or are building a small network, ask whether a proxy server program for Internet sharing is included with your home or small-office networking kit.

Chapter 7

Parallel Ports, Printers, Scanners, and Drives

Parallel Port Connectors

Three different types of parallel port connectors are defined by the IEEE-1284 parallel port standard. In Figure 7.1, the DB-25 connector used on PCs for parallel cables (also called Type A) is on the left. The Centronics 36 connector (also called Type B) is in the middle. Virtually every parallel-interface printer, from the oldest dot-matrix to the newest laser printer, uses the Type B connector. Hewlett-Packard introduced the Type C connector and has added it to most of its recent laser printers, although it still uses the Type B connector as well. Type C is a high-density connector that uses a cable with an integral clip, as opposed to the clumsy, easy-to-lose wire clips used on the Type B port.

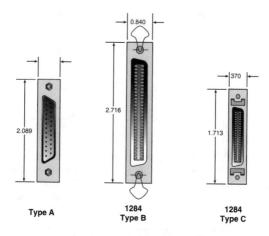

| Type A | 1284 Type B | 1284 Type C |

Figure 7.1 The three types of IEEE-1284 parallel port connectors.

You can see these connectors, along with all the others on the back of your system, in Chapter 14, "Connector Quick Reference."

Parallel Port Performance

As printers have gotten faster and more devices are attached to parallel ports, the need for increasing parallel port speed has become more and more apparent. High-speed laser and inkjet printers, tape backup drives, CD-RW drives, and parallel port-to-SCSI converters can all benefit from using the fastest parallel port modes available on your system.

Use the following tables to help determine whether your parallel ports are set to the fastest standard supported by your printers or other parallel port devices. On most computers, you adjust these parallel port settings through the CMOS/BIOS configuration screens. If the port is on an expansion card, you might use jumper blocks or a setup program to change the settings.

Table 7.1 summarizes the various types of parallel ports, their input and output modes, speed, and hardware settings.

Table 7.1   Parallel Port Types as Defined by IEEE-1284

Parallel Port Type	Input Mode	Output Mode	Input/ Output Speed	Comments
SPP (Standard Parallel Port)	Nibble (4 bits)	Compatible	Input: 50KB/ second Output: 150KB/second	4-bit input, 8-bit output
	Compatible (8 bits)	Input/Output	Bidirectional 8-bit I/O: 150KB/second	Byte
EPP (Enhanced Parallel Port)	EPP	EPP	Input/Output: 500KB– 2MB/sec	8-bit I/O, uses IRQ
ECP (Enhanced Capabilities Port)	ECP	ECP	Input/Output: 500KB– 2MB/sec	8-bit I/O, uses IRQ and DMA

EPP Versus ECP Modes

Both EPP and ECP ports are part of the IEEE-1284 bidirectional parallel port standard, but they are not identical. Use the following table to understand how they differ, and consult your parallel port device manuals to see which mode is best for your system.

Port Type	IRQ Usage	DMA Usage	Designed For	Notes
EPP	Yes (Table 7.2)	No	Tape drives, CD-ROM, LAN adapters	Version 1.7 predates IEEE-1284 standard; IEEE-1284 version often called EPP 1.9

Port Type	IRQ Usage	DMA Usage	Designed For	Notes
ECP	Yes (Table 7.2)	DMA 3 (Standard) DMA 1 (Optional; default on some Packard-Bell models)	High-speed printers, scanners	Many systems offer an EPP/ECP port setting for best results with all types of parallel port devices

Some older parallel printers don't recommend either mode and might print erratically if EPP or ECP modes are enabled. and ECP ports

Prerequisites for EPP and ECP Modes

To use these advanced modes, you must

- Enable the appropriate mode on the parallel port (see previous section)

- Use a parallel cable rated for IEEE-1284 uses

The IEEE-1284–compatible printer cable transports all signal lines to the printer, is heavily shielded, and produces very reliable printing with old and new printers alike in any parallel port mode. IEEE-1284 cables can also be purchased in a *straight-through* version for use with printer-sharing devices.

Parallel Port Configurations

Table 7.2 lists the standard parallel port settings. While add-on multi-I/O or parallel port cards can offer additional settings, other settings will work only if software can be configured to use them.

Table 7.2 Parallel Interface I/O Port Addresses and Interrupts			
Standard LPTx	Alternate LPTx	I/O Ports	IRQ
LPT1	—	3BC-3BFh	IRQ 7
LPT1	LPT2	378-37Ah	IRQ 7 (LPT1) IRQ 5 (LPT2)
LPT2	LPT3	278h-27Ah	IRQ 5

Testing Parallel Ports

The most reliable way to test printer ports is to use a parallel port testing program along with the appropriate loopback plug. This method isolates the port and allows the system to capture output back as input. Parallel port testing programs are included in major diagnostic programs, such as Norton Utilities, CheckIt, AMIDiag, QA+ family, MicroScope 2000, and many others.

Building a Parallel Loopback Plug

Several loopback plugs are used for parallel ports because of the different testing procedures performed by the various diagnostic programs. If you have the correct pinouts, you can build your own, or you can purchase them directly from the diagnostic software company, either with the software or separately.

Most use the IBM style loopback, but some use the style that originated in the Norton Utilities diagnostics. *Check with your diagnostic software vendor to see which of these loopback designs is the correct one for your system, or if a different design is needed.*

The following wiring is necessary to construct your own loopback or wrap plugs to test a parallel port:

- IBM 25-Pin Parallel (Male DB25P) Loopback Connector (Wrap Plug). Connect the following pins:

  1 to 13

  2 to 15

  10 to 16

  11 to 17

- Norton Utilities 25-Pin Parallel (Male DB25P) Loopback Connector (Wrap Plug). Connect the following pins:

  2 to 15

  3 to 13

  4 to 12

  5 to 10

  6 to 11

Troubleshooting Parallel Ports

Table 7.3   Resolving Parallel Port Problems

Symptoms	Cause(s)	Solution
Device on port not recognized; can't configure printer; printer won't print	Wrong parallel-port setting	Check device manual; probably need to change port to EPP, ECP, or EPP/ECP mode.
	Wrong cable	If you're using EPP or ECP, you must use an IEEE-1284 cable.

Table 7.3	Resolving Parallel Port Problems Continued	
Symptoms	**Cause(s)**	**Solution**
	Switchbox between device and computer	All cables and switchbox must be IEEE-1284–compliant; remove switchbox and connect directly to device. If it works, replace non-compliant switchbox or cables.
	IRQ or I/O port address conflict	EPP and ECP require a non-shared IRQ; use Windows 9x Device Manager to see whether IRQ for LPT (parallel) port is conflicting with another device; also check I/O port address and DMA.
	Device not powered on	Power on device before starting computer.
	Port defective	Use loopback and test software to verify data going out port is readable.

Printers

Printers can be attached to your computer in a variety of ways. Major interfaces used for printers include those listed in Table 7.4.

Table 7.4	Printer Interface Standards and Recommended Uses		
Interface Type Required	**Benefits**	**Drawbacks**	**Operating System**
Parallel (LPT)	Relatively fast, especially if EPP or ECP modes are used. Supported by virtually any application that can print. No port speed or setup options required in most cases. Standard cable works with virtually any PC and printer combination.	Regular printer cable length restricted to 10 feet due to signalloss. Daisy-chaining with other peripherals doesn't always work. Printer must be last device on daisy-chain.	Works with any operating system.
Serial (RS-232/COM)	Standard cable can reach up to 50 feet; use line drivers and phone cable to reach hundreds of feet. Printer can work with terminals, PCs, or Macintoshes with appropriate cable.	Serial port speed, word length, and stop bits must be set for both printer and application for printing to work. Very slow graphics printing. Different printers require custom cabling.	Works with any operating system, but is obsolete for PC use.

Table 7.4   Printer Interface Standards and Recommended Uses Continued

Interface Type Required	Benefits	Drawbacks	Operating System
USB	Faster than most parallel port modes. Devices can be daisy-chained through hubs in any order. Hot-swappable; printer can be moved to any USB-based system. Many devices are cross-platform–compatible with both PCs and Macs.	Driver problems causing difficulty for many USB-based[2] printers, especially certain HP inkjet models.	Requires Windows 98, Windows 2000, or Windows Me[1].
PC Card	Provides power to printer; no electrical cord needed. Allows design of very compact printers for use with notebook computers.	Fragile PC Card can be broken or damaged. Printers with this interface can't work with desktop computers; might need to remove a PC Card from the notebook computer to enable printing.	Varies with printer.
Network	Enables sharing of a single, high-performance printer among many clients. Fast networks allow printing about as fast as local printing. Can "print" offline to queue and release when printer becomes available.	Requires network cards and config-uration. Low-cost, host-based printers can't be networked.	Works with any network operating system; check printer for limitations.

1. *Windows 95 OSR2.1 also includes USB support, but many USB devices will not work with that version. Windows Me can use Windows 98 drivers, but a different driver is required for Windows 2000. More USB devices support Windows 98/Me than 2000.*

2. *I recommend you purchase printers that can also be used with parallel ports in case of prob-lems with USB slupport.*

Printers also can be interfaced by IEEE-1394 and SCSI ports, but these implementations are used primarily by Macintosh systems with high-end inkjet or laser printers in graphic arts environments.

Use Tables 7.5 and 7.6 to help you keep your printer running reli-ably.

Hewlett-Packard PCL Versions

Use Table 7.5 to determine which printer control language (PCL) features a printer offers, based on the version of HP-PCL it sup-ports. You also can use this table to choose compatible printers in case you don't have exactly the right driver for a given HP-PCL printer or compatible.

Table 7.5 lists major printer models that support various versions of PCL. It is not exhaustive; check your printer's manual for details about its PCL version and features.

Table 7.5   Hewlett-Packard Printer Control Language (PCL) Versions

Version	Date	Models	Benefits
PCL 3	1984	LaserJet LaserJet Plus	Full page formatting; vector graphics.
PCL 4	1985	LaserJet Series II LaserJet IIP series	Added typefaces; downloadable macros; support for larger bitmapped fonts and graphics.
PCL 5	1990	LaserJet III, IIID, IIIP, IIIsi	Scalable typefaces; outline fonts; HP-GL/2 (vector) graphics; font scaling.
PCL 5e	1992	LaserJet 4, 4M, 4L, 4ML, 4P, 4MP, 4 Plus, 4M Plus, 5P, 5MP, 5L, 5L-FS, 5Lxtra, 6L, 6Lxi, 6Lse, 6P, 6MP, 6Psi, 6Pse	600dpi support; bidirectional communication between printer and PC; additional fonts for Microsoft Windows.
PCL 5c	1994	Color LaserJet Color LaserJet 5, 5M	Color extensions
PCL 6	1996	LaserJet 4000 LaserJet 2100	Faster graphics printing and return to application; better WYSIWYG printing; faster graphics printing; less network traffic; better document fidelity and full backward-compatibility with PCL 5 and earlier versions; uses object-oriented printer commands. PCL 6 requires a Windows 9x/NT/3.1 printer driver; non-Windows operating systems can use a PCL 6 printer as a PCL 5e printer.

Comparing Host-Based to PDL-Based Printers

Most printers use a page description language (PDL). PDL-based printers receive commands from applications or the operating system that describe the page to the printer, which then renders it before printing. More and more low-cost printers are using a host-based printing system in which the computer renders the page instead of the printer.

Use Table 7.6 to determine which type of printer is suitable for your users.

Table 7.6 PDL Versus Host-Based Printers

Printer Type	Feature	Benefit	Drawback
PDL (includes HP-PCL and compatibles, PostScript)	Page rendered in printer	Printer can be used independently of a PC or particular operating system; MS-DOS support	Higher cost because brains are inside the printer
Host-based	Page rendered by computer	Lower cost because brains are inside the PC, not the printer	Printer must be married to a computer with a compatible operating system and minimum performance requirements; non-Windows support is chancy; often can't be networked

Use Table 7.7 to determine the simplest way to test a printer. Note that host-based printers *must* have their drivers installed before they can print.

Table 7.7 Testing Printers

Printer Type	Test Method
Non-PostScript printer using PDL or escape sequences (HP-PCL, compatibles, dot-matrix, inkjet)	Enter DIR>LPTI from a command prompt (MS-DOS or Windows 9x/Me); printer will print directory listing.
PostScript printer	You must send PostScript commands to the printer directly to test it without drivers. You can use PostScript printer test in Microsoft MSD or install correct drivers and use test print. (Windows 9x/NT/2000/ME offer a printer test at the end of the driver install process. This test can also be performed at any time through the printer's icon in the Printer's folder.)
Host-based printer	Install correct drivers and then use test print as earlier.

Printer Hardware Problems

Use Table 7.8 to track down problems and solutions with printers (any interface type).

Table 7.8 Troubleshooting Printer Problems

Symptom	Printer Type	Cause(s)	Solutions
Fuzzy printing	Laser	Damp paper	Use paper stored at proper temperature and humidity.

	Printer		
Symptom	**Type**	**Cause(s)**	**Solutions**
	Inkjet	Wrong paper type or printer settings	Use inkjet-rated paper; check print setting and match settings and resolution to paper type; make sure you're using correct side of paper (look for a "print this side first" marking on the package).
	Inkjet	Cartridge clogged or not seated correctly	Reseat cartridge; run cleaning utility; remove Canon cartridge from unit and clean printhead.
White lines through printed text or graphics	Inkjet	Some nozzles clogged	Use nozzle-cleaning routine on printer or utility program in printer driver to clean; retest afterwards.
			On Canon, HP, and other printers with removable printheads, clean printhead with alcohol and foam swab.
			On Epson and other models with fixed printhead, use cleaning sheet to clean printhead.
			On any model, replace printer cartridge if three cleaning cycles and tests don't clear up clogging.
	Impact dot-matrix	Pins in printhead stuck or broken	Remove printhead and clean with alcohol and foam swab; retest.
			If pins are bent or broken, repair or replace printhead.
			Check head gap and adjust to avoid printhead damage; widen head gap for envelopes, labels, and multipart forms; adjust back to regular position for normal paper.
			Change ribbon; discard ribbons with snags or tears.
Variable print density	Laser	Toner unevenly distributed in drum or toner cartridge	Remove toner cartridge and shake from side to side; check printer position and ensure it's level; check for light leaks; replace toner cartridge or refill toner.
Fuzzy white lines on pages	Laser	Dirty corotrons (corona wires)	Clean corotrons per manufacturer recommendation.
Pages print solid black	Laser	Broken charger corotron	Replace toner cartridge if it contains corotron, or repair printer.
Pages print solid white	Laser	Broken transfer corotron	Repair transfer corotron.

Table 7.8   Troubleshooting Printer Problems Continued

Table 7.8   Troubleshooting Printer Problems Continued

Symptom	Printer Type	Cause(s)	Solutions
Sharp, vertical white lines	Laser	Dirty developer unit	Clean developer if separate; replace toner cartridge if it contains developer unit.
Regularly spaced spots	Laser	Spots less than 3 inches apart indicate dirty fusing roller	Clean fusing roller.
		Widely spaced spots, or one per page, indicates scratched or flawed drum	Replace drum and fuser cleaning pad.
Gray print	Laser	Worn-out drum	Replace drum (most common with separate drum and toner supply) background.
Loose toner	Laser	Fusing roller not hot enough	Service fusing roller.
Solid vertical black line	Laser	Toner cartridge nearly empty	Shake toner cartridge to redistribute toner.
		Scratched drum	Replace drum or toner cartridge.
Paper jams and misfeeds	Laser and inkjet	Incorrect paper loading; paper too damp; paper wrinkled; paper too heavy/thick for printer	Use paper that is in proper condition for printing; don't overfill paper tray; don't dog-ear paper when loading it.
Envelope jams	Laser and inkjet	Incorrect paper loading; failure to set laser printer to use rear paper exit tray; printer can't handle envelopes	Check correct envelope handling procedures; consider using labels to avoid envelopes.
Blank pages between printed pages	Laser and inkjet	Paper stuck together; paper is damp or wrinkled	Riffle paper before loading paper tray; make sure all paper is the same size.
Blank page between print jobs	Laser and inkjet	Print spooler set to produce a blank divider page	Change print spooler setting.

Table 7.8 Troubleshooting Printer Problems Continued

Symptom	Printer Type	Cause(s)	Solutions
Error light on printer flashes; printer ejects partial page (might require you to press page-eject button)	Laser	Memory or overflow printer overrun error	Reduce graphics resolution; simplify a PostScript page; reduce number of fonts; check printer memory size is accurately set; run printer self-test to determine amount of RAM onboard; add RAM to printer.
Error light blinks; no page ejected or printed	Laser	Various causes	Look up blink code in printer documentation and take appropriate action. Error codes vary with printer model; check manufacturer's Web site for a list of codes if the user manual is missing.
LCD panel on printer displays error code or message	Laser	Various causes	Look up error code or message in manual and take appropriate action. Error codes vary with printer model; check manufacturer's Web site for a list of codes if the user manual is missing. Many less-expensive models use signal lights (see previous).

Printer Connection Problems

Use Table 7.9 to determine the cause and cure for problems with your printer connection.

Table 7.9 Troubleshooting Printer Connections

Symptom	Printer Type Or Port Type	Cause(s)	Solutions
Gibberish printing	Any	PDL used for print job doesn't match printer	Make sure print job is sent to correct printer; check default printer value; check port used for printer; check switchbox for proper printer selection; replace switchbox with LPT2 card or with USB-parallel cable.
		Damaged cable	Look for damaged pins or insulation; use pinouts for each port type to test cable with a loop back plug or with a multimeter with CONT (continuity) function; retest with known-working cable.
	Serial port	Incorrect speed, word length, parity, and stop bits	Both serial port on computer and printer must be set to match.

Table 7.9   Troubleshooting Printer Connections Continued

Symptom	Printer Type Or Port Type	Cause(s)	Solutions
			Use DOS MODE or Windows COM Port properties sheet to set serial port on computer.
			Printer configuration varies; might involve use of DIP switches, jumper blocks, printer setup panel, or software configuration program; see printer manual.
		Incorrect cable pinout	No such thing as a "universal" RS-232 printer cable; check pinouts at both computer and printer end; rewire or reorder cable as needed.
	PostScript laser	PostScript preamble not properly received	Check cable; check serial port configuration; reload drivers.
Printer not available	Any	Print job has timed out; computer is using offline mode to spool jobs	Check for paper out; reload paper. Check printer cable or serial port settings; look for IRQ conflicts and correct them; set switchbox to automatic mode, or lock it to computer you want to print from.
	USB port	Printer may not be detected by Device Manager	Check Device Manager; remove and reattach printer and recheck. See Chapter 8 for other USB troubleshooting tips.
Printer doesn't notify Windows of paper out, jams, out of toner or ink, etc.	Laser and inkjet	IEEE-1284 connection not working	Ensure port and cable(s) and switchbox are all IEEE-1284 (EPP or ECP or EPP/ECP); check cable connection; CMOS/BIOS configuration. Install ECP LPT port driver in Windows.
Intermittent or failed communications with printer	Any	Bad switchbox or cables	Use direct connection to printer; check cables; replace rotary-dial manual switchbox with autosensing switchbox.
	Parallel port	Device daisy-chain with printer	Use printer only; change order of daisy-chain; avoid use of Zip, scanner, and printer on single LPT port.

Table 7.9	Troubleshooting Printer Connections Continued		
Symptom	Printer Type Or Port Type	Cause(s)	Solutions
	USB port	Hub or driver problems	See Chapter 8 for USB troubleshooting tips.
Port busy; printer goes offline	Laser and inkjet	ECP port prints too fast for printer	Use Windows 9x/Me Control Panel to load standard LPT driver in place of ECP driver; change setting in BIOS to EPP or bidirectional.

If your USB printer can also be used as a parallel printer, use the parallel (LPT) port if you cannot solve print quality or reliability problems when you use it in USB mode.

Printer Driver and Application Problems

Printers use driver software to communicate with operating systems and applications. Use Table 7.10 to solve problems with drivers and applications.

Table 7.10	Troubleshooting Printer Drivers and Applications		
Symptom	Printer Type	Cause(s)	Solutions
Prints okay from command prompt (DIR>LPT1), but not from applications	Any	Printer driver damaged or buggy	Reload printer driver and test; reinstall printer driver; switch to compatible new version that can be downloaded.
Form-feed light comes on, but nothing prints	Laser	Incomplete page sent to printer	Normal behavior for Print-Screen or envelope printing; eject paper manually; otherwise, reinstall driver.
Incorrect fonts print	Laser or inkjet	Printer using internal fonts instead of TrueType	Check driver setting to determine which fonts will be used.
Incorrect page breaks	Any	Printer changed between document composition and printing	If you change printers or plan to use a fax modem to print your document, select the printer and scroll through your document first to check page breaks due to differences in font rendering and so on; correct as needed.
Page cut off on left, right, top, or bottom edges	Laser or inkjet	Margins set beyond printable area of printer	Reset document margins; use "print to fit" to scale page or document to usable paper size; check for proper paper size set in printer properties.

Troubleshooting Parallel Port and Other Types of Scanners

Scanners are among the most popular add-ons to computers, but they can cause plenty of problems for users. Use Table 7.11 to help make scanning trouble-free.

Table 7.11	Scanner Troubleshooting		
Interface Type	**Problem**	**Causes**	**Solution**
Parallel	Slow scanning speed	Wrong port setting	Use ECP or EPP mode per scanner.
	Scanner not recognized	Problems with daisy-chain when scanner used with non-printer devices or as third item (printer, scanner, and anything else)	Shuffle order of scanner and non-printing device; check port settings; try scanner by itself; install second parallel port; make sure SCSI/Parallel scanner set for parallel mode; check device driver setup during boot; and set SCSI/Parallel scanner for SCSI mode; check cable.
SCSI	Scanner not recognized	Termination set wrong; wrong SCSI ID; no drivers installed	Terminate scanner only if last device in SCSI daisy-chain; look for switch or terminating plug and check operation; check SCSI IDs already in use and select an unused number; install TWAIN or ISIS drivers as well as SCSI drivers; check cable.
USB	Scanner not recognized	USB port not working or not present	Enable USB port in BIOS or install card; check port for IRQ conflict; use Windows 98, ME, or 2000 to avoid support problems with Windows 95B; get updated drivers; check cable.
All	Scanner worked with Windows 95, but not after Windows 98 upgrade	TWAIN.DLL file was replaced by Windows 98	Use Windows 98's Version Conflict Manager to determine if TWAIN.DLL was replaced; use the original version (backed up by VCM).
	Scanner not recognized	Scanner turned off when system booted	Turn on scanner, open Windows 9x/Me/2000's Device Manager and refresh devices; if this doesn't work, leave the scanner on and reboot the system.

Table 7.11	Scanner Troubleshooting Continued		
Interface Type	**Problem**	**Causes**	**Solution**
	Acquire command in Photoshop or other programs won't launch scanner	TWAIN or ISIS drivers not properly installed or registered in system Registry; scanner turned off	Verify scanner detected by system; if scanner works with its own software (not launched from another application), reinstall drivers and verify Acquire command works.
	Graphics look distorted during scan	Wrong scanning mode set for document	Use Table 7.12 to determine best scanning mode by document type.

Use Table 7.12 as a quick reference to help determine the best scanning mode for your documents.

Table 7.12	Recommended Scanning Modes for Document Types			
Document Type	**Color Photo**	**Drawing**	**Text**	**B&W Photo Scanning Mode**
Line Art	No	Yes	Yes	No
OCR	No	No	Yes	No
Grayscale	No	Yes[1]	No	Yes
Color photo	Yes	No	No	Yes[2]
Color halftone	Yes[3]	No	No	No
Color drawing	No	Yes	No	No
256-color	No	Yes	No	No
Copy/fax	Yes[4]	Yes[4]	Yes[4]	Yes[4]

1. *Recommended only for drawings containing pencil shading and ink wash effects*

2. *Use to convert color to black and white if photo-editing software conversion is unavailable or produces inferior results*

3. *Adjust halftone options to match output device's requirements*

4. *Use to prepare scanned image for sending as fax or when image will be photocopied; converts all tones to digital halftones*

Parallel Port Drives

Parallel ports were originally designed for printing, but have been pressed into service for many different tasks, including tape, optical, and removable-media drives.

Use Table 7.13 to help you get the most from parallel port interface drives.

Table 7.13	Troubleshooting Parallel Port Drives	
Drive Type	**Problem**	**Solution**
Any drive type	Drive not detected in Device Manager or backup program	Check power and tighten cables; refresh Device Manager.
		Restart system if necessary; rerun drive installation software or tape backup installation software.
Any drive type	Slow operation	Use fastest parallel port mode (EPP or ECP) available.
		Use drive or backup program setup utility to adjust speed of port.
CD-R/CD-RW drive	Buffer underruns; can't make CD-Rs reliably	Use fastest parallel port mode (EPP or ECP) available.
		Reduce write speed.
		Avoid using computer for other tasks while making CD-R.
		Use packet-writing with CD-Rs to reduce load on CPU if media will be used on computers that can accept multisession CD-Rs.

Chapter 8

USB and IEEE-1394 Ports and Devices

Universal Serial Bus

The *Universal Serial Bus (USB)* port is a dual-speed connection running at 1.5Mbps or 12Mbps, which enables up to 127 devices of many different types to be connected to a single port. The USB port is well on its way to replacing the traditional serial, parallel, and PS/2 ports on new and forthcoming systems, and it is already being used for a wide variety of devices. Use this section to help you detect and configure USB ports effectively.

USB Port Identification

Figures 8.1 and 8.2 help you identify USB devices and ports.

Figure 8.1   This icon is used to identify USB cables, connectors, and peripherals.

Pinout for the USB Connector

Table 8.1 shows the pinout for the USB connector.

Table 8.1	USB Connector Pinout		
Pin	Signal Name	Color	Comment
1	VCC	Red	Cable power
2	– Data	White	
3	+ Data	Green	
4	Ground	Black	Cable ground

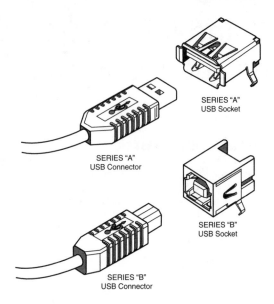

SERIES "A"
USB Socket

SERIES "A"
USB Connector

SERIES "B"
USB Socket

SERIES "B"
USB Connector

Figure 8.2   USB Series A and Series B plugs and receptacles.

Typical USB Port Locations

The location of USB ports varies with the system. On late-model desktop and tower computers using baby-AT motherboards, you might find one or two USB ports on a card bracket in the rear of the computer. The ports might be mounted on an add-on card or cabled out from motherboard ports.

Most systems using ATX, NTX, or similar motherboards—as well as late-model LPX-based systems—will have one or two USB ports on the rear of the case next to other ports.

Some consumer-oriented, late-model systems have one USB port on the front, sometimes located next to a 9-pin serial port. These ports are located in the front of the computer for easier connection of digital cameras and card readers for digital image downloading.

Adding USB Ports to Your Computer

If your computer doesn't have USB ports onboard, use one of the following options to add them:

- Purchase USB header cables to extend motherboard USB cable connectors to the outside of the case.

- Purchase and install a USB host adapter card.

Even if your baby-AT system has connectors for USB header cables, changes in the USB spec make installing an up-to-date USB host adapter card a better idea for many users.

Prerequisites for Using USB Ports and Peripherals

Before you buy or try to install a USB peripheral, make sure your system meets the requirements shown in Table 8.2. Some adjustments or updates to the system configuration might be necessary.

Table 8.2 Prerequisites for Use of USB Ports/Peripherals		
Requirement	**Reason**	**Notes**
Windows 98 Windows 2000 Windows Millennium Edition	Built-in support for USB peripherals	Windows 95B OSR 2.1 and above have USB support, but many peripherals require Win98 or above.
Working USB ports	Many systems shipped with disabled USB ports	Check BIOS and enable there if necessary; some systems might require header cables to bring the USB connector to the rear of the system.

You can download the free USB Ready utility program at `www.usb.org/data/usbready.exe` to check your system's USB readiness at both hardware and software levels.

Verify that the peripheral you are installing is designed for your operating system. Although USB ports themselves are found on both PC and Macintosh systems, some USB devices are for use only on PCs or Macintoshes, not both types of systems.

Troubleshooting USB Ports

USB ports built into the computer (also called *root hubs*) are becoming the primary external device connection for an increasing number of PCs. While USB devices are plug and play, requiring (and allowing!) no configuration, persistent problems with USB devices are common for many users. Use the following tips to help you achieve reliable USB operation:

- Check Prerequisites from Table 8.2.

- If devices don't work when plugged into an external hub, plug them into the root hub (USB connector on the system); if they work when attached to the root hub, upgrade the external hub's firmware, attach a power supply to it, or replace it.

- If a new device isn't detected, remove other USB devices, plug in the new device first, and then reattach the other USB devices.

- Check the power usage for the USB bus in the Power dialog box of the operating system.

- Verify that the USB device is drawing no less than 50mA and no more than 500mA.

- Use the Windows Device Manager to verify proper operation of the USB port; adjust IRQ settings if necessary to avoid conflicts with other devices.

- Install the latest USB device drivers for the device and the operating system; USB devices that work in Windows 98 might not be supported by other versions of Windows.

- If a printer doesn't work properly with the "correct" USB driver, try using a compatible driver for an older model as a workaround.

- Install the latest firmware for the USB device; bad firmware creates "ghost" versions of devices in the Device Manager when the device is unplugged and reattached.

- Verify that the USB root hub (port) is assigned an IRQ; normally IRQ 9 is used if available. Make sure IRQ steering is working if all available IRQs are already assigned to other ports.

- Use high-speed (heavily shielded) cabling for high-speed devices, such as printers, scanners, and network connections.

- Separate low-speed from high-speed devices by attaching them to separate USB ports.

- Assign USB controllers to Controller ID 1 if not detected by the game.

- Use the smallest number of hubs possible; some versions of Windows can't use over 5 USB hubs (some devices double as hubs).

- Before you purchase a USB device, verify device driver support for your operating system; Windows 2000 supports USB devices, but many vendors are slow about supplying USB drivers for Windows 2000.

- When possible, buy devices that can be connected by either a USB port or a so-called "legacy" port (PS/2 keyboard/mouse port, serial port, parallel port, or SCSI port) to enable you to use the device even if you have problems with your USB ports or peripherals.

Using USB Hubs with Legacy (Serial, Parallel, and PS/2) Ports

A number of products on the market enable you to connect various legacy products to USB ports. The most economical way to connect serial, parallel, or PS/2-port products is through the use of a multi-purpose hub that also features multiple USB ports.

You can also purchase serial-to-USB or parallel-to-USB converter cables, but these are less flexible and more expensive if you need to connect multiple legacy devices to a system.

Check the list of supported legacy devices before you buy a con-verter cable or multi-purpose port. USB hubs with PS/2 and serial ports normally support legacy devices such as modems, keyboards, and mice; USB hubs with parallel ports normally support printers. If you use other types of parallel devices, such as drives or scanners, you will need an actual parallel port to connect them. However, because daisy-chaining multiple parallel devices can be difficult, moving the printer to a multi-purpose USB hub can free up the LPT port for use by these other devices.

Online Sources for Additional USB Support

- Linux USB Device Support and Status

  http://www.qbik.ch/usb/devices/

- USB News and Troubleshooting Sites

  http://www.usbman.com/

  http://www.usbworkshop.com/

  http://www.usb.org

USB 2.0

USB 2.0 is a backward-compatible extension of the USB 1.1 specifica-tion that uses the same cables, connectors, and software interfaces, but which runs 40 times faster than the original 1.0 and 1.1 versions.

All existing USB 1.1 devices will work in a USB 2.0 bus because USB 2.0 supports all the slower-speed connections. USB data rates are shown in Table 8.3.

Table 8.3   USB Data Rates

Interface	Megabits per Second	Megabytes per Second
USB 1.1 low-speed	1.5Mbit/sec	0.1875MByte/sec
USB 1.1 high-speed	12Mbit/sec	1.5MByte/sec
USB 2.0	480Mbit/sec	60MByte/sec

The support of higher-speed USB 2.0 peripherals requires using a USB 2.0 hub. You can still use older USB 1.1 hubs on a 2.0 bus, but any peripherals or additional hubs connected downstream from a 1.1 hub will operate at the slower 1.5MByte/sec USB 1.1 maximum speed. Devices connected to USB 2.0 hubs operate at the maximum speed of the device, up to the full USB 2.0 speed of 60MBytes/sec.

When communicating with an attached USB 2.0 peripheral, the 2.0 hub simply repeats the high-speed signals; however, when communicating with USB 1.1 peripherals, a USB 2.0 hub buffers and manages the transition from the high speed of the USB 2.0 host controller (in the PC) to the lower speed of a USB 1.1 device. This feature of USB 2.0 hubs means that USB 1.1 devices can operate along with USB 2.0 devices and not consume any additional bandwidth.

IEEE-1394

The so-called *FireWire* or *iLINK* interface pioneered by Apple is also available for Windows/Intel–type computers. Despite the fact that IEEE-1394 ports are seldom standard equipment at present, the performance features they offer suggest that they will become a part of the "twenty-first century PC" for many users.

Figure 8.3 shows you how to recognize an IEEE-1394 connector plug, cable, and socket.

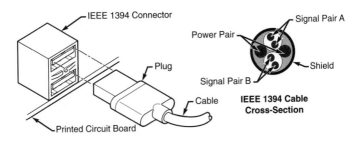

Figure 8.3   IEEE-1394 cable, socket, and connector plug.

Adding IEEE-1394 Ports to Your Computer

While most recent systems have USB ports onboard, IEEE-1394 ports are rare among PCs, but are more common on Macintosh systems.

A wide variety of IEEE-1394 host adapters are available for purchase. Most host adapters provide one or more 6-pin IEEE-1394 ports, provide an adapter for 4-pin IEEE-1394 devices, and use a single 32-bit PCI slot. Adaptec's AHA-8945 and HotConnect Ultra 8945 products combine Ultra SCSI and IEEE-1394 on a single 32-bit PCI slot.

IEEE-1394, like USB, also supports hubs for sharing a single port among multiple devices, although the hubs are different.

Resource Requirements for IEEE-1394 Host Adapters

Regardless of the number of IEEE-1394 ports, an IEEE-1394 host adapter card uses only one IRQ and one I/O port address. The IRQ used by the host adapter should not be shared with other devices. If necessary, take advantage of IRQ steering for PCI cards with Windows 98, 2000, and ME to have other PCI cards share an IRQ to free up an IRQ for the IEEE-1394 host adapter. If your host adapter also has a SCSI port onboard, the SCSI port will also require an IRQ and I/O port address.

The PCI slot you choose for the IEEE-1394 host adapter must support bus-mastering if the host adapter uses this feature. Consult your system or motherboard documentation and your host adapter documentation to see whether this is a requirement for you. You might need to move existing PCI cards around to satisfy this requirement.

Comparing USB and IEEE-1394

Because of the similarity in both the form and function of USB and 1394, some confusion has existed about the two. Table 8.3 summarizes the differences between the two technologies.

Table 8.3 Comparing IEEE-1394 and USB Technologies		
	IEEE-1394 (i.LINK) (FireWire)	**USB 1.1**
PC-Host Required	No	Yes
Maximum Number of Devices	63	127
Hot-Swappable	Yes	Yes
Maximum Cable Length Between Devices	4.5 meters	5 meters
Current Transfer Rate	200Mbps (25MB/sec)	12Mbps (1.5MB/sec) or 1.5Mbps
Future Transfer Rates	400Mbps (50MB/sec) 800Mbps (100MB/sec) 1Gbps+ (125MB/sec+)	480Mbps (USB 2.0)
Typical Devices	DV Camcorders High-Res. Digital Cameras HDTV Set-Top Boxes High-Speed Drives High-Res. Scanners Printers	Keyboards Mice Joysticks Low-Resolution Digital Cameras Low-Speed Drives Modems Printers Low-Res. Scanners

The main difference is speed. Currently, IEEE-1394 offers a data transfer rate that is more than 16 times faster than that of USB 1.1, but which is less than half as fast as USB 2.0. This speed differential might change in the future as higher speed versions of IEEE-1394 debut and faster versions of USB are introduced. In the future, PCs might frequently include both USB and IEEE-1394 interfaces. Together, these two buses can replace most of the standard connections found on the back of a typical PC.

USB 1.1 is clearly designed for low-speed peripherals, such as keyboards, mice, modems, and printers, whereas USB 2.0 can be used to connect most high-speed external devices. 1394 will be used to connect mostly high-performance digital video electronics products.

Another important benefit of 1394 is that a PC host connection is not required. Thus, 1394 can be used to directly connect a Digital Video (DV) camcorder and a DV-VCR for dubbing tapes or editing.

USB ports are standard on all recent desktop and notebook computers because Intel has added USB support to all its motherboard chipsets since 1996. However, IEEE-1394 ports must be added by means of an adapter card because the motherboard chipsets for PCs don't support this interface.

Troubleshooting IEEE-1394 Host Adapters and Devices

- **Host adapter is installed but doesn't work**—Make sure that your system has loaded the correct IEEE-1394 driver for the host adapter. Some host adapters don't use the Windows-provided TI chipset driver.

- **Wrong driver is installed for host adapter**—If you have installed the wrong driver, remove the IEEE-1394 host adapter listing from the Windows Device Manager, have the driver CD or disk supplied with the host adapter handy, restart the system, and have the computer search for the best driver. It will find the driver on the disk or CD-ROM and install it.

- **Choppy video during digital editing**—Use UDMA Bus-mastering drivers with ATA/IDE hard disks to provide smooth flow of digital video; install and enable as necessary (see Chapter 4, "SCSI and IDE Hard Drives and Optical Drives," for details).

- **4-wire devices aren't recognized**—Whereas 6-wire devices get power from the IEEE-1394 bus, 4-wire devices require their own power supply; ensure that it's connected and turned on.

- **Device "disappears" from Windows Device Manager after being connected**—The connected device is probably using power management; after the device's power management is enabled, this is normal. Use the device's power management controls to disable power management while the device is connected to the computer.

- **Device displays a yellow ! in Device Manager or isn't displayed**—Windows 2000 provides support for only host adapters that support OpenHCI (OHCI). Adaptec and other brands that use non-OHCI drivers must install their own drivers to work. Update the drivers or remove the device and reinstall it, providing the correct drivers to correct the problem.

IEEE-1394 and Linux

Linux kernel versions 2.2 and 2.3 support IEEE-1394. To download the support files or for more information about supporting IEEE-1394 devices under Linux, go to the following address:

```
linux1394.sourceforge.net/index.html
```

Online Sources for Additional IEEE-1394 Support

- IEEE-1394 Products

    ```
    www.firewire-1394.com/
    ```

    ```
    www.askfor1394.com
    ```

- IEEE-1394 Trade Association

    ```
    www.1394ta.org
    ```

Chapter 9

Keyboards, Mice, and Input Devices

Keyboard Designs

The primary keyboard types are as follows:

- 101-key Enhanced keyboard
- 104-key Windows keyboard
- 83-key PC and XT keyboard (obsolete)
- 84-key AT keyboard (obsolete)

> **Note**
>
> If you need information about the 83-key PC and XT keyboard or 84-key AT keyboard, see Chapter 7 of *Upgrading and Repairing PCs, 10th Anniversary Edition*—included in PDF format on the 12th Edition CD-ROM.

The 101-Key Enhanced Keyboard

This keyboard design serves as the basis for virtually all current-model keyboards.

101-Key Versus 102-Key Keyboards

Foreign language versions of the Enhanced keyboard include 102 keys and a slightly different layout from the 101-key U.S. versions.

The 104-Key Windows Keyboard

The Microsoft Windows keyboard specification outlines a set of new keys and key combinations. The familiar 101-key layout has now grown to 104 keys, with the addition of left and right Windows keys and an Application key. These keys are used for operating-system and application-level keyboard combinations, similar to today's Ctrl and Alt combinations. (Figure 9.2 shows the standard Windows keyboard layout, including the three new keys.)

Using Windows Keys

Table 9.1 shows a list of all the Windows 9x, Windows NT 4, and Windows 2000 key combinations that can be performed with the

104-key Windows keyboard. These keyboard shortcuts can be useful, especially if your mouse stops working or you want to work more quickly with the Windows desktop.

Table 9.1   Windows Key Combinations

Key Combination	Resulting Action
WIN+R	Opens Run dialog box
WIN+M	Minimize All
Shift+WIN+M	Undo Minimize All
WIN+F1	Opens Help
WIN+E	Opens Windows Explorer
WIN+F	Find Files or Folders
Ctrl+WIN+F	Find Computer
WIN+Tab	Cycles through taskbar buttons
WIN+Break	Opens System Properties dialog box
Application key	Displays a context menu for the selected item

When a 104-key Windows keyboard is used with Microsoft IntelliType Software installed, the additional key combinations shown in Table 9.2 can be used.

Table 9.2   Additional Key Combinations

Key Combination	Resulting Action
WIN+L	Logs off Windows
WIN+P	Opens Print Manager
WIN+C	Opens the Control Panel
WIN+V	Opens Clipboard
WIN+K	Opens Keyboard Properties dialog box
WIN+I	Opens Mouse Properties dialog box
WIN+A	Opens Accessibility Options (if installed)
WIN+spacebar	Displays the list of IntelliType hotkeys
WIN+S	Toggles the Caps Lock key on and off

Keyboard-Only Commands for Windows 9x/NT4/2000/Me with Any Keyboard

If your mouse stops working, or if you want to work more quickly, use the keys shown in Table 9.3 to perform common Windows actions.

Table 9.3   Keyboard Commands for Windows 9x/NT4/2000/Me

Key Combination	Resulting Action
F1	Starts Windows Help.
F10	Activates menu bar options.
Shift+F10	Opens a context menu (shortcut menu) for the selected item.
Ctrl+Esc	Opens the Start menu. Use the arrow keys to select an item.
Ctrl+Esc, Esc	Selects the Start button. Press Tab to select the taskbar, or press Shift+F10 for a context menu.
Alt+Tab	Switches to another running application. Hold down the Alt key and then press the Tab key to view the task-switching window.
Shift	Press down and hold the Shift key while you insert a CD-ROM to bypass the AutoPlay feature.
Alt+spacebar	Displays the main window's System menu. From the System menu, you can restore, move, resize, minimize, maximize, or close the window.
Alt+- (Alt+hyphen)	Displays the Multiple Document Interface (MDI) child window's System menu. From the MDI child window's System menu, you can restore, move, resize, minimize, maximize, or close the child window.
Ctrl+Tab	Switches to the next child window of an MDI application.
Alt+<underlined letter in menu>	Opens the corresponding menu.
Alt+F4	Closes the current window.
Ctrl+F4	Closes the current MDI window.
Alt+F6	Switches between multiple windows in the same program. For example, when Notepad's Find dialog box is displayed, Alt+F6 switches between the Find dialog box and the main Notepad window.

Here are the Windows dialog box keyboard commands:

Key Combination	Resulting Action
Tab	Moves to the next control in the dialog box.
Shift+Tab	Moves to the previous control in the dialog box.
Spacebar	If the current control is a button, this keyboard command clicks the button. If the current control is a check box, it toggles the check box. If the current control is an option button, it selects the option button.
Enter	Equivalent to clicking the selected button (the button with the outline).
Esc	Equivalent to clicking the Cancel button.

Key Combination	Resulting Action
Alt+<underlined letter in dialog box item>	Moves to the corresponding item.
Ctrl+Tab/ Ctrl+Shift+Tab	Moves through the property tabs.

These are the keyboard combinations for Windows Explorer tree controls:

Key Combination	Resulting Action
Numeric Keypad *	Expands everything under the current selection.
Numeric Keypad +	Expands the current selection.
Numeric Keypad -	Collapses the current selection.
Right arrow	Expands the current selection if it is not expanded; otherwise, goes to the first child.
Left arrow	Collapses the current selection if it is expanded; otherwise, goes to the parent.

Here are the general Windows folder/shortcut controls:

Key Combination	Resulting Action
F4	Selects the Go To a Different Folder box and moves down the entries in the box (if the toolbar is active in Windows Explorer).
F5	Refreshes the current window.
F6	Moves among panes in Windows Explorer.
Ctrl+G	Opens the Go To Folder tool (in Windows 95 Windows Explorer only).
Ctrl+Z	Undoes the last command.
Ctrl+A	Selects all the items in the current window.
Backspace	Switches to the parent folder.
Shift+click	Selects the Close button. (For folders, closes the current folder plus all parent folders.)

These are general folder and Windows Explorer shortcuts for a selected object:

Key Combination	Resulting Action
F2	Renames object.
F3	Finds all files.
Ctrl+X	Cuts.
Ctrl+C	Copies.

Key Combination	Resulting Action
Ctrl+V	Pastes.
Shift+Del	Deletes selection immediately, without moving the item to the Recycle Bin.
Alt+Enter	Opens the property sheet for the selected object.
To copy a file	Press down and hold the Ctrl key while you drag the file to another folder.
To create a shortcut	Press down and hold Ctrl+Shift while you drag a file to the desktop or a folder.

Standard Versus Portable Keyboards

Table 9.4 lists the differences in configuration and system setup for standard versus portable keyboards.

Table 9.4   Standard and Portable Keyboards Compared

Feature	Standard	Portable
Key size	Full-sized keys on entire keyboard	Full-sized keys on typing keys only; directional and function keys usually smaller
Cursor keys	Inverted-T layout standard	Inverted-T layout seldom used; makes "blind" cursor movements difficult
Numeric keypad	Separate keys at right of directional keys	Embedded into right-hand alphanumerics; should disable numlock in BIOS to avoid keying errors; might require use of F*n* key to use
Add-on keypad	Not needed	Popular option for number-intensive uses; must plug into external port

Keyswitch Types

The most common type of keyswitch is the mechanical type, available in the following variations:

- Pure mechanical
- Foam element
- Rubber dome
- Membrane

Table 9.5 compares user feel, repair, and servicing issues for these keyswitch types.

Table 9.5   Mechanical Keyswitch Types Compared

| | Keyswitch Type | | | |
Feature	Pure Mechanical	Foam	Rubber-Dome	Membrane
Tactile feedback	Usually a click	Minimal feedback	Soft click	No click
Durability and serviceability	High: 20-million keystroke rating	Variable: Contacts can corrode; easy to clean	High: Rubber dome protects contacts from corrosion	Extreme: No moving parts, sealed unit for harsh industrial environments

The pure mechanical type of keyboard, often using Alps keyswitches, is second only to the keyboards using capacitive switches in terms of tactile feedback and durability. Capacitive keyswitches are rated for up to 25 million keystrokes. Traditionally, the only vendors of capacitive keyswitch keyboards have been IBM and the inheritors of its keyboard technology, Lexmark and Unicomp.

Cleaning a Foam-Element Keyswitch

Figure 9.1 shows a foam-element keyswitch, often found in keyboards sold by Compaq and keyboards manufactured by Keytronics.

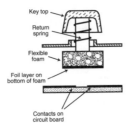

Figure 9.1   A typical foam-element mechanical keyswitch.

The foil contacts at the bottom of the key and the contacts on the circuit board often become dirty or corroded, causing erratic key operation. Disassemble the keyboard to gain access to the foil pads, clean them, and treat them with Stabilant 22a from DW Electrochemicals to improve the switch-contact quality.

If you need to clean or repair a keyboard, you'll find much more information in Chapter 17 of *Upgrading and Repairing PCs, 12th Edition*, from Que.

Adjusting Keyboard Parameters in Windows

To modify the default values for the typematic repeat rate and delay parameters in any version of Windows, open the Keyboard icon in the Control Panel. In Windows 9x/Me/NT/2000, the controls are located on the Speed tab. The Repeat Delay slider controls the amount of times a key must be pressed before the character begins to repeat, and the Repeat Rate slider controls how fast the character repeats after the delay has elapsed. Use the test box to see the effect of the changes you make before you apply them.

> **Note**
>
> The increments on the Repeat Delay and Repeat Rate sliders in the Keyboard Control Panel correspond to the timings given for the MODE command's RATE and DELAY values. Each mark in the Repeat Delay slider adds about 0.25 seconds to the delay, and the marks in the Repeat Rate slider are worth about one character per second each.

Keyboard Layouts and Scan Codes

Figure 9.2 shows the keyboard numbering and character locations for the 101-key Enhanced keyboard. Table 9.6 shows each of the three scan code sets for each key in relation to the key number and character. Scan Code Set 1 is the default; the other two are rarely used. Figure 9.3 shows the layout of a typical foreign language 102-key version of the Enhanced keyboard—in this case, a U.K. version.

Knowing these key number figures and scan codes is useful when you are troubleshooting stuck or failed keys on a keyboard. Diagnostics can report the defective keyswitch by the scan code, which varies from keyboard to keyboard on the character it represents and its location.

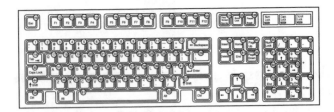

Figure 9.2 101-key Enhanced keyboard key number and character locations (U.S. version).

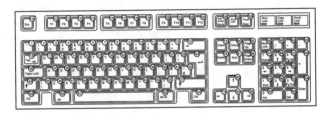

Figure 9.3 102-key Enhanced keyboard key number and character locations (U.K. English version).

Table 9.6 101-/102-Key (Enhanced) Keyboard Key Numbers and Scan Codes

Key Number	Key/Character	Scan Code Set 1	Scan Code Set 2	Scan Code Set 3
1	`	29	0E	0E
2	1	2	16	16
3	2	3	1E	1E
4	3	4	26	26
5	4	5	25	25
6	5	6	2E	2E
7	6	7	36	36
8	7	8	3D	3D
9	8	9	3E	3E
10	9	0A	46	46
11	0	0B	45	45
12	-	0C	4E	4E
13	=	0D	55	55
15	Backspace	0E	66	66
16	Tab	0F	0D	0D
17	Q	10	15	15
18	W	11	1D	1D

Table 9.6   101-/102-Key (Enhanced) Keyboard Key Numbers and Scan Codes Continued

Key Number	Key/Character	Scan Code Set 1	Scan Code Set 2	Scan Code Set 3
19	E	12	24	24
20	R	13	2D	2D
21	T	14	2C	2C
22	Y	15	35	35
23	U	16	3C	3C
24	I	17	43	43
25	O	18	44	44
26	P	19	4D	4D
27	[	1A	54	54
28	]	1B	5B	5B
29	\ (101-key only)	2B	5D	5C
30	Caps Lock	3A	58	14
31	A	1E	1C	1C
32	S	1F	1B	1B
33	D	20	23	23
34	F	21	2B	2B
35	G	22	34	34
36	H	23	33	33
37	J	24	3B	3B
38	K	25	42	42
39	L	26	4B	4B
40	;	27	4C	4C
41	`	28	52	52
42	# (102-key only)	2B	5D	53
43	Enter	1C	5A	5A
44	Left Shift	2A	12	12
45	\ (102-key only)	56	61	13
46	Z	2C	1A	1A
47	X	2D	22	22
48	C	2E	21	21
49	V	2F	2A	2A
50	B	30	32	32
51	N	31	31	31
52	M	32	3A	3A
53	,	33	41	41
54	.	34	49	49

Key Number	Key/Character	Scan Code Set 1	Scan Code Set 2	Scan Code Set 3
55	/	35	4A	4A
57	Right Shift	36	59	59
58	Left Ctrl	1D	14	11
60	Left Alt	38	11	19
61	Spacebar	39	29	29
62	Right Alt	E0, 38	E0, 11	39
64	Right Ctrl	E0, 1D	E0, 14	58
75	Insert	E0, 52	E0, 70	67
76	Delete	E0, 53	E0, 71	64
79	Left arrow	E0, 4B	E0, 6B	61
80	Home	E0, 47	E0, 6C	6E
81	End	E0, 4F	E0, 69	65
83	Up arrow	E0, 48	E0, 75	63
84	Down arrow	E0, 50	E0, 72	60
85	Page Up	E0, 49	E0, 7D	6F
86	Page Down	E0, 51	E0, 7A	6D
89	Right arrow	E0, 4D	E0, 74	6A
90	Num Lock	45	77	76
91	Keypad 7 (Home)	47	6C	6C
92	Keypad 4 (Left arrow)	4B	6B	6B
93	Keypad 1 (End)	4F	69	69
95	Keypad /	E0, 35	E0, 4A	77
96	Keypad 8 (Up arrow)	48	75	75
97	Keypad 5	4C	73	73
98	Keypad 2 (Down arrow)	50	72	72
99	Keypad 0 (Ins)	52	70	70
100	Keypad *	37	7C	7E
101	Keypad 9 (PgUp)	49	7D	7D
102	Keypad 6 (Left arrow)	4D	74	74
103	Keypad 3 (PgDn)	51	7A	7A
104	Keypad . (Del)	53	71	71
105	Keypad -	4A	7B	84
106	Keypad +	4E	E0, 5A	7C

Table 9.6   101-/102-Key (Enhanced) Keyboard Key Numbers and Scan Codes Continued

Table 9.6   101-/102-Key (Enhanced) Keyboard Key Numbers and Scan Codes Continued

Key Number	Key/Character	Scan Code Set 1	Scan Code Set 2	Scan Code Set 3
108	Keypad Enter	E0, 1C	E0, 5A	79
110	Escape	1	76	8
112	F1	3B	5	7
113	F2	3C	6	0F
114	F3	3D	4	17
115	F4	3E	0C	1F
116	F5	3F	3	27
117	F6	40	0B	2F
118	F7	41	83	37
119	F8	42	0A	3F
120	F9	43	1	47
121	F10	44	9	4F
122	F11	57	78	56
123	F12	58	7	5E
124	Print Screen	E0, 2A, E0, 37	E0, 12, E0, 7C	57
125	Scroll Lock	46	7E	5F
126	Pause	E1, 1D, 45, E1, 9D, C5	E1, 14, 77, E1, F0, 14, F0, 77	62

The additional keys on a 104-key Windows keyboard have their own unique scan codes. Table 9.7 shows the scan codes for the new keys.

Table 9.7   104-Key Windows Keyboard New Key Scan Codes

New Key	Scan Code Set 1	Scan Code Set 2	Scan Code Set 3
Left Windows	E0,5B	E0, 1F	8B
Right Windows	E0,5C	E0, 27	8C
Application	E0,5D	E0, 2F	8D

Keyboard Connectors

While some of the newest systems offer color-coded keyboard connectors and cables, the best way to recognize the keyboard connector is still to know what it looks like. Two common standards exist, and low-cost adapters are available to switch a device using one standard to a connector using the other standard. The keyboard connector standards are as follows:

- **5-pin DIN connector**—Used on most PC systems with Baby-AT form factor motherboards.

- **6-pin mini-DIN connector**—Used on PS/2 systems and most PCs with LPX, ATX, and NLX motherboards.

- **USB connector**—Used on "legacy-free" systems that lack PS/2, serial, or parallel ports.

Figure 9.4 and Table 9.8 show the physical layout and pinouts of the respective keyboard connector plugs and sockets for the DIN and mini-DIN connector. Refer to Chapter 8, "USB and IEEE-1394 Ports and Devices," for USB connectors.

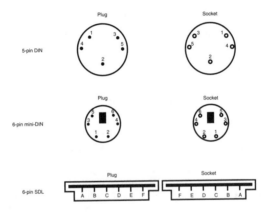

Figure 9.4 Keyboard and mouse connectors.

Keyboard Connector Signals

Table 9.8 lists the keyboard connector signals for three common keyboard connectors.

Table 9.8 Keyboard Connector Signals

Signal Name	5-Pin DIN[1]	6-Pin Mini-DIN	6-Pin SDL[2]
Keyboard Data	2	1	B
Ground	4	3	C
+5v	5	4	E
Keyboard Clock	1	5	D
Not Connected	—	2	A

Table 9.8	Keyboard Connector Signals Continued		
Signal Name	5-Pin DIN[1]	6-Pin Mini-DIN	6-Pin SDL[2]
Not Connected	—	6	F
Not Connected	3	—	—

1. DIN = German Industrial Norm (Deutsche Industrie Norm), a committee that sets German dimensional standards.

2. SDL = Shielded Data Link, a type of shielded connector created by AMP and used by IBM and others for keyboard cables. It is used inside the keyboard housing to attach the cable to the keyboard's electronics, and the other end of the cable will have the DIN or mini-DIN connector to attach to the computer.

USB Keyboard Requirements

USB (Universal Serial Bus) devices have become increasingly popular, and over the next few years are expected to replace serial, parallel, keyboard, and mouse port connectors with this single, versatile, sharable port (refer to Chapter 8 for more information about USB).

To use a keyboard connected via the USB port, you must meet three requirements:

- Have a USB port in the system

- Run Microsoft Windows 98, Windows Me, or Windows 2000 (all of which include USB keyboard drivers)

- Have USB Legacy support present and enabled in your system BIOS

USB Legacy support means your motherboard ROM BIOS includes drivers to recognize a USB keyboard. Without USB Legacy support in the BIOS, you can't use a USB keyboard when in MS-DOS or when installing Windows on the system for the first time. Also, if the Windows installation fails and requires manipulation outside Windows, the USB keyboard will not function unless it is supported in the BIOS. Virtually all 1998 and newer systems with USB ports include a BIOS with USB Legacy (meaning USB Keyboard) support.

Keyboard Troubleshooting and Repair

Keyboard errors are usually caused by two simple problems. Other more difficult, intermittent problems can arise, but they are much less common. The most frequent problems are as follows:

- Defective cables

- Stuck keys

Use Table 9.9 to help you troubleshoot a defective keyboard.

Table 9.9	Keyboard Troubleshooting	
Problem	**Symptoms**	**Solution**
Defective cable	No keyboard operation; all keys produce errors or wrong characters.	Swap keyboard with known, working spare. If problem isn't repeated, original keyboard is the problem.
		Replace cable with spare (if available, check "scrap" keyboards or vendor spare parts lists) or replace keyboard.
		Test cable with Digital Multimeter (DMM) with continuity tester; each wire (see pinouts previously) should make a connection, even when you wiggle the cable. Replace failed cable.
Stuck key	"Stuck key error" or 3xx error onscreen during POST.	Look up scancode from table in this chapter to determine which key is stuck. Clean keyswitch.
Damaged motherboard keyboard connector	Known-working keyboards don't work when plugged in.	For a simple test of the motherboard keyboard connector, you can check voltages on some of the pins. Measure the voltages on various pins of the keyboard connector. To prevent possible damage to the system or keyboard, turn off the power before disconnecting the keyboard. Then, unplug the keyboard and turn the power back on. Make measurements between the ground pin and the other pins according to Table 9.10.
		Repair or replace motherboard if voltage fails specifications.
USB Keyboard works in Windows 98, 2000, or Me, but not in MS-DOS or at startup	USB Legacy mode not enabled in BIOS/CMOS configuration.	Connect standard keyboard, start computer, start BIOS/CMOS configuration, enable USB Legacy mode, save changes, and shut down computer.
		Reconnect USB keyboard and retry; keyboard should now function at all times.

Keyboard Connector Voltage and Signal Specifications

Use Table 9.10 along with a digital multimeter (DMM) to determine whether your keyboard connector is working correctly.

Table 9.10	Keyboard Connector Specifications		
DIN Connector Pin	Mini-DIN Connector Pin	Signal	Voltage
1	5	Keyboard Clock	+2.0v to +5.5v
2	1	Keyboard Data	+4.8v to +5.5v
3	—	Reserved	—
4	3	Ground	—
5	4	+5v Power	+2.0v to +5.5v

If your measurements do not match these voltages, the motherboard might be defective. Otherwise, the keyboard cable or keyboard might be defective. If you suspect that the cable is the problem, the easiest thing to do is replace the keyboard cable with a known good one. If the system still does not work normally, you might have to replace the entire keyboard or the motherboard.

Keyboard Error Codes

Some BIOSs use the following 3*xx*-series numbers to report keyboard errors. These error codes will be displayed onscreen during the startup process. Look up the error code and fix the problem.

Table 9.11 lists some standard POST and diagnostics keyboard error codes.

Table 9.11	Keyboard POST Codes
Error Code	Description
3*xx*	Keyboard errors.
301	Keyboard reset or stuck-key failure (XX 301; XX = scan code in hex).
302	System unit keylock switch is locked.
302	User-indicated keyboard test error.
303	Keyboard or system-board error; keyboard controller failure.
304	Keyboard or system-board error; keyboard clock high.
305	Keyboard +5v error; PS/2 keyboard fuse (on motherboard) blown.
341	Keyboard error.

Table 9.11	Keyboard POST Codes Continued
Error Code	**Description**
342	Keyboard cable error.
343	Keyboard LED card or cable failure.
365	Keyboard LED card or cable failure.
366	Keyboard interface cable failure.
367	Keyboard LED card or cable failure.

Mice and Pointing Devices
Mouse Motion Detection Methods

The most common type of mouse mechanism is the opto-mechanical, used by Logitech and many other vendors. Dirt on the mouse ball or rollers, or fuzz in the light paths will cause skipping and erratic mouse cursor operation.

Microsoft sells mice based on both mechanical (roller-type) technology and a new optical technology called IntelliEye. The IntelliMouse Optical and IntelliMouse with IntelliEye detect the mouse's motion with a high-speed purely CMOS-based optical sensor that, unlike the old optical mouse designs from Mouse Systems, doesn't require a special pad or special mousing surface. For those who prefer a different color to Microsoft's IntelliEye Red, Logitech's new MouseMan Wheel and Wheel Mouse feature a translucent blue bottom and similar optical detection features.

Although some stores display these mice on a mirrored surface, don't use a mirror or glass as a mousing surface. Your pants leg, airline tray table, or old school tie will work well, though.

Pointing Device Interface Types

The connector used to attach your mouse to the system depends on the type of interface you are using. Mice are most commonly connected to your computer through the following three interfaces:

- Serial port

- Dedicated motherboard mouse port (PS/2 port)

- USB port

Most mice that attach to the USB port can also be adapted to the PS/2 mouse port. Many serial mice are shipped with a PS/2 adapter, too.

The serial port can be seen in Chapter 6, "Serial Ports and Modems." The PS/2 mouse port is the same mechanical connector as the keyboard 6-pin mini-DIN shown earlier in this chapter, but you cannot interchange the mouse and keyboard.

A fourth connector type, the 9-pin mini-DIN bus-mouse connector, is found on the back of a dedicated bus-mouse interface card or on some old ATI video cards. Bus mice are now considered obsolete, and most cannot be adapted to other types of ports.

Note

Microsoft sometimes calls a bus mouse an *Inport mouse*, which is its proprietary name for a bus mouse connection.

Wireless Mouse Types

The following are the two methods for interfacing wireless mice:

- Radio Control

- Infra-Red(IR)

Radio-controlled mice are sold by Logitech, Microsoft, and other companies. The radio receiver plugs in to the standard mouse interface(s) listed previously, and the mouse is cordless, using a small battery to power its radio transmitter. Older versions of these mice were very bulky when compared to corded mice, but new wireless mice are about the same size as their corded cousins.

IR mice are rare, and are most often combined with IR keyboards. The IR receiver plugs in to the standard mouse (and keyboard) connector, and requires a clear line-of-site between the mouse and the receiver.

Software Drivers for the Mouse

Depending on the operating system you're using or the operating mode, you might need to manually load a driver, or it might be loaded automatically for you. Use Table 9.12 to determine what's needed for your mouse.

Table 9.12   Mouse Drive Type and Location by Operating System

Operating System	Driver Type	Loading Method	Notes
Windows 9x, NT, 2000, Me	32-bit .DRV and .VXD	Automatically detected and installed	Most mice with PS/2 ports can use standard Microsoft driver, although third-party drivers provide support for scroll wheels, third buttons, and so on.
MS-DOS mode under Windows 9x/Me	Uses Windows 32-bit driver	Automatically supported in windowed and full-screen modes	In window, can use mouse to mark text for the Windows Clipboard.
MS-DOS, including Windows 9x command prompt (not MS-DOS mode)	Mouse.com or Device= mouse.sys	Run MOUSE from command line or Autoexec.bat or Add device= mouse.sys to Config.sys	New versions of Mouse.com from Microsoft and Logitech can load into UMB RAM above 640KB with little conventional memory used.

Mice under Linux are configured through the kernel (for use with standard text-based displays). Xfree86-based graphical user interfaces (*window managers*) require that you specify the device name and mouse protocol used by your mouse or other pointing device. See the manual for your Linux distribution and window manager for details.

Alternative Pointing Devices

Table 9.13 provides an overview of pointing devices used as alternatives to normal mice, including those used with notebook computers.

Table 9.13   Alternative Pointing Devices

Device	Where Located	How Operated	Tips and Notes
Glidepoint Developed by Alps Electric (also called touchpad)	Flat surface below spacebar on notebook PCs; might be separate device or on right side of keyboard on desktop PCs	Move finger across surface; use left and right buttons beneath spacebar, or tap/ double-tap with finger in place of click/double-click.	Most commonly used built-in mouse alternative; also available for desktop PCs. Requires you to move hand from keyboard; depends on skin moisture and resistance. Accuracy can be a problem.

Table 9.13	Alternative Pointing Devices Continued		
Device	**Where Located**	**How Operated**	**Tips and Notes**
			If you prefer to use a "real" mouse, disable the touchpad in the BIOS, because it can still be active on some machines, even when a mouse is installed.
Trackpoint Developed by IBM	Small "eraserhead" pointing stick located in middle of keyboard	Gently press surface of "eraser" in the direction you want to go.	Very fast operation because it's on the keyboard. Licensed by Toshiba as "Accupoint" and also found on some IBM/Lexmark/Unicomp keyboards and on some other notebook computer brands.
Trackball	Rollerball placed below spacebar on notebook computer; also available integrated into desktop keyboards or as separate devices	Roll ball with fingers or thumb to move mouse pointer in desired direction.	Popular for some users who have comfort or ergonomic issues with mice; are available in ergonomic shapes as separate devices.

Keep in mind that many notebook computer users use "real" mice or trackballs when they have room.

Mouse Troubleshooting

If you are experiencing problems with your mouse, you must look in only two general places—hardware or software. Because mice are basically simple devices, looking at the hardware takes very little time. Detecting and correcting software problems can take a bit longer, however.

Use Table 9.14 to keep your mouse or pointing device in top condition.

Table 9.14	Troubleshooting Mouse and Pointing Device Problems	
Symptom	**Problem**	**Solution**
Jerky mouse pointer.	Dirt and dust on rollers and ball or sensor.	Remove retainer plate on bottom of mouse, remove ball, and clean ball and rollers with non-abrasive solvents such as contact lens cleaner. Blow dust away from wheels and sensor. Reassemble and test.

Table 9.14   Troubleshooting Mouse and Pointing Device Problems Continued

Symptom	Problem	Solution
		Remove trackball ball from sensor and clean as above.
		Replace TrackPoint eraserhead with a new cap.
Mouse pointer freezes when another device (modem, and so on) is used.	IRQ conflict.	If mouse is PS/2, be sure no other device is using IRQ 12. If mouse is serial, check for modem on same IRQ as mouse. COM 1/3 share IRQ 4; COM 2/4 share IRQ 3 by default. See Chapter 6 for information on avoiding mouse/modem conflicts.
		If mouse is bus, check its IRQ usage and try to find an unused IRQ for bus card.
		Use Windows Device Manager if available to find IRQ information.
Mouse won't work at all.	Defective mouse.	Replace the original mouse with a known-working similar spare. If it works, replace the original mouse for good.
	Defective port.	Any mouse plugged in to the port won't work. First, check to see whether port is disabled. If the port is not disabled, use add-on port card or replace motherboard.
	Disabled COM, USB, or PS/2 port.	Check BIOS or motherboard jumpers and enable if IRQ used by port isn't already in use.
	Radio-controlled mouse has a dead battery.	Check battery in mouse; replace if dead or weak.
	Wrong channel set on mouse or receiver.	Mouse and receiver must be set to same channel; adjust channels on both devices to solve interference problems.
	Infra-red mouse can't "see" IR receiver.	Check line-of-site issues for IR mouse and receiver.
Mouse works as PS/2, but not as serial.	Mouse designed for PS/2 port only.	Most "bundled" mice are designed for the PS/2 port only. Retail mice are designed to be used with adapters. Get a mouse built for the serial port.

Table 9.14   Troubleshooting Mouse and Pointing Device Problems Continued

Symptom	Problem	Solution
Mouse locks up when accessed by Microsoft MSD or other diagnostic.	Bad mouse.	To verify mouse is the problem, run MSD/I to bypass initial detection. Detect computer and other information; then detect mouse. If the mouse is at fault, you'll lock up your system. Turn off system, replace with known-working mouse, and repeat. If replacement mouse works okay, you've solved the problem.
Standard left and right mouse buttons work, but middle or scroll buttons don't work.	Incorrect mouse configuration.	A dual-emulation mouse with a PC/MS slider on the bottom must be set to PC (Mouse Systems) mode to activate the middle button. Most Logitech mice can use the Microsoft driver, but Microsoft mice don't support three buttons. Use the correct driver for the mouse.
	Button not programmed.	Use mouse setup program to verify that the middle button is set to work, and check its function.
	Mouse drivers out of date.	Original scrolling mouse drivers would work only in Web browsers and a few other applications. Download and install new drivers.

Chapter 10

Video and Audio

Selecting a Monitor Size

Table 10.1 shows the monitor's advertised diagonal screen size, along with the approximate diagonal measure of the actual active viewing area for the most common display sizes.

Table 10.1	Advertised Screen Size Versus Actual Viewing Area
Monitor CRT Size (in Inches)	**Actual Viewing Area (in Inches)**
12	10 1/2
14	12 1/2
15	13 1/2
16	14 1/2
17	15 1/2
18	16 1/2
19	17 1/2
20	18 1/2
21	19 1/2

The size of the actual viewable area varies from manufacturer to manufacturer but tends to be approximately 1 1/2 inches less than the actual screen size. However, you can adjust some monitors—such as some models made by NEC, for example—to display a high-quality image that completely fills the tube from edge to edge. Other makes can fill the screen also, but some of them do so only by pushing the monitor beyond its comfortable limits. The result is a distorted image that is worse than the monitor's smaller, properly adjusted picture.

This phenomenon is a well-known monitor-purchasing issue, and as a result, most manufacturers and vendors have begun advertising the size of the active viewing area of their monitors along with the screen size. This makes it easier for consumers to compare what they are paying for.

Monitor Resolution

Resolution is the amount of detail a monitor can render. This quantity is expressed in the number of horizontal and vertical picture elements, or *pixels*, contained in the screen. The greater the number of pixels, the more detailed the images. Pixels also are referred to as *pels*, which is short for picture elements. The resolution required depends on the application. Character-based applications (such as DOS command-line programs) require little resolution, whereas graphics-intensive applications (such as desktop publishing and Windows software) require a great deal.

CRTs Versus LCDs

CRTs can handle a wide range of resolutions, but LCD panels of any type must use scaling to change to resolutions other than their native setting.

Common Monitor Resolutions

Table 10.2 shows standard resolutions used in PC video adapters and the terms commonly used to describe them.

Table 10.2	Monitor Resolutions	
Resolution	**Acronym**	**Standard Designation**
640×480	VGA	Video graphics array
800×600	SVGA	Super VGA
1,024×768	XGA	Extended graphics array
1,280×1,024	UVGA	Ultra VGA

However, the terms SVGA, XGA, and UVGA have fallen into disuse. The industry now describes screen resolutions by citing the number of pixels. Nearly all the video adapters sold today support the 640×480, 800×600, and 1,024×768 pixel resolutions at several color depths, and most now support 1,280×1,024 and higher as well.

> **Note**
>
> To understand this issue, you might want to try different resolutions on your system. As you change from 640×480 to 800×600 and 1024×768, you'll notice several changes to the appearance of your screen.

At 640×480, text and onscreen icons are very large. Because the screen elements used for the Windows desktop and software menus are at a fixed pixel width and height, you'll notice that they shrink in size onscreen as you change to the higher resolutions. Some recent versions of Windows, starting with Windows 98, let you select a large icons option in the Display properties sheet. This enables you to use high-resolution selections (which help you see more of your document) and still have large, legible icons.

Table 10.3 shows the minimum-size monitors I recommend to properly display the resolutions that users typically select.

Table 10.3	Resolution and Monitor Size Recommendations
Resolution	**Minimum Recommended Monitor**
640×480	13-inch
800×600	15-inch
1,024×768	17-inch
1,280×1,024	21-inch

LCD Versus CRT Display Size

LCD panels, especially all-digital units, provide high-quality displays that are always crisp and perfectly focused. Plus, their dimensions are fully usable and can comfortably display higher resolutions than comparably sized CRTs. Table 10.4 provides common CRT screen sizes and the comparable LCD display panel sizes.

Table 10.4	CRT Versus LCD Usable Screen Size Comparison	
CRT Monitor Size Display (in Inches)	**CRT Viewing Area (in Inches)**	**Comparable LCD (Also Viewing Area in Inches)**
14	12.5	12.1
15	13.5	13.3, 13.7
16	14.5	14.1, 14.5
17	15.5	15, 15.1
19	17.5	17, 17.1
20	18.5	18.1

As you can see, a 15-inch LCD actually provides a usable viewing area similar to a 17-inch CRT.

Monitor Power Management Modes

One of the first energy-saving standards for monitors was VESA's Display Power Management Signaling (DPMS) spec, which defines the signals a computer sends to a monitor to indicate idle times. The computer or video card decides when to send these signals.

In Windows 9x and 2000, you need to enable this feature if you want to use it because it's turned off by default. To enable it, open the Display properties in the Control Panel, switch to the Screen Saver tab and make sure the Energy Star low-power setting and Monitor shutdown setting are checked. You can adjust how long the system remains idle before either the monitor picture is blanked or the monitor shuts down completely. Windows Me defaults to suspend after 10 minutes, but timings can be adjusted with any of these versions of Windows.

Table 10.5 summarizes the DPMS modes.

Table 10.5	Display Power Management Signaling				
State	**Horizontal**	**Vertical**	**Video**	**Power Savings**	**Recovery Time**
On	Pulses	Pulses	Active	None	Not applicable
Standby	No pulses	Pulses	Blanked	Minimal	Short
Suspend	Pulses	No pulses	Blanked	Substantial	Longer
Off	No pulses	No pulses	Blanked	Maximum	System dependent

Microsoft and Intel developed a more broadly based power management specification called APM (advanced power management), and Microsoft developed an even more advanced power management specification called ACPI (advanced configuration and power interface) for use with Windows 98 and beyond. Table 10.6 summarizes the differences between DPMS, APM, and ACPI.

Table 10.6	Power Management Standards Compared		
Standard	**Devices Controlled**	**How Implemented**	**Notes**
DPMS	Monitor and video card	Drivers for display and video card; must be enabled by operating system, such as Windows 9x/2000/Me via Control Panel	DPMS will work along-side APM or ACPI; user defines timer intervals for various modes listed.
APM	Monitor, hard disks, other peripherals	Implemented in BIOS; enabled in BIOS and in operating system (Windows 9x/2000/Me via Control Panel)	User defines timer intervals for various devices in BIOS or operating system.

Table 10.6	Power Management Standards Compared Continued		
Standard	**Devices Controlled**	**How Implemented**	**Notes**
ACPI	All APM peripherals plus other PC and consumer devices	Implemented in BIOS; support must be present in BIOS and devices; supports automatic power-up and power-off for PC and consumer devices including printers, stereos, CDs, and others	If ACPI support is present in the BIOS when Windows 98/Me/ 2000 is first installed, Windows ACPI drivers are installed; update BIOS before instal- ling Windows if ACPI support is not present in BIOS.

VGA Video Connector Pinouts

Illustrations of all the following connectors can be seen in Chapter 14, "Connector Quick Reference."

VGA DB-15 Analog Connector Pinout

Virtually all displays in use today are descended from the 1987-vintage IBM VGA display introduced with the IBM PS/2s. The con-nector pinout is shown in Table 10.7.

Table 10.7	Standard 15-Pin VGA Connector Pinout	
Pin	**Function**	**Direction**
1	Red Video	Out
2	Green Video	Out
3	Blue Video	Out
4	Monitor ID 2	In
5	TTL Ground	—-_ (monitor self-test)
6	Red Analog Ground	-_
7	Green Analog Ground	-_
8	Blue Analog Ground	-_
9	Key (Plugged Hole)	-_
10	Sync Ground	-_
11	Monitor ID 0	In
12	Monitor ID 1	In
13	Horizontal Sync	Out
14	Vertical Sync	Out
15	Monitor ID 3	In

On the VGA cable connector that plugs into your video adapter, pin 9 is often pinless. Pin 5 is used only for testing purposes, and pin 15 is rarely used (these are often pinless as well). To identify the type of monitor connected to the system, some manufacturers use the presence or absence of the monitor ID pins in various combinations.

Digital Flat Panel Pinouts

The Digital Flat Panel (DFP) is a Video Electronic Standards Association specification for digital video displays, especially LCD panels. It was adopted in February 1999, but it already has been superseded for most uses by the DVI standard, discussed in the next section. The DFP supports a maximum resolution of 1280×1024 and transmits only digital signals. The DFP connector has two rows of edge connectors.

Table 10.8 provides the pinouts for DFP. DFP panels can be adapted to the newer DVI by the use of an adapter cable because both standards use the same TDMS PanelLink digital transfer protocol.

Table 10.8	**DFP Pinouts**	
Pin #	**Signal**	**Description**
1	TX1+	TDMS Positive Differential output, channel 1
2	TX1-	TDMS Negative Differential output, channel 1
3	SHLD1	Shield for TDMS channel 1
4	SHLDC	Shield for TDMS clock
5	TXC+	TDMS Positive Differential output, reference clock
6	TXC-	TDMS Negative Differential output, reference clock
7	GND	Logic ground
8	+5V	Logic +5V power supply from host
9	No Connect 9	No connection
10	No Connect 10	No connection
11	TX2+	TDMS Positive Differential output, channel 2
12	TX2-	TDMS Negative Differential output, channel 2
13	SHLD2	Shield for TDMS channel 1
14	SHLD0	Shield for TDMS channel 0
15	TX0+	TDMS Positive Differential output, channel 0
16	TX0-	TDMS Negative Differential output, channel 0
17	No Connect 17	No connection
18	HPD	Host Plug Detection (+5v DC to host)

Table 10.8	DFP Pinouts Continued	
Pin #	Signal	Description
19	DDC_DAT	DDC2B Data
20	DDC_CLK	DDC2B Clock

Digital Visual Interface Pinouts

The Digital Visual Interface (DVI) connector is used on an increasing number of LCD display panels as well as some CRT monitors. Many of the newest high-performance video cards feature either the DVI-D (digital only) or DVI-I (digital and analog) version of this connector. DVI can support either high-resolution (dual-link, which is above 1280×1024 resolution) or low-resolution (single-link, which has a maximum of 1280×1024 resolution) displays. DVI connectors use three rows of square pins, with pin 14 (power) recessed.

Dual-link displays use all the connectors shown in Table 10.9, whereas single-link displays omit some connectors.

Video cards that have only a DVI-I connector usually come with a special video cable that can connect to either analog VGA or DVI digital display types.

Table 10.9 lists the pin assignments used by both DVI-D and DVI-I connectors.

Table 10.9	DVI-I and DVI-D Pinouts	
Row #	Pin #	How It Is Used
1	1	TMDS Data 2-
	2	TMDS Data 2+
	3	TMDS Data 2/4 Shield
	4	TMDS Data 4-
	5	TMDS Data 4+
	6	DDC Clock
	7	DDC Data
	8	Analog Vertical Sync
2	9	TMDS Data 1-
	10	TMDS Data 1+
	11	TMDS Data 1/3 Shield
	12	TMDS Data 3-
	13	TMDS Data 3+
	14	+5V Power
	15	Ground (+5, Analog H/V Sync)
	16	Hot Plug Detect

Table 10.9	**DVI-I and DVI-D Pinouts Continued**	
Row #	Pin #	How It Is Used
	17	TMDS Data 0-
	18	TMDS Data 0+
3	19	TMDS Data 0/5 Shield
	20	TMDS Data 5-
	21	TMDS Data 5+
	22	TMDS Clock Shield
	23	TMDS Clock+
	24	TMDS Clock-

DVI-I also has the following MicroCross/high-speed pins, which are shown in Table 10.10.

Table 10.10	**DVI-I Additional Connectors**
C1	Analog Red Video Out
C2	Analog Green Video Out
C3	Analog Blue Video Out
C4	Analog Horizontal Sync
C5	Analog Common Ground Return (Red, Green, Blue Video Out)

VGA Video Display Modes

Depending on the application, you might need to identify a desired mode by the BIOS mode numbers listed in this section.

Table 10.11 lists the video modes of the chips and technologies 65554 SVGA graphics accelerator, a typical chipset used today.

Table 10.11	**Chips and Technologies 65554 Graphics Accelerator Chipset Video Modes**				
BIOS Mode	Mode Type	Resolution	Character	Colors (Displayed from Palette)	Scan Freq. (Hor./Vert.)
0, 1	VGA Text	40×25 char	9×16	16KB/256KB	31.5KHz/70Hz
2, 3	VGA Text	80×25 char	9×16	16KB/256KB	31.5KHz/70Hz
4, 5	VGA Graph	320×200 pels	8×8	4KB/256KB	31.5KHz/70Hz
6	VGA Graph	640×200 pels	8×8	2KB/256KB	31.5KHz/70Hz
7	VGA Text	80×25 char	9×16	Mono	31.5KHz/70Hz
D	VGA Graph	320×200 pels	8×8	16KB/256KB	31.5KHz/70Hz
E	VGA Graph	640×200 pels	8×8	16KB/256KB	31.5KHz/70Hz
F	VGA Graph	640×350 pels	8×14	Mono	31.5KHz/70Hz

BIOS Mode	Mode Type	Resolution	Character	Colors (Displayed from Palette)	Scan Freq. (Hor./Vert.)

Table 10.11   Chips and Technologies 65554 Graphics Accelerator Chipset Video Modes Continued

BIOS Mode	Mode Type	Resolution	Character	Colors (Displayed from Palette)	Scan Freq. (Hor./Vert.)
10	VGA Graph	640×350 pels	8×14	16KB/256KB	31.5KHz/70Hz
11	VGA Graph	640×480 pels	8×16	2KB/256KB	31.5KHz/60Hz
12	VGA Graph	640×480 pels	8×16	16KB/256KB	31.5KHz/60Hz
13	VGA Graph	320×200 pels	8×8	256KB/256KB	31.5KHz/70Hz
20	SVGA Graph	640×480 pels	8×16	16KB/256KB	31.5KHz/60Hz 37.6KHz/75Hz 43.2KHz/85Hz
22	SVGA Graph	800×600 pels	8×8	16KB/256KB	37.9KHz/60Hz 46.9KHz/75Hz 53.7KHz/85Hz
24	SVGA Graph	1024×768 pels	8×16	16KB/256KB	35.5KHz/87Hz* 48.5KHz/60Hz 60.0KHz/75Hz 68.8KHz/85Hz
28	SVGA Graph	1280×1024 pels	8×16	16KB/256KB	35.5KHz/87Hz* 35.5KHz/60Hz
30	SVGA Graph	640×480 pels	8×16	256KB/256KB	31.5KHz/60Hz 37.6KHz/75Hz 43.2KHz/85Hz
32	SVGA Graph	800×600 pels	8×16	256KB/256KB	37.9KHz/60Hz 46.9KHz/75Hz 53.7KHz/85Hz
34	SVGA Graph	1024×768 pels	8×16	256KB/256KB	35.5KHz/87Hz* 48.5KHz/60Hz 60.0KHz/75Hz 68.8KHz/85Hz
38	SVGA Graph	1280×1024 pels	8×16	256KB/256KB	35.5KHz/87Hz* 35.5KHz/60Hz
40	SVGA Graph	640×480 pels	8×16	32KB/32KB	31.5KHz/60Hz 37.6KHz/75Hz 43.2KHz/85Hz
41	SVGA Graph	640×480 pels	8×16	64KB/64KB	31.5KHz/60Hz 37.6KHz/75Hz 43.2KHz/85Hz
42	SVGA Graph	800×600 pels	8×16	32KB/32KB	37.9KHz/60Hz 46.9KHz/75Hz 53.7KHz/85Hz

Table 10.11   Chips and Technologies 65554 Graphics Accelerator Chipset Video Modes Continued

BIOS Mode	Mode Type	Resolution	Character	Colors (Displayed from Palette)	Scan Freq. (Hor./Vert.)
43	SVGA Graph	800×600 pels	8×16	64KB/64KB	37.9KHz/60Hz 46.9KHz/75Hz 53.7KHz/85Hz
44	SVGA Graph	1024×768 pels	8×16	32KB/32KB	48.5KHz/60Hz
45	SVGA Graph	1024×768 pels	8×16	64KB/64KB	48.5KHz/60Hz
50	SVGA Graph	640×480 pels	8×16	16MB/16MB	31.5KHz/60Hz
52	SVGA Graph	800×600 pels	8×16	16MB/16MB	37.9KHz/60Hz

Interlaced displays draw half the screen lines in a single pass. Lines 1, 3, 5, 7, and so forth are drawn in one pass of the electron gun. The second pass draws lines 2, 4, 6, 8, and so on. Interlacing was once common, but is now rare because of improvements in monitor design. Any interlaced display will be prone to eye-straining flicker. Flicker can be minimized by using a dark-glass glare screen.

From the standpoint of user comfort, you should use this type of information, supplied with both graphics cards and monitors, to select the most comfortable viewing settings. Comfortable viewing comes from the optimal combination of resolution, color depth, and vertical refresh rates.

In deciding whether a video card is suitable for a particular task, or whether it's obsolete and should be replaced, the amount of video RAM on the card is a critical factor.

Video RAM

Video adapters rely on their own onboard memory that they use to store video images while processing them. The amount of memory on the adapter determines the maximum screen resolution and color depth that the device can support.

Most cards today come with at least 4MB, and many have 8MB or more. Although adding more memory is not guaranteed to speed up your video adapter, it can increase the speed if it enables a wider bus (from 64 bits wide to 128 bits wide) or provides non-display memory as a cache for commonly displayed objects. It also enables the card to generate more colors and higher resolutions.

Many different types of memory are used on video adapters today. These memory types are summarized in Table 10.12.

Table 10.12   Memory Types Used in Video Display Adapters

Memory Type	Definition	Relative Speed	Use
FPM DRAM	Fast Page-Mode RAM	Slow	Low-end ISA cards; obsolete
VRAM[1]	Video RAM	Very fast	Expensive; rare today
WRAM[1]	Window RAM	Very fast	Expensive; rare today
EDO DRAM	Extended Data Out DRAM	Moderate	Low-end PCI-bus
SDRAM	Synchronous DRAM	Fast	Midrange PCI/AGP
MDRAM	Multibank DRAM	Fast	Infrequently used; rare
SGRAM	Synchronous Graphics DRAM	Very fast	High-end PCI/AGP
DDR SDRAM[2]	Double Data-Rate Synchronous DRAM	Very Fast	High-end AGP

1. *VRAM and WRAM are dual-ported memory types that can read from one port and write data through the other port. This improves performance by reducing wait times for accessing the video RAM.*

2. *DDR SDRAM can send and receive signals on both the rising and falling parts of a cycle, effectively doubling its speed over normal SDRAM. Because it is otherwise similar to conventional SDRAM, several vendors have introduced faster DDR SDRAM versions of existing video cards.*

Memory, Resolution, and Color Depth

For maximum realism in such tasks as full-motion video playback, videoconferencing, and photo-editing, a color depth of 24 bits (over 16 million colors) is desirable at the highest comfortable display resolution possible with your monitor.

Use Tables 10.13 and 10.14 to determine whether your video card has the required memory to display some of the most commonly used screen resolutions and color depths.

Table 10.13   Video Display Adapter Minimum Memory Requirements—2-D Operation

Resolution	Color Depth	Number of Colors	RAM on Video Card	Memory Required
640×480	4-bit	16	256KB	153,600 bytes
640×480	8-bit	256	512KB	307,200 bytes
640×480	16-bit	65,536	1MB	614,400 bytes
640×480	24-bit	16,777,216	1MB	921,600 bytes
800×600	4-bit	16	256KB	240,000 bytes
800×600	8-bit	256	512KB	480,000 bytes
800×600	16-bit	65,536	1MB	960,000 bytes
800×600	24-bit	16,777,216	2MB	1,440,000 bytes

Table 10.13   Video Display Adapter Minimum Memory Requirements—2-D Operation Continued

Resolution	Color Depth	Number of Colors	RAM on Video Card	Memory Required
1,024×768	4-bit	16	512KB	393,216 bytes
1,024×768	8-bit	256	1MB	786,432 bytes
1,024×768	16-bit	65,536	2MB	1,572,864 bytes
1,024×768	24-bit	16,777,216	4MB	2,359,296 bytes
1,280×1,024	4-bit	16	1MB	655,360 bytes
1,280×1,024	8-bit	256	2MB	1,310,720 bytes
1,280×1,024	16-bit	65,536	4MB	2,621,440 bytes
1,280×1,024	24-bit	16,777,216	4MB	3,932,160 bytes

From this table, you can see that a video adapter with 2MB can display 65,536 colors in 1,024×768 resolution mode, but for a true color (16.8M colors) display, you would need to upgrade to 4MB or reduce resolution to 800×600.

Although many of the newest video cards on the market today have memory sizes of 8MB, 16MB, or even 32MB, this additional memory will not be used for 24-bit color in high resolutions for 2-D graphics unless the display resolution exceeds 1,280×1,024 at 24-bit color. The additional RAM is used for 3-D texture mapping and display caching.

Use Table 10.14 to determine whether you have sufficient display memory for the desired 3-D video operation.

Table 10.14   Video Display Adapter Memory Requirements—3-D Operation

Resolution	Color Depth	On-Board Video RAM	Actual Memory Required
640×480	16-bit	2MB	1.77MB
640×480	32-bit[1]	4MB	2.93MB
800×600	16-bit	4MB	2.76MB
800×600	32-bit[1]	8MB	4.58MB
1,024×768	16-bit	8MB	4.50MB
1,024×768	32-bit[1]	8MB	7.50MB
1,280×1,024	16-bit	8MB	7.50MB

1. Although 3-D adapters typically operate in a 32-bit mode, this does not necessarily mean that they can produce more than the 16,277,216 colors of a 24-bit true color display. Many video processors and video memory buses are optimized to move data in 32-bit words, and they actually display 24-bit color while operating in a 32-bit mode, instead of the 4,294,967,296 colors that you would expect from a true 32-bit color depth.

Determining the Amount of RAM on Your Display Card

Because the size of video memory is increasingly important to most computer users, it's useful to know how much memory your display card has onboard.

Table 10.15 summarizes some methods you can use.

Table 10.15 Methods for Determining the Amount of RAM on a Video Card		
Method	**Benefits**	**Cautions**
Use memory/resolution table earlier and adjust video settings to options requiring 1MB, 2MB, 4MB, and 8MB.	If the settings work (a reboot is often required), you have at least that much RAM on your video card.	Method assumes that video card is set correctly by system; often can't be used to detect memory above 4MB because of driver limitations.
Use third-party system diagnostics to probe video card.	Universal solution for organizations with mixed display card standards.	Must use up-to-date diagnostics; might be confused by shared memory technologies found on low-cost systems.
Use diagnostics provided by video card or video chipset maker to probe video card.	Best source for technical information.	Must use different programs for different chipsets.

Given the low cost and high performance of today's video cards, you should seriously consider replacing any video card with less than 8MB of display memory onboard because even the least powerful cards in use today far outstrip top-end models of just a couple of years ago.

Local-Bus Video Standards

If you are in the market for a new video card, you need to consider your upgrade options. All video cards worth considering use a so-called local-bus technology, which uses a high-speed connection to the CPU that bypasses the slow ISA standard in use for many years. The major current standards are PCI (Peripheral Component Interconnect) and AGP (Advanced Graphics Port). The original local-bus standard, VL-Bus (the VESA Local-Bus), became outdated when the 486 CPU was replaced by Pentium-class CPUs.

PCI and AGP have some important differences, as Table 10.16 shows.

Table 10.16 Local Bus Specifications		
Feature	**PCI**	**AGP**
Theoretical maximum	132MB/sec[1]	533MB/sec throughput (2X) 1.06GB/sec throughput (4X)
Slots[2]	4/5 (typical)	1
Plug and Play support	Yes	Yes
Cost	Slightly higher	Slightly higher than PCI
Ideal use	High-end 486, Pentium, P6	Pentium II, III, Celeron, AMD K6, K7

1. At the 66MHz bus speed and 32 bits. Throughput will be higher on the 100MHz system bus.

2. More slots are possible through the use of PCI bridge chips.

Obviously, of the three local-bus standards, AGP is the fastest, but only very recent systems offer AGP video. Use Table 10.17 to determine what your best video upgrade is, depending on your system.

Table 10.17 Best Video Upgrades by CPU and Slot Type			
CPU	**Slot Type**	**Best Option**	**Notes**
486	VL-Bus	No current video cards available in VL-Bus; obsolete.	Buy used or surplus; replace motherboard; retire system.
486	PCI	Buy any low-cost PCI card with at least 4MB of RAM.	Verify that card will work with 486; some require Pentium.
Pentium, K6 MII	PCI	Buy PCI card with at least 8MB of RAM; look for DVD playback, TV out as desirable features.	Choose a card with a chipset that can be used as secondary video in case you move to AGP later by upgrading to a new motherboard or by moving the card to a system with AGP.
Pentium II/ III/Celeron K6/Athlon Duron	AGP	Buy AGP card with 16MB or more RAM; should support AGP 2X or faster speed; look for DVD playback, TV out as desirable features; DVI option desirable for display upgrades.	AGP upgrade is available only on systems with AGP slot. Many low-cost systems have AGP video on mother-board only; must use PCI for upgrade (see previous table entry).

Table 10.18 lists motherboard chipsets that support AGP. Note that the use of this chipset doesn't guarantee that every system using this chipset on its motherboard will be capable of accepting an AGP card because integrated AGP video is common on many low-cost systems today.

Table 10.18	AGP Support by Chipset	
Manufacturer	**Chipset**	**CPUs Supported**
Intel	440LX, 440EX, 440ZX-66	Celeron
	440BX, 440ZX	Pentium II, Pentium III, Celeron
	820[1]	Pentium III, Pentium II
Ali	Aladdin Pro II	Pentium II
	Aladdin V	Socket 7
Via	Apollo VP3	Socket 7
	Apollo MVP3	Socket 7
	Apollo Pro 133A[1]	Pentium II/III/Celeron
	Apollo Pro 133	Pentium II/III/Celeron
	Apollo Pro Plus	Pentium II/III/Celeron
	Apollo KX133[1]	AMD Athlon
SiS	SiS5591/5595	Socket 7
	SiS600/5595	Pentium II
	SiS5600/5595	Pentium II

1. *These chipsets support AGP version 2.0, which supports AGP 4x speed. Others listed support AGP version 1.0, which supports AGP 1x and 2x speeds.*

RAMDAC

The speed of the RAMDAC (the digital-to-analog converter) is measured in MHz; the faster the conversion process, the higher the adapter's vertical refresh rate. Table 10.19 shows the effect of faster RAMDAC chips on typical video card chipsets. As RAMDAC speed increases, higher resolutions with higher vertical refresh rates are supported.

Table 10.19 Typical Chipset and RAMDAC Speed Pairings and Their Effects on Resolution and Refresh Rates			
Chipset	**RAMDAC Speed**	**Maximum Resolution**	**Refresh Rate**
Matrox G200	250MHz	1920×1200 (2-D) 1920×1080 (3-D)	70Hz (2D)
Matrox G400MAX	360MHz	2048×1536 (2-D/3-D)	85Hz (2-D) 75Hz (3-D)

Note
In some cases, the maximum resolutions and refresh rates listed for any video card might require a RAM upgrade or the purchase of a video card with more RAM.

Refresh Rates

The speed of the RAMDAC affects the vertical refresh rate. The refresh rate (also called the *vertical scan frequency*) is the rate at which the screen display is rewritten. This is measured in hertz (Hz). A refresh rate of 72Hz means that the screen is refreshed 72 times per second. A refresh rate that is too low causes the screen to flicker, contributing to eyestrain. A *flicker-free refresh rate* is a refresh rate high enough to prevent you from seeing any flicker; eliminating flicker reduces eyestrain. The flicker-free refresh rate varies with the resolution of your monitor setting (higher resolutions require a higher refresh rate) and must be matched by both your monitor and your display card.

Low-cost monitors often have refresh rates that are too low to achieve flicker-free performance for most users, and thus can lead to eyestrain.

Table 10.20 compares two typical 17-inch CRT monitors and a typical mid-range graphics card.

Although the Matrox Millennium G200 video card supports higher refresh rates than either monitor, rates higher than the monitor can support cannot be used safely because rates in excess of the monitor's maximum refresh rate can damage the monitor.

Table 10.20 Refresh Rates Comparison			
Resolution	**G200 Video Card Vertical Refresh**	**LG 760SC (17") Monitor Vertical Refresh (Maximum)**	**LG 790SC (17") Monitor Vertical Refresh (Maximum)**
1024×768	60–140	87Hz[1]	124Hz[1]
1,280×1024	60–100Hz[1]	65Hz	93Hz[1]
1,600×1200	52–85Hz[1]	Not supported	80Hz[1]

1. Rates above 72Hz will be flicker free for many users; the VESA standard for flicker-free refresh is 85Hz or above.

For a user who wants to run at resolutions above 1,024×768, the monitor with the higher refresh rate is preferable.

Adjusting the Refresh Rate of the Video Card

The refresh rate of the video card can be adjusted in several ways:

- With older cards, a command-line program or separate Windows program was often provided.

- With recent and new cards, the standard display properties sheet offers a selection of refresh rates.

In any case, you need to know the allowable refresh rates for the monitor before you can make an appropriate selection. If your

Windows installation uses an unknown, Default Monitor, or Super VGA display type, rather than a particular brand and model of monitor, you will be prevented from selecting the higher, flicker-free refresh rates. Install the correct driver for your monitor model to get the highest refresh rates.

Comparing Video Cards with the Same Chipset

Many manufacturers create a line of video cards with the same chipset to sell at different pricing points. Why not save some dollars and get the cheapest model? Why not say "price is no object" and get the most expensive one? When you're faced with various cards in the chipsetX family, look for differences such as those shown in Table 10.21.

Table 10.21	**Comparing Video Cards with the Features You Need**
Feature	**Effect on You**
RAMDAC speed	Less-expensive cards in a family often use a slower RAMDAC. Buy the card with the fastest RAMDAC, especially for use with 17-inch or larger monitors. Faster RAMDACs are often paired with SGRAM or DDR SRAM, which are the fastest types of RAM currently found on video cards.
Amount of RAM	Although AGP video cards can use *AGP memory* (a section of main memory borrowed for texturing), performing as much work as possible on the card's own memory is still faster. PCI cards must perform all functions within their own memory. Less-expensive cards in a chipset family often have lower amounts of memory onboard, and most current model cards aren't expandable. Buy a card with enough memory (8MB–16MB or more) for your games or applications—today and tomorrow.
Memory type	High-end video cards frequently use the new SGRAM (Synchronous Graphics RAM) or DDR SRAM (Double-Data-Rate Synchronous DRAM), with regular SDRAM as a popular choice for mid-range video cards. Choose DDR SRAM, SGRAM, and then SDRAM, in order of preference when possible.
Memory and core	Many suppliers adjust the recommended speed of graphics controllers in an effort to provide users with maximum performance. If you have questions about the rated speed of a controller, check the chip supplier's Web site. Many reputable companies do use overclocked parts, but the best vendors supply large heat sinks or even powered fans to avoid overheating.
TV tuner	You can save some money by having it built in, but it's not as important as the other issues listed earlier.

Setting Up Multiple Monitor Support in Windows 98/Me/2000

Windows 98 was the first version of Windows to include a video display feature that Macintosh systems have had for years: the capability to use multiple monitors on one system. Windows 98 and Windows Me support up to nine monitors (and video adapters), each of which can provide a different view of the desktop. You can display a separate program on each monitor, use different resolutions and color depths, and enjoy other features.

On a multi-monitor Windows 98 or Windows Me system, one display is always considered to be the *primary* display. The primary display can use any PCI or AGP VGA video adapter that uses a Windows 98 mini-driver with a linear frame buffer and a packed (non-planar) format, meaning that most of the brand-name adapters sold today are eligible. Additional monitors are called *secondaries* and are much more limited in their hardware support.

Video cards with the Permedia chipset (not the later Permedia NT and Permedia 2) can't be used in a multiple-monitor configuration.

The following list of video card chipsets with the specified Microsoft Windows 98 or Me drivers can be used in any combination of primary or secondary adapters. Unlisted chipsets also can work as primary adapters. This list is condensed from Microsoft's Knowledge Base article #Q182/7/08 (check it for updates):

- **ATI**—Mach 64 GX and beyond, including 3-D cards, Rage Pro series, Xpert series, and others using the ATIM64.drv or ATIR3.drv

- **S3**—765 (Trio64V+) S3MM.drv

> **Note**
>
> Only certain updates work. These are 40, 42, 43, 44, 52, 53, and 54. Note that if the card is at one of these updates, Windows 98 recognizes the card as a Trio 64V+, provided the Microsoft driver is used. If the card is not at one of these updates, it is recognized as a Trio 32/64. Some OEM drivers don't care which update is present; be sure to note carefully which Microsoft driver Windows 98 selects when you use this card.
>
> Other S3 chipsets include the Trio64V2 and various Diamond, STB, Hercules, Number Nine, and other cards using the Virge or newer chipsets.

- **Cirrus**—5436, Alpine, 5446, and other cards using the CIRRUSMM.drv

- **Tseng**—Cards with the ET6000 chipset

- **Trident**—9685/9680/9682/9385/9382/9385 chipsets

Windows 2000 also provides multiple-monitor support, but with some differences from Windows 98/Me, as seen in Table 10.22.

Windows Version	Number of Adapters/ Monitors Supported	How Compatible Cards Are Listed	Finding Compatible Cards
Table 10.22 Comparing Windows 98/Me and Windows 2000 Multiple-Monitor Support			
98/Me	10	By chipset	On Microsoft's Web site
2000	9	Brand and model	HCL listing on CD-ROM

As of the initial release of Windows 2000, some of the major brands with products on the multiple-monitor approved list include:

- 3DFX
- 3Dlabs
- Creative Labs
- Diamond Multimedia
- ELSA
- Matrox
- Number Nine
- nVidia
- SiS 300 compatible
- STB

Windows 2000's Hardware Compatibility List is organized by graphics card brand and model, rather than by chipset (check the Windows 2000 CD-ROM Hardware Compatibility List for details). This list is likely to change as Windows 2000 support becomes more widespread, but unfortunately the online version of the Windows 2000 HCL doesn't provide an updated list of cards that support multiple-monitor configurations. You should check with your video card or chipset manufacturer for the latest information on Windows 2000 and multiple-monitor support issues.

Some video card manufacturers, including Appian and Matrox, make video cards that can support two or more monitors with a single card, avoiding the problems of using multiple cards for multiple-monitor support.

Useful third-party Web sites for multiple-monitor support include the following:

www.realtimesoft.com/multimon/

www.digitalroom.net/techpub/multimon.html

System Configuration Issues for Multiple-Monitor Support

If the BIOS on your computer does not let you select which device should be the primary VGA display, it decides based on the order of the PCI slots in the machine; AGP slots on most systems have a lower priority than PCI slots. You should, therefore, install the primary adapter in the highest-priority PCI slot. Because many systems do not list the slot priority in their documentation, you might need to experiment by switching the cards around between different PCI expansion slots.

After the hardware is in place, you can configure the display for each monitor from the Display Control Panel's Settings page. The primary display is always fixed in the upper-left corner of the virtual desktop, but you can move the secondary displays to view any area of the desktop you want. You also can set the screen resolution and color depth for each display individually.

Video Card and Chipset Makers Model Reference
3-D Chipsets

As with standard 2-D video adapters, several manufacturers of popular 3-D video chipsets exist and many more manufacturers of video adapters that use them exist.

> **Note**
>
> See Chapter 15 of *Upgrading and Repairing PCs, 12th Edition*, for an exhaustive listing of current 3-D chipsets and the boards on which they are found.

Multimedia Devices

When choosing TV, video-out, or video capture options for your PC, use Table 10.23 to help you decide which solution is best for you.

Table 10.23   Multimedia Device Comparison

Device Type	Pros	Cons
Graphics card w/ built-in TV tuner	Convenience, single-slot solution.	Upgrading requires card replacement.
TV-tuner attachment	Allows upgrade to existing graphics cards; might be movable to newer models.	Can't be used with all graphics cards.

Table 10.23	Multimedia Device Comparison Continued	
Device Type	**Pros**	**Cons**
Parallel-port attachment	Universal use on desktop or notebook computer; inexpensive.	Frame rate limited by speed of port.
USB-port attachment	Easy installation on late-model, USB-equipped computers with Windows 98/Me/2000.	Might not work on Windows 95B OSR 2.x with USB; requires active USB port.
Dedicated ISA or PCI interface card	Fast frame rate for realistic video; doesn't require disconnecting parallel printer; works with any graphics card.	High resource requirements (IRQ and so on) on some models; ISA nearly obsolete; requires internal installation.
IEEE-1394 (FireWire, iLINK) connection to digital video	No conversion from analog to digital needed; all-digital image is very high quality without compression artifacts (blocky areas) in video; fast throughput.	Requires IEEE-1394 interface card and IEEE-1394 digital video source; new and expensive; card requires internal installation.

Troubleshooting Video Capture Devices

Table 10.24 provides some advice for troubleshooting problems with video capture devices.

Table 10.24	Troubleshooting Video Capture Devices	
Device Type	**Problem**	**Solution**
Parallel-port attachment	Can't detect device, but printers work okay.	Check port settings; device might require IEEE-1284 settings (EPP and ECP); change in BIOS; make sure device is connected directly to port; avoid daisy-chaining devices unless device specifically allows it; check Windows 9x Device Manager for IRQ conflicts.
TV tuners (built-in graphics card or add-on)	No picture.	Check cabling; set signal source correctly in software.
All devices	Video capture is jerky.	Frame rate is too low; increasing it might require capturing video in a smaller window; use fastest parallel-port setting you can.
	Video playback has pauses, dropped frames.	Hard disk might be pausing for thermal recalibration; use AV-rated SCSI hard drives or new UDMA EIDE drives; install correct bus-mastering EIDE drivers for motherboard chipset to speed things up.

Table 10.24   **Troubleshooting Video Capture Devices Continued**

Device Type	Problem	Solution
USB devices	Device can't be detected or doesn't work properly.	Use Windows 98 or above; late versions of Windows 95 have USB drivers, but they often don't work; if you use a USB hub, make sure it's powered.
Interface cards (all types)	Card can't be detected or doesn't work.	Check for IRQ conflicts in Windows Device Manager; consider setting card manually if possible.
All devices	Capture or installation problems.	Use the newest drivers available; check manufacturer's Web site for updates, FAQs, and so on.

Testing a Monitor with Common Applications

Even without dedicated test and diagnostics software, you can use the software accessories (WordPad, Paint, and so on) that come with Microsoft Windows to test a monitor for picture quality.

One good series of tasks is as follows:

- Draw a perfect circle with a graphics program. If the displayed result is an oval, not a circle, this monitor will not serve you well with graphics or design software.

- Using a word processor, type some words in 8- or 10-point type (1 point equals 1/72 inch). If the words are fuzzy or if the black characters are fringed with color, select another monitor.

- Turn the brightness up and down while examining the corner of the screen's image. If the image blooms or swells, it is likely to lose focus at high brightness levels.

- Display a screen with as much white space as possible and look for areas of color variance. This might indicate a problem only with that individual unit or its location, but if you see it on more than one monitor of the same make, it can be indicative of a manufacturing problem; or it could indicate problems with the signal coming from the graphics card. Move the monitor to another system equipped with a different graphics card model and retry this test to see for certain whether it's the monitor or video card.

- Load Microsoft Windows to check for uniform focus. Are the corner icons as sharp as the rest of the screen? Are the lines in the title bar curved or wavy? Monitors usually are sharply focused at the center, but seriously blurred corners indicate a poor design. Bowed lines can be the result of a poor video adapter, so don't dismiss a monitor that shows those lines without using another adapter to double-check the effect.

- A good monitor will be calibrated so that rays of red, green, and blue light hit their targets (individual phosphor dots) precisely. If they don't, you have bad convergence. This is apparent when edges of lines appear to illuminate with a specific color. If you have good convergence, the colors will be crisp, clear, and true, provided there isn't a predominant tint in the phosphor.

- If the monitor has built-in diagnostics (a recommended feature), try them as well to test the display independent of the graphics card and system to which it's attached.

Use Table 10.25 to troubleshoot specified problems.

Table 10.25   Troubleshooting Display Problems

Symptom	Cause	Solution
No Picture	LED indicates power-saving mode (flashing green or yellow by power switch).	Move the mouse or press Alt+Tab on the keyboard and wait up to one minute to wake up the system if the system is turned on.
	LED indicates normal mode.	Check monitor and video data cables; replace with known, working spare.
		Turn off monitor; reset mode switch to correct setting (analog for VGA).
		Check brightness and contrast control; adjust as necessary.
No picture; no power lights on monitor	No power flowing to monitor.	Cycle monitor off and on in case power management has kicked in; check power cable and replace; check surge protector and replace; replace monitor and retest.
Jittery picture quality	LCD monitors display not adjusted.	Use display-adjustment software to reduce or eliminate pixel jitter and pixel swim.
	Cables loose.	Check cables for tightness at the video card and the monitor (if removable).
	Defective main or extender cable.	Remove the extender cable and retest with the monitor plugged directly into the video card; if the extended cable is bad, replace it; if the main cable is bad, replace it.
	Jitter is intermittent.	Check for interference; microwave ovens near monitors can cause severe picture distortion when turned on.

Table 10.25	Troubleshooting Display Problems Continued	
Symptom	**Cause**	**Solution**
	CRT monitor—wrong refresh rate.	Check settings; reduce refresh rate until acceptable picture quality is achieved.
		Use onscreen picture adjustments until an acceptable picture quality is achieved.
	Intermittent—not due to external interference.	If the problem can be fixed by waiting or gently tapping the side of the monitor, the monitor power supply is probably bad or has loose connections internally; service or replace the monitor.
Picture in DOS, not Windows	Incorrect or corrupted Windows video driver.	Boot Windows 9x in Safe Mode; boot Windows 2000 in Enable VGA Mode. If these display modes work, delete current video card from Device Manager and restart system to reinstall drivers. If incorrect drivers are selected by Windows, manually choose correct drivers in Device Manager.

Audio I/O Connectors

Sound cards, or built-in audio chips, provide another significant part of modern PCs' multimedia capabilities. Learning the correct uses for the basic input/output connectors will help you as you set up typical sound-equipped computers. See Chapter 14 for examples of these connectors.

- **Stereo line out or audio out connector**—The line out connector is used to send sound signals from the audio adapter to a device outside the computer, such as stereo speakers, a headphone, or a stereo system. Some adapters provide two jacks for line out: one for the left channel and the other for the right channel.

- **Stereo line or audio in connector**—With the line in connector, you can record or mix sound signals from an external source, such as a stereo system or VCR, to the computer's hard disk.

- **Speaker/headphone connector**—The speaker/headphone connector is provided on most audio adapters, but not necessarily all of them. Some systems use line out instead. When the adapter provides both a speaker/headphone and a line out connector, the speaker/headphone connector provides an amplified signal that can power your headphones or small bookshelf speakers. Most adapters can provide up to four watts of power to drive your speakers. The signals that the adapter sends through the line out connector are not amplified. The line out connector generally provides better sound reproduction because it relies on the external amplifier built in to your stereo system or speakers, which is typically more powerful than the small amplifier on the audio adapter.

- **Microphone or mono in connector**—The mono in connector is used to connect a microphone for recording your voice or other sounds to disk. This microphone jack records in mono, not in stereo, and is therefore not suitable for high-quality music recordings. Many audio adapter cards use Automatic Gain Control (AGC) to improve recordings. This feature adjusts the recording levels on-the-fly. A 600-ohm to 10KB-ohm dynamic or condenser microphone works best with this jack. Some inexpensive audio adapters use the line in connector instead of a separate microphone jack.

- **Joystick connector**—The joystick connector is a 15-pin, D-shaped connector that can connect to any standard joystick or game controller. Sometimes the joystick port can accommodate two joysticks if you purchase an optional Y-adapter.

- **MIDI connector**—Audio adapters typically use the same joystick port as their MIDI connector. Two of the pins in the connector are designed to carry signals to and from a MIDI device, such as an electronic keyboard. In most cases, you must purchase a separate MIDI connector from the audio adapter manufacturer that plugs into the joystick port and contains the two round, 5-pin DIN connectors used by MIDI devices, plus a connector for a joystick. Because their signals use separate pins, you can connect the joystick and a MIDI device at the same time. You need this connector only if you plan to connect your PC to external MIDI devices. You can still play the MIDI files found on many Web sites by using the audio adapter's internal synthesizer.

- **Internal pin-type connector**—Most audio adapters have an internal pin-type connector that you can use to plug an internal CD-ROM drive directly into the adapter, using a small, round cable. This connection enables you to channel audio signals from the CD-ROM directly to the audio adapter, so you can play the sound through the computer's speakers. This connector does not carry data from the CD-ROM to the system bus; it only provides the CD-ROM drive with direct audio access to the speakers. If your adapter lacks

this connector, you can still play CD audio through the computer speakers by connecting the CD-ROM drive's headphone jack to the audio adapter's line in jack with an
external cable.

Tip

The line in, line out, and speaker connectors on an audio
adapter all use the same 1/8-inch mini-jack socket. The three
jacks are usually labeled, but when setting up a computer on or
under a desk, these labels on the back of the PC can be difficult
to read. One of the most common reasons a PC fails to produce
any sound is that the speakers are plugged into the wrong
socket.

If your sound card, microphone, and speakers aren't color-coded,
do it yourself. See Chapter 1, "General Technical Reference," for the
PC99 standards for color-coding for audio and other ports.

Connectors for Advanced Features

Many of the newest sound cards are designed for advanced gaming,
DVD audio playback, and sound production uses, and have additional connectors:

- **MIDI In/MIDI Out**—Some advanced sound cards don't
  require you to convert the game port (joystick port) to MIDI
  interfacing by offering these ports on a separate external
  connector. This permits you to use a joystick and have an
  external MIDI device connected at the same time. Its typical
  location is in an external device.

- **SPDIF (also called SP/DIF) In and SPDIF Out**—The
  Sony/Philips Digital Interface Format connector receives digital audio signals directly from compatible devices without
  converting them to analog format first. Its typical location is
  in an external device. SPDIF interfaces are also referred to by
  some vendors as Dolby Digital interfaces.

- **CD SPDIF**—Connects compatible CD-ROM drives with
  SPDIF interfacing to the digital input of the sound card. Its
  typical location is on the side of the audio card.

- **TAD In**—Connects modems with Telephone Answering
  Device support to the sound card for sound processing of
  voice messages. Its typical location is on the side of the
  audio card.

- **Digital DIN Out**—This supports multi-speaker digital speaker systems. Its typical location is in an external device.

- **Aux In**—Provides input for other sound sources, such as a TV tuner card. Its typical location is on the side of the audio card.

- **I2S In**—This enables the sound card to accept digital audio input from an external source, such as 2-channel decoded AC-3 from DVD decoders and MPEG-2 Zoom Video. Its typical location is on the side of the audio card.

Sound Quality Standards

Many sound card owners never record anything, but if you like the idea of adding sound to a Web site or presentation, you should know the quality and file size impact that typical sound settings will have. The Windows 9x/2000/Me standard sound quality settings are shown in Table 10.26.

Table 10.26   Windows 9x/2000/Me Sound File Resolutions

Resolution	Frequency	Bandwidth	File Size
Telephone quality	11,025Hz	8-bit mono	11KB/sec
Radio quality	22,050Hz	8-bit mono	22KB/sec
CD quality	44,100Hz	16-bit stereo	172KB/sec

Note that the higher the sound quality, the larger the file size. The file sizes are for .WAV files saved with the Windows Sound Recorder's default settings. If you want to add sound effects or speech to a Web site, you should get a program such as Real Networks's RealProducer, which is capable of compressing sound as much as 100:1 while still maintaining reasonable quality.

Many new sound cards also support a 48KHz standard designed to match the requirements of DVD audio playback and Dolby AC-3 audio compression technologies. This frequency must be set manually in Sound Recorder if you need to record at this high frequency level.

Configuring Sound Cards

Traditionally, sound cards have been one of the toughest single installation tasks because they use three of the four settings possible for an add-on card: IRQ, DMA, and I/O port addressing. The rule of thumb is: "The sound card first!"—no matter what else you need to install.

PCI Versus ISA Sound Cards

PCI cards have become the best choice recently for all types of upgrades, including sound cards. Compared to ISA cards, PCI cards are faster, have a lower CPU utilization rate, and use fewer hardware resources (see Table 10.27). Compare the configuration of the Sound Blaster 16 card with the native configuration for an Ensoniq-chipset PCI sound card.

Table 10.27 Default Resource Assignments for ISA and PCI Sound Card in Native and Emulation Modes				
Card **Onboard Device**	**IRQ**	**I/O**	**DMA** **(16 Bit)**	**DMA** **(8 Bit)**
Sound Blaster 16—ISA Bus				
Audio	5	220h-233h	5	1
MIDI Port	—	330h-331h	—	—
FM Synthesizer	—	388h-38Bh	—	—
Game Port	—	200h-207h	—	—
Ensoniq Audio PCI—PCI Bus Native Mode				
Audio	11	DC80-DCBFh	—	—
Game Port	—	200h-207h	—	—
Ensoniq Audio PCI—PCI Bus Legacy (SB Pro) Mode				
Audio	7*	DC80-DCBFh	—	—
MIDI Port	—	330h-331h	—	—
FM Synthesizer	—	388h-38Bh	—	—
(Ensoniq SoundScape)	—	0530-0537h	—	—
Game Port	—	200h-207h	—	—

*Shared IRQ with printer port; allowed by Ensoniq driver

While the Ensoniq Audio PCI card uses only one IRQ and one I/O port address in its native mode, if you have software (mostly older Windows and DOS game/educational titles) that requires Sound Blaster Pro compatibility, the Legacy settings must also be used. However, if you are *not* running Sound Blaster–specific software (all your software is native Windows 9x, for example), you might be able to disable the Legacy mode for a PCI-based sound card.

Multifunction (Modem and Sound) Cards

Multifunction cards that use DSP (digital signal processor) technology, such as IBM Mwave-based cards, can be very difficult to install in today's IRQ-starved systems. These cards typically combine a modem plus a Sound Blaster–compatible sound card. They also typically require an IRQ and one or more I/O port address ranges for the DSP as well as the normal settings seen previously and in Chapter 6, "Serial Ports and Modems," for the sound card and modem functions.

These cards also might require a very complex software installation process for the DSP, sound, modem, and soft wavetable sound samples. Because they are resource hungry, often have limited modem speeds, and are usually ISA based, I recommend replacing these types of multifunction cards with separate PCI-based sound and modem cards if possible.

Troubleshooting Audio Hardware
Hardware (Resource) Conflicts

You might notice that your audio adapter doesn't work (no sound effects or music), repeats the same sounds over and over, or causes your PC to freeze. This situation is called a *device*, or *hardware*, conflict centering around IRQ, DMA, and I/O port address settings in your computer (see Chapter 2, "System Components and Configuration").

Detecting Resource Conflicts

Use Table 10.28 to help you determine resource conflicts caused by your sound card.

Table 10.28	Resolving Sound Card Resource Conflicts		
Problem	**Symptom**	**How to Detect**	**Solution**
Sound card using same IRQ as another device.	Skipping, jerky sound, or system lockups.	Use Windows Device Manager. For other systems, use IRQ and DMA card, as described in Chapter 2.	For PnP device: Disable automatic configuration for conflicting device and try to set card manually through direct alteration of settings or by choosing alternative configurations.
Sound card and another device using the same DMA channel.	No sound at all from sound card.		For non-PnP device: Move conflicting device to another setting to allow sound card to use defaults.

Table 10.28 Resolving Sound Card Resource Conflicts Continued			
Problem	**Symptom**	**How to Detect**	**Solution**
PCI-slot sound card works okay with Windows, but not MS-DOS apps.	Windows software plays; DOS software doesn't play card; can't detect card.	Check for Legacy or SB settings in the Windows 9x Device Manager.	If no Legacy support is installed, install it. Follow instructions carefully for using the card with older software. You might need to run Setup program or TSR before starting DOS program. You might need software patch from game developer. In extreme cases, you might need to use an actual SB Pro/16 card alongside your PCI sound card and use it instead.
Some DOS and Windows software works, but some can't use card.	Error messages about incorrect card settings.	Check card or Legacy software settings; alternative settings work okay for some programs, but not others.	Software expects SB default settings; use settings in preceding table for Sound Blaster 16 (all but DMA 5 apply to SB Pro).
DSP-equipped card, such as IBM Mwave, not installed properly or out of resources.	Multifunction sound and modem card doesn't work.	Check Windows 9x Device Manager for DSP host configuration.	Mwave and similar cards require basic SB settings as in previous entry, plus serial (COM) port setting resources for the DSP! Reinstall card with all drivers.
PnP card on a non-PnP system was working, but has now stopped in these files.	PnP enumerator program in startup process probably removed or damaged.	Check CONFIG.SYS or AUTOEXEC.BAT for driver; use REM to create labels before and after driver commands.	Reinstall software and test; upgrade BIOS to PnP mode if possible.

Most Common Causes of Hardware Conflicts with Sound Card

The most common causes of system resource conflicts are the following:

- SCSI host adapters
- Network interface cards

- Bus mouse adapter cards

- Serial port adapter cards for COM3 or COM4

- Parallel port adapter cards for LPT2

- Internal modems

- Scanner interface cards

All these cards use IRQ, DMA, and I/O port addresses, which in some cases can overlap with default or alternative sound card settings.

Freeing Up IRQ 5 for Sound Card Use While Still Printing

If you are using an LPT2 port card for a slow-speed device, such as a dot-matrix or low-end inkjet printer, you can often free up its default IRQ 5 by disabling EPP/ECP/IEEE-1284 modes. These modes require use of an IRQ (ECP also uses a DMA channel). Reverting to standard printing will cause most LPT ports to use only I/O port addresses. This will enable you to use the port for printing and its IRQ 5 for a sound card.

Other Sound Card Problems

Like the common cold, audio adapter problems have common symptoms. Table 10.29 will help you diagnose sound card problems.

Table 10.29	Diagnosing Sound Card Problems	
Symptom	**Cause**	**Solution**
No sound.	Incorrect or missing speaker wires.	Plug speakers into the correct jack (stereo line out/speaker out).
	No power to amplified speakers.	Turn on; attach to AC adapter or use fresh batteries.
	Mono speaker attached to stereo plug.	Use stereo speaker or headset.
	Mixer settings too low.	Adjust master volume setting; turn off mute option.
	Sound card might not be working.	Test with diagnostic software and sounds provided.
	Sound card hardware needs to be reset.	Power down, then on again, or use reset button to restart PC.
	Some games play, but others don't.	Check hardware defaults as above; verify correct version of Windows DirectX or other game API is installed.

Table 10.29 Diagnosing Sound Card Problems Continued

Symptom	Cause	Solution
Mono Sound.	Mono plug in stereo jack.	Use stereo speaker jack.
	Incorrectly wired speakers.	Check color coding.
	Audio card in left-channel mono fail-safe mode because of driver problem.	Reload drivers and test stereo sound.
	Speakers with independent volume controls might be set differently.	Adjust volume to match on both.
Low volume.	Speakers plugged into headphone jack.	Use higher powered speaker jack if separate jacks are provided.
	Mixer settings too low.	Boost volume in mixer.
	Hardware volume control (thumbwheel) on sound card turned too low.	Adjust volume on card.
	Speakers not powered or require more power.	Power speakers, add amplifier, or replace speakers.
Scratchy sound.	Audio card picking up interference from other cards.	Move away from other cards.
	ISA sound card might be dropping signals during hard disk access.	Normal problem due to high CPU utilization of ISA card; use PCI sound card instead.
	Interference from monitor causing interference.	Move speakers farther away. Put subwoofers on the floor to maximize low-frequency transmission and to keep their big magnets away from the monitor.
	Poor quality FM-synthesis music from sound card.	Change to wavetable sound card; check wavetable settings.
Computer won't start after card installation.	Card not seated tightly in expansion slot.	Remove card, reinsert, and restart PC.
IOS Error displayed during Windows 95 startup; system locked up.	Sound card software clashes with Windows Input/Output System (IOS).	Check with sound card vendor for an IOS fix program; might be supplied on install disk; start Windows 9x in Safe mode to locate and install.
Joystick doesn't work.	Duplicate joystick ports on sound card and another card causing I/O port address conflict.	Disable sound card joystick port.
	Computer too fast for inexpensive joystick port.	Buy high-speed joystick port; disable port on sound card; install replacement joystick port card.
		Slow down computer with de-turbo button or BIOS routine.

Table 10.29   Diagnosing Sound Card Problems Continued

Symptom	Cause	Solution
Can't play DVD audio or MP3 files, or use SPDIF connections.	Hardware resource not enabled on sound card.	Enable hardware resource.
	Wrong playback program for media type.	Use correct playback program.
	Volume set too low in sound card mixer program.	Adjust volume for correct playback device in sound mixer program; check volume and power to speakers.
	Cabling incorrect.	Adjust cabling.

Chapter 11

Networking

Client/Server Versus Peer-to-Peer Networking

Table 11.1 compares the features of client/server networking (such as with Novell NetWare, Windows NT Server, and Windows 2000) with peer-to-peer networking (such as with Windows for Workgroups, Windows 9x, Windows Me, and Windows NT Workstation). This table will help you decide which type of network is appropriate for your situation.

> **Note**
>
> Networking is an enormous topic. The following content serves as a reference for field technicians and other professionals. If you need more in-depth information about networking, see Chapter 19 of *Upgrading and Repairing PCs, 12th Edition,* or pick up a copy of *Upgrading and Repairing Networks, Second Edition.*

Table 11.1	Comparing Client/Server and Peer-to-Peer Networking	
Item	**Client/Server**	**Peer-to-Peer**
Access control	Via user/group lists of permissions; single password provides user access to only the resources on his/her list; users can be given several different levels of access.	Via password lists by resource; each resource requires a separate password; all-or-nothing access; no centralized user list.
Security	High, because access is controlled by user or by group identity.	Low, because knowing the password gives anybody access to a shared resource.
Performance	High, because server doesn't waste time or resources handling workstation tasks.	Low, because servers often act as workstations.
Hardware cost	High, because of specialized design of server, high-performance nature of hardware, redundancy features.	Low, because any workstation can become a server by sharing resources.
Software cost	License fees per workstation user are part of the cost of the Network Operating System server software (Windows NT and Windows 2000 Server, Novell NetWare).	Free; all client software is included with any release of Windows 9x, Windows NT Workstation, Windows 2000 Professional, or Windows Me.

Table 11.1 Comparing Client/Server and Peer-to-Peer Networking Continued		
Item	**Client/Server**	**Peer-to-Peer**
Backup	Centralized when data is stored on server; allows use of high-speed, high-capacity tape backups with advanced cataloging.	Left to user decision; usually mixture of backup devices and practices at each workstation.
Redundancy	Duplicate power supplies, hot-swappable drive arrays, and even redundant servers are common; network OS normally capable of using redundant devices automatically.	No true redundancy among either peer "servers" or clients; failures require manual intervention to correct with high possibility of data loss.

If you choose any form of Ethernet network hardware for your peer-to-peer network, you can upgrade to a client/server network later by adding a server with the appropriate network operating system. Your existing network cards, cables, and other hardware can still be used with the new server.

Choosing Network Hardware and Software

In this section, you'll receive a detailed checklist of the hardware and software you need to build your network. Although many options are available on the market for network hardware, this discussion assumes that you will be choosing Fast Ethernet hardware that can also work with standard Ethernet networks ("dual-speed" 10/100 cards and hubs). This is the most popular and cost-effective network currently available.

First, start with the number of computers you plan to network together. You need the items discussed in the following section to set up your network.

NIC

One network interface card (NIC) is required for every computer on the network. To simplify technical support, buy the same model of NIC for each computer in a peer-to-peer workgroup network. Today, the best price-performance combination is Fast Ethernet (100BASE-TX) NICs. You should choose dual-speed (10/100) versions of these cards to enable interconnection with standard 10Mbps Ethernet networks.

You should record the brand name and model number of the NIC(s) you are using, as well as the driver version or source. Use Table 11.2 as a guide.

Table 11.2 NIC Location and Information Worksheet					
NIC Location and Computer ID	**Brand Name**	**Model #**	**Cable Type(s)**	**Speed**	**Driver Source or Version**

UTP Cable

Each NIC must be connected by a cable long enough to reach comfortably between the NIC and the hub, which connects multiple computers. Use Table 11.3 as a guide for recording necessary information regarding your cabling. Your cabling should be Category 5 or better.

Table 11.3 UTP Cable Worksheet		
Computer ID	**Cable Length**	**Wiring Standard**

You need only one hub for the typical workgroup network.

Hub

Buy a hub of the correct speed with at least enough RJ-45 ports for each computer on the network; for expansion, buy a hub with a couple of empty ports. Use the worksheet shown in Table 11.4 as a guide for recording information about your hub or hubs. Dual-speed 10/100 Ethernet/Fast Ethernet hubs will enable you to connect with existing standard Ethernet networks.

Table 11.4 Hub Worksheet					
Hub #	**Brand**	**Model#**	**# of Ports**	**Uplink?**	**Speed(s)**

Software

Start by using the built-in networking software supplied with your version of Windows. Any recent version of Windows contains network client and simple peer-server software. Your workgroup network can contain any combination of the following:

- Windows for Workgroups 3.11
- Windows 95
- Windows 98

- Windows 2000 Professional

- Windows NT 4.0 Workstation

- Windows Me

Table 11.5 shows the basic configuration you'll need to complete for any client (accessing services on another PC) and server (sharing services with other PCs) using these versions of Windows.

Table 11.5 Minimum Network Software for Peer-to-Peer Networking		
Item	Client	Server
Windows network client	Yes	No
NetBEUI protocol	Yes	Yes
File and print sharing for Microsoft Networks	No	Yes
NIC installed and bound to previous protocols and services	Yes	Yes
Workgroup identification (same for all PCs in workgroup)	Yes	Yes
Computer name (each PC needs a unique name)	Yes	Yes

Any system that will be used as both a client and a server must have the components from *both* columns installed.

Depending on how you plan to use the computer, one or both of the following might also need to be installed:

- If the computer is going to access a Novell NetWare client/server network, the IPX/SPX protocol must also be installed and configured.

- If the computer is going to be used to access the Internet or any other TCP/IP-based network, the TCP/IP protocol must also be installed.

Note that Windows 2000 and Windows Me do *not* install the NetBEUI protocol by default. You must specify it when you set up the network features of either version of Windows if you want to use Direct Cable Connection or create a simple workgroup network. Windows 2000 and Windows Me use TCP/IP as their default network protocol.

Use the Network icon in the Windows Control Panel to choose your network settings. You'll need the following software to set up the network:

- Operating system CDs, disks, or hard-disk image files

- NIC drivers

Network Protocols

The second most important choice you must make when you create your network is which network protocol you will use. The network protocol affects with which types of computers your network can connect.

The three major network protocols are TCP/IP, IPX/SPX, and NetBEUI. Unlike data-link protocols, though, network protocols are not tied to particular hardware (NIC or cable) choices. Network protocols are software and can be installed or removed to any computer on the network at any time as necessary.

Table 11.6 summarizes the differences between these protocols.

Protocol	Included in Protocol Suite	Best Used for	Notes
Table 11.6 Overview of Network Protocols and Suites			
IP	TCP/IP	Internet and large networks	Also used for dial-up Internet access; native protocol suite of Windows 2000, Windows Me, and Novell NetWare 5.x
IPX	IPX/SPX	Networks with Novell 4.x and earlier servers	Used by NetWare 5.x for certain special features only
NetBEUI	N/A	Windows 9x, Me, 2000, or Windows for Workgroups peer networks	Can't be routed between networks; simplest network protocol; also used with Direct Cable Connection NIC-less "networking"

All the computers on any given network must use the same network protocol or protocol suite to communicate with each other.

IP and TCP/IP

IP stands for Internet Protocol; it is the network layer of the collection of protocols (or protocol suite) developed for use on the Internet and commonly known as *TCP/IP* (Transmission Control Protocol/Internet Protocol).

Later, the TCP/IP protocols were adopted by the UNIX operating systems, and they have now become the most commonly used protocol suite on PC LANs. Virtually every operating system with networking capabilities supports TCP/IP, and it is well on its way to displacing all the other competing protocols. Novell NetWare 5 and Windows 2000 both use TCP/IP as their native protocol for most services.

Selecting a Network Data-Link Protocol (Specification)

Regardless of the type of network (client/server or peer-to-peer) you select, you can choose from a wide variety of network data-link protocols, also known as *specifications*. The most common ones in use for PCs are listed here. Use Table 11.7 to understand the requirements, limitations, and performance characteristics of the major types of network data-link protocols.

Table 11.7   Network Data-Link Protocols Summary

Network Type	Speed	Max Number of Stations	Cable Types	Notes
ARCnet	2.5Mbps	255 stations	RG-62 coax UTP[1]/Type 1 STP[2]	Obsolete for new installations; was used to replace IBM 3270 terminals (which used the same coax cable).
Home PNA 1.0	1Mbps	N/A	RJ-11 phone cable	Easy home-based networking via parallel-port connections or internal ISA, PCI, or PC Card NICs or USB port; replaced by Home PNA 2.0.
Home PNA 2.0	10Mbps	N/A	RJ-11 phone cable	Easy, faster home-based networking via PCI or PC Card NICs or USB port.
Ethernet	10Mbps	Per segment: 10BASE-T-2 10BASE-2-30 10BASE-5-100 10BASE-FL-2	UTP[1] Cat 3 (10BASE-T), Thicknet (coax; 10BASE-5), Thinnet (RG-58 coax; 10BASE-2), Fiber optic (10BASE-F)	Being replaced by Fast Ethernet; can be interconnected with Fast Ethernet by use of dual-speed hubs and switches; use switches and routers to overcome "5-4-3" rule in building very large networks.
Fast Ethernet	100Mbps	Per segment: 2	Cat 5 UTP[1]	Fast Ethernet can be interconnected with standard Ethernet through use of dual-speed hubs, switches, and routers.

Table 11.7	**Network Data-Link Protocols Summary Continued**			
Network Type	**Speed**	**Max Number of Stations**	**Cable Types**	**Notes**
Gigabit Ethernet	1000Mbps	Per segment:	2 Cat 5 UTP	Gigabit Ethernet can be interconnected with Fast and/or standard Ethernet through use of dual-speed hubs, switches and routers.
Token Ring	4Mbps or 16Mbps	72 on UTP[1] 250-260 on type 1 STP[2]	UTP[1], Type 1 STP[2], and Fiber optic	High price for NICs[3] and MAUs[4] to interconnect clients; primarily used with IBM mid-size and mainframe systems.

1. UTP = Unshielded Twisted Pair
2. STP = Shielded Twisted Pair
3. NIC = Network Interface Card
4. MAU = Multiple Access Unit

Network Cable Connectors

Several types of network cable connectors are available. Table 11.8 summarizes these and indicates which ones are in current use.

Table 11.8	**Network Cable Connectors**	
Connector Type	**Used By**	**Notes**
DB-15	Thick Ethernet	Used a "vampire tap" cable from the connector to attach to the main cable; obsolete.
DB-9	Token Ring	Obsolete.
BNC	RG-62 ARCnet (obsolete), RG-58 Thin Ethernet	Thin Ethernet uses T-connector to enable pass-through to another station or a terminating resistor to indicate end of network segment. Obsolete in most installations; BNC still used in small networks or to connect hubs.
RJ-45	Newer Token-Ring, 10BASE-T Ethernet, Fast Ethernet, Gigabit Ethernet	Twisted-pair cabling overwhelming favorite for most installations.

While virtually all newly installed networks today with conventional cables use twisted-pair cabling, many networks are mixtures of twisted-pair and older cabling types. Token-Ring Network Interface cards and Ethernet cards with all three of the popular

Ethernet connector types remain in wide use. When a network interface card has more than one connector type, you might need to use the card's setup program to select which connector to use.

Wire Pairing for Twisted-Pair Cabling

For large, multi-office installations, network cables are usually built from bulk cable stock and connectors. Because the twisted-pair cabling has eight wires, many pairings are possible. If you are adding cable to an existing installation, you should match the wire pairings already in use. However, the most popular wiring standard is the AT&T 258A standard detailed in Table 11.9. You can buy pre-built cabling that matches this standard or build your own.

Table 11.9 RJ-45 Connector Wire Pairing and Placement AT&T 258A Standard		
Wire Pairing	**Wire Connected to Pin #**	**Pair Used For**
White/blue and blue	White/blue - #5 Blue - #4	Not used[1]
White/orange and orange	White/orange - #1 Orange - #2	Transmit
White/green and green	White/green - #3 Green - #6	Receive
White/brown - brown	White/brown - #7 Brown - #8	Not used[1]

1. *This pair is not used with 10BASE-T or Fast Ethernet 100BASE-TX, but all four pairs are used with Fast Ethernet 100BASE-T4 and with Gigabit Ethernet 1000BASE-TX standards.*

Thus, a completed cable that follows the AT&T 268A (also called the EIA/TIA 568B) standard should look similar to the following when viewed from the flat side of the RJ-45 connector (from left to right): orange/white, orange, green/white, blue, blue/white, green, brown/white, brown.

Making Your Own UTP Cables

You will need the following tools and supplies to build your own Ethernet cables:

- UTP cable (Category 5 or better)

- RJ-45 connectors

- Wire stripper

- RJ-45 crimping tool

You can buy all the previous tools for a single price from many different network-products vendors. If you are working with a network with a wiring closet, you will also want to add a punchdown tool to your kit.

Before you create a "real" cable of any length, follow these procedures and practice on a short length of cable. RJ-45 connectors and bulk cable are cheap; network failures are not.

Follow these steps for creating your own twisted-pair cables:

1. Determine how long your UTP cable should be. You'll want to allow adequate slack for moving the computer and for avoiding strong interference sources. Keep the maximum distances for TP cables (listed later in this chapter) in mind.

2. Roll out the appropriate length of cable.

3. Cut the cable cleanly from the box of wire.

4. Use the wire stripper to strip the insulation jacket off the cable to expose the TP wires; you'll need to rotate the wire about 1 1/4 turns to strip away all of the jacket. If you turn it too far, you'll damage the wires inside the cable.

Caution

Don't strip the UTP wires themselves; just the jacket!

---

5. Check the outer jacket and inner TP wires for nicks; adjust the stripper tool and repeat steps 3 and 4 if you see damage.

6. Arrange the wires according to the AT&T 268B/EIA 568B standard listed previously.

7. Trim the wire edges so the eight wires are even with one another and are slightly less than 1/2" past the end of the jacket. If the wires are too long, crosstalk (wire-to-wire interference) can result; if the wires are too short, they can't make a good connection with the RJ-45 plug.

8. With the clip side of the RJ-45 plug facing away from you, push the cable into place. Verify that the wires are arranged according to the EIA/TIA 568B standard *before* you crimp the plug on to the wires. Adjust the connection as necessary.

9. Use the crimping tool to squeeze the RJ-45 plug on to the cable. The end of the cable should be tight enough to resist being removed by hand.

10. Repeat steps 4—9 for the other end of the cable. Recut the end of the cable if necessary before stripping it.

11. Label each cable with the following information:

    • Wiring standard

    • Length

    • End with crossover (if any)

    • _____ (blank) for computer ID

Note

The cables should be labeled at both ends to make matching the cable with the correct computer easy and to facilitate troubleshooting at the hub. Check with your cable supplier for suitable labeling stock or tags you can attach to each cable.

An excellent online source for this process, complete with illustrations, is http://www.duxcw.com/digest/Howto/network/cable/.

Network Cabling Distance Limitations

Network distance limitations must be kept in mind when creating a network. If you find that some users will be "out of bounds" because of these limitations, you can use repeaters, routers, or switches to reach distant users.

Table 11.10 lists the distance limitations of various kinds of LAN cable.

In addition to the limitations shown in the table, keep in mind that you cannot connect more than 30 computers on a single Thinnet Ethernet segment, more than 100 computers on a Thicknet Ethernet segment, more than 72 computers on a UTP Token-Ring cable, and more than 260 computers on an STP Token-Ring cable.

Table 11.10 Network Distance Limitations			
Network Adapter	**Cable Type**	**Maximum**	**Minimum**
Ethernet	Thin[1]	607 ft.	20 in.
	Thick (drop cable)[1]	164 ft.	8 ft.
	Thick (backbone)[1]	1,640 ft.	8 ft.
	UTP	328 ft.	8 ft.

Table 11.10 Network Distance Limitations Continued			
Network Adapter	Cable Type	Maximum	Minimum
Token Ring	STP	328 ft.	8 ft.
	UTP	148 ft.	8 ft.
ARCnet[1] (passive hub)		393 ft.	Depends on cable
ARCnet[1] (active hub)		1,988 ft.	Depends on cable

1. Indicates obsolete for new installations; may be found in existing installations.

Cabling Standards for Fast Ethernet

Thanks to low costs for cabling, network interface cards, and now hubs, Fast Ethernet networks can be built today at a cost comparable to conventional Ethernet networks. Note that the distance limitations given for 100BASE-TX (the most common type) are the same as for 10BASE-T. Consider using 100BASE-FX fiber-optic cable with media converters for longer runs.

Table 11.11 lists the cabling standards for Fast Ethernet.

Table 11.11 100BASE-T Cabling Standards		
Standard	Cable Type	Segment Length
100BASE-TX	Category 5 (2 pairs)	100 meters
100BASE-T4	Category 3, 4, or 5 (4 pairs)	100 meters
100BASE-FX	62.5/125[1] multimode 400 meters (2 strands)	

1. First figure is core diameter; second figure is cladding diameter; both in micrometers

Properly constructed Fast Ethernet 100BASE-TX Category 5 cable can be certified for Gigabit Ethernet operation. Gigabit Ethernet uses all four wire pairs.

Specialized Network Options

The following sections cover specialized networks you might encounter, including the Home PNA networking and wireless networking standards.

What About Home Networking?

So-called *SOHO (small-office/home-office)* users want networks for Internet connection sharing, printer sharing, and file transfer. To avoid the cabling problems and protocol configuration and setup issues of traditional Ethernet networks, the Home Phoneline Network Association (HomePNA) established the HomePNA 1.0 and faster 2.0 standards for using existing phone wiring for networking.

The advantages include

- Easy setup for technical novices because of the integrated nature of the hardware and software

- Choice of internal (card-based) or external (parallel port or USB-based) solutions

- No rewiring needed; uses the phone lines in the home or home office

The disadvantages include

- Difficult to have a portable computer set up to use both HomePNA and standard Ethernet-based networking; special dual-purpose devices are required

- Low speed: HomePNA 2.0 is still just 10Mbps

- Can't turn HomePNA-based network into a client/server network later

Wireless Networking Standards

Wireless networking, once considered a narrow "niche" technology hampered by a lack of standards, is now becoming a major network type.

Star-Topology Wireless Networks

The following networks use a star topology: Wireless NICs send signals to an access point, which relays the signal to the receiving computer. By using multiple access points in a building or campus environment, users can stay connected as they move from room to room or building to building. The NICs automatically switch to the strongest signal from an access point; thus, this type of wireless network is similar in concept to cellular phone networks. The networks are as follows:

- **IEEE 802.11b**—The leading industry standard is IEEE 802.11b, a wireless Ethernet standard designed to interconnect easily with standard Ethernet 10BASE-T networks. It runs at 11Mbps and uses the same 2.4GHz wavelength used by cellular phones and other communications devices. IEEE 802.11b is supported by a number of leading network hardware vendors, and products from different vendors can be mixed and matched just as conventional "wired" Ethernet products can be.

- **RadioLAN Wireless MobilLINK**—The proprietary Radio-LAN Wireless MobilLINK runs at 5.8GHz for faster performance. It can't connect directly to IEEE 802.11b devices, but can be connected to standard 10BASE-T Ethernet networks.

Point-to-Point Wireless Networks

Each wireless client sends its signal directly to the receiving client. This is much slower, but also much simpler and less expensive than star-topology wireless LANs. The following standards use a point-to-point topology:

- **HomeRF**—HomeRF is a home-oriented network standard that runs at just 1.6Mbps currently, but future versions will run at 10Mbps. It also can be connected to standard Ethernet networks by means of a wireless bridge. HomeRF products running at 1.6Mbps are available now.

- **Bluetooth**—Bluetooth is a very short-range, slow-speed (400Kbps) standard primarily designed for data interchange between appliance devices, such as pagers, PDAs, and wireless phones, as well as notebook computers. Bluetooth-enabled devices should become available in late 2000.

Both HomeRF and Bluetooth use the same 2.4GHz frequency as IEEE 802.11b, so interference between these types of networks is possible.

Table 11.12 provides an overview of the various wireless network standards currently in use.

Table 11.12   Comparison of Current Wireless Networks

Network	Rated Speed	Logical Topology	Connects with 10BASE-T Ethernet via	Maximum Number of PCs per Access Point	Average Cost per User[5]
IEEE 802.11b	11Mbps	Logical Star (requires access point)	Access point	Varies by brand and model; up to 2048	$525[1,2]
RadioLAN	10Mbps[3]	Logical Star (requires access point)	Wireless BackboneLINK (access point)	128	$600[2]
HomeRF[4]	1.6Mbps	Point-to-Point	Symphony Cordless Ethernet Bridge	10	$139

1. *Average price of products from Cisco, Lucent, and 3Com as of 2000.*

2. *Price includes access point (required).*

3. *Actual throughput of RadioLAN compared to average of IEEE 802.11b products is about 25% faster due to higher radio frequency used.*

4. *Figures for Proxim Symphony, first HomeRF product available.*

5. *Average cost per user based on a four-station network with two PCI desktop and two notebook PCs and one access point (if needed).*

Wireless Network Configuration and Selection Issues

Wireless NICs require an IRQ and I/O port address range, just as conventional NICs do. Other configuration and product selection issues include the following:

- **NIC Card Type**—With most wireless networks, you can choose PCI-based NICs for desktop computers and PC Card—based NICs for notebook computers. Although the speed of current wireless networks also permits the use of ISA cards, you should avoid these because this 16-bit card design is obsolete.

- **Network Security and Encryption**—For maximum security, select wireless network products that support either of these features:

  - A seven-digit security code called an ESSID; wireless devices without this code can't access the network

  - A list of authorized MAC numbers (each NIC has a unique MAC); a wireless device not on the MAC list can't access the network

These features must be enabled to be effective. Also, use the strongest data encryption your network supports. Many of the early versions of IEEE 802.11b network devices supported only the "weak" 40-bit encryption when introduced, but installable updates to "strong" 128-bit encryption should be available later. You should switch to strong encryption as soon as possible to provide another layer of network security.

TCP/IP Network Protocol Settings

TCP/IP is taking over the computing world, replacing the hodge-podge of competing protocols used earlier in networking (NetBIOS, NetBEUI, and IPX/SPX). TCP/IP is the standard protocol of the World Wide Web, as well as of the latest network operating systems from Novell (NetWare 5) and Microsoft (Windows 2000). Even though it's used by both dial-up (modem) users and LAN workstations, the typical configurations in these situations have virtually nothing in common. Use Table 11.13 as a guide to what must be set, and remember to record the settings your TCP/IP connections use.

Table 11.13   TCP/IP Properties by Connection Type—Overview

TCP/IP Property Tab	Setting	Modem Access ("Dial-Up Adapter")	LAN Access ("XYZ Network Card")
IP Address	IP Address	Automatically assigned by ISP	Specified (get value from network administrator)
WINS[1] Configuration	Enable/Disable WINS Resolution	Disabled	Indicate server or enable DHCP[2] to allow NetBIOS over TCP/IP
Gateway	Add Gateway/ List of Gateways	None (PPP is used to connect modem to Internet)	IP address of to Gateway used connect LAN to Internet
DNS[3] Configuration	Enable/Disable Host Domain	Usually disabled, unless proxy server used by ISP	Enabled, with host and domain specified (get value from network administrator)

1. WINS = Windows Internet Naming Service; used on NT servers to automatically manage the association of workstation names and locations to IP addresses; used with DHCP (see note 2)

2. DHCP = Domain Host Configuration Protocol; sets up IP addresses for PCs connected to an NT network

3. DNS = Domain Name System; matches IP addresses to Web site names through the use of name servers

TCP/IP Protocol Worksheet

Use the worksheet shown in Table 11.14 to track TCP/IP settings for either network card or dial-up connections. The settings are based on the Networks icon in Windows 9x. The first worksheet is blank; the second worksheet lists typical (fictitious) settings for a workstation on a LAN.

Table 11.14   TCP/IP Protocol Settings Worksheet

IP Address

Address	Subnet	Automatically assigned			

WINS Configuration

Enable/ Disable	Primary WINS Server	Secondary WINS Server	Scope ID	Use DHCP for WINS Resolution	

Gateway (list in order; top = first)

First	Second	Third	Fourth	Fifth	Sixth

Bindings That Will Use This Protocol (list)

Advanced (list)

Use TCP/IP as Default

Table 11.14 TCP/IP Protocol Settings Worksheet Continued

IP Address

		DNS Configuration			
Disable/ Enable DNS	Host	Domain			
First DNS Server	Second DNS Server	Third DNS Server	Fourth DNS Server	Fifth DNS Server	Sixth DNS Server
First Domain Suffix	Second Domain Suffix	Third Domain Suffix	Fourth Domain Suffix	Fifth Domain Suffix	Sixth Domain Suffix

Table 11.15 shows how TCP/IP protocols could be set up to enable Internet access via a LAN in an office building. If you use TCP/IP for both Internet and LAN access as your only protocol, your settings will vary.

Table 11.15 Completed TCP/IP Protocol Settings Worksheet—LAN Connection

IP Address

Address	Subnet	Automatically assigned	Notes
192.168.0.241	255.255.255.0	No	If automatically assigned = "Yes", no values are used for either address or subnet

WINS Resolution

Enable/ Disable	Primary WINS Server	Secondary WINS Server	Scope ID	Use DHCP for WINS resolution	Notes
Disable	(blank)	(blank)	(blank)	(blank)	If "disable", no values for other fields

Gateway (list in order; top=1st)

First	Second	Third	Fourth	Fifth	Sixth
192.168.0.1	192.168.0.2	(blank)	(blank)	(blank)	(blank)

Bindings That Will Use this Protocol (list)

Client for Microsoft Networks enabled	File and Print Sharing for Microsoft Networks* disabled	Note *This is a very dangerous setting. While this may be listed as an option, do not enable it if you use another protocol for your LAN. Enabling this setting would allow anybody on the Web access to your system!

Advanced (list)

Use TCP/IP as Default	Other value(s)	Note *This network also uses NetBEUI for internal LAN communications; if TCP/IP were the only protocol, it would be enabled as default.
disabled*	(none)	

Table 11.15   Completed TCP/IP Protocol Settings Worksheet—LAN Connection Continued

DNS Configuration

Disable/ Enable DNS	Host (list)	Domain			
Enabled	smithy	Biz-tech.com			
First DNS Server	Second DNS Server	Third DNS Server	Fourth DNS Server	Fifth DNS Server	Sixth DNS Server
192.168.0.1	(none)	(none)	(none)	(none)	(none)
First Domain Suffix	Second Domain Suffix	Third Domain Suffix	Fourth Domain Suffix	Fifth Domain Suffix	Sixth Domain Suffix
(none)	(none)	(none)	(none)	(none)	(none)

Troubleshooting Networks

Use Tables 11.16 and 11.17 to help you find solutions to common networking problems.

Troubleshooting Network Software Setup

Table 11.16   Troubleshooting Network Software Setup

Problem	Symptoms	Solution
Duplicate computer IDs.	You get a "duplicate computer name" message at startup.	Make sure that every computer on the network has a unique ID (use Control Panel, Network Identification to view this information). Set the ID before connecting to the network.
Workgroup name doesn't match.	You don't see other workstations in Network Neighborhood.	Make sure that every computer that's supposed to be working together has the same workgroup name.
		Different workgroup names actually create different workgroups, and you'd need to access them by browsing via "Entire Network."
Shared resources not available.	You can't access drives, printers, or other shared items.	Make sure that shared resources have been set for any servers on your network (including "peer servers" on Windows 9x).
		If you can't share a resource through Windows Explorer on the peer server, make sure that File and Printer Sharing has been installed.
Changes to configuration don't show up.	Network doesn't work after making changes.	Did you reboot? Any change in the Network icon in Windows 9x Control Panel requires a system reboot.
		Did you log in? Any network resources can't be accessed unless you log in when prompted. You can use Start, Shutdown, Close all Programs, and log in as a new user to recover quickly from a failure to log in.

Troubleshooting Networks in Use

Table 11.17 Troubleshooting Networks On-the-Fly

Problem	Symptoms	Solution
Connection to network not working for one user	Other users can use shared printers, drives, and so on.	First, have the user use Start, Close All Programs and log in as new user. Pressing Cancel or Esc instead of logging in keeps the user off the network.
		Use Network Neighborhood to browse other computers on network. If browse won't work, make sure correct Network name is listed in properties and that correct protocols and protocol config-urations are present. All com-puters in a workgroup must use same the workgroup name and protocol(s).
		Next, check cable connections at the server and workstation.
		Check NIC for proper opera-tion. Use diagnostics software provided with most cards to test NVRAM, interrupt, loop-back, and send/receive signal functions. Use the diagnostics on two NICs on the same net-work to send and receive sig-nals from each other.
		Use Windows 9x or 2000's Device Manager and check NIC's properties. If any resource conflicts are present, card won't work. Note that IRQ steering on PCI cards with recent chipsets enables multi-ple devices to share an IRQ without a conflict.
Connection to network not working for multiple users	No one can access network.	Loose terminators or BNC T-connectors will cause trouble for all workstations on Thinnet cable segment.
		Hub power or equipment fail-ure will cause trouble for all stations using UTP.
Have read-only access instead of full access	Can't save files to shared drive.	If you save your passwords in a password cache, entering the read-only password instead of the full-access password will limit your access with peer servers.

Table 11.17   Troubleshooting Networks On-the-Fly Continued

Problem	Symptoms	Solution
Have read-only access instead of full access	Can't save files to shared drive.	Try un-sharing the resource and try to re-share it, or have the user of that peer server set up new full-access and read-only passwords. Or, don't use password caching by unchecking the Save Password box when you log in to a shared resource. With a client/server network with user lists and rights, check with your network administrator because he or she will need to change the rights for you.

Troubleshooting TCP/IP

Use Table 11.18, in addition to the TCP/IP information presented earlier, to troubleshoot a TCP/IP connection on either a LAN or dial-up connection.

Windows 2000 uses a single networking wizard to configure both types of network connections. With other versions of Windows, TCP/IP configuration for LANs takes place in the Network icon in Control Panel, whereas modems are configured through the Dial-Up Networking properties sheet for a given dial-up connection.

Web browsers that communicate through proxy servers or gateways with the Internet also might require special configuration options. Use the Internet icon in Control Panel to adjust Microsoft Internet Explorer TCP/IP settings. With Netscape Navigator/Communicator, use Edit, Preferences, Advanced, Proxies to adjust proxy server settings.

Table 11.18   Troubleshooting TCP/IP Connections

Problem	Symptoms	Solution
Incorrect settings in network properties.	Can't connect to any TCP/IP resources.	Get correct TCP/IP settings from administrator and enter; restart PC.
Problem with server type or PPP version.	Can't keep connection running in Dial-Up Networking.	Might have wrong version of PPP running (classic CompuServe uses CISPPP instead of normal PPP); change server type in properties under Dial-Up Networking, not Networks.
Duplicate IP addresses.	Error message indicates "the (TCP/IP) interface has been disabled" during startup.	Duplicate IP addresses will disable both TCP/IP and NetBEUI networking if NetBEUI is being transported over TCP/IP.

Table 11.18 Troubleshooting TCP/IP Connections Continued		
Problem	**Symptoms**	**Solution**
One user to an IP address.	Can't share the Web.	If you're trying to share your Internet connection, use software such as Artisoft's Ishare or check with your networking hardware vendor for their recommendations. If your LAN uses a proxy server for connection, some sharing products might not work.
		Windows 98 Second Edition, Windows 2000 Professional, and Windows Me can all be configured as a gateway to enable Internet sharing from a cable modem, dial-up modem, ISDN, or DSL modem connection. For details, see Chapter 6, "Serial Ports and Modems."
	Browser can't display Web pages.	To verify that the TCP/IP connection works, open an MS-DOS window and type **PING** *websitename* (replace *websitename* with a particular IP address or Web site). If PING indicates that signals are returning, check the proxy settings in the browser. If PING can't connect, recheck your TCP/IP settings for the NIC or modem and retry after making changes.

Direct Cable Connections
Null Modem and Parallel Data-Transfer Cables

A *null modem cable* is a special cable that has its circuits crossed so the transmit data (TD) pin on each serial port connector leads to the receive data (RD) pin on the other. A cable that connects the systems' parallel ports in this way is called a *parallel data-transfer cable*. Cables such as these are usually available at computer stores that sell cables. They are sometimes called *LapLink* cables, after one of the first software products to introduce the concept of the direct cable connection. The cables supplied with FastLynx and other data-transfer programs for MS-DOS and Windows 3.x/9x/Me will also work. A good rule of thumb is this: If the cable works for LapLink or the MS-DOS INTERLNK file transfer utility, you can use it for Direct Cable Connection, as well.

You also can build your own null modem or parallel data-transfer cable using the wiring diagrams that follow. Table 11.19 shows the pins you must connect for a serial cable, using either DB-9 (9-pin) or DB-25 (25-pin) connectors. Table 11.20 shows the connections for a parallel port cable. The parallel cable is slightly harder to build, but is recommended because of its much higher transfer speed and because it will not interfere with existing modems and mouse drivers on computers.

Table 11.19   3-Wire Serial Null Modem Cable Pinouts

PC#1	DB-9	DB-25	DB-25	DB-9	PC#2
TD	3	2 <———>	3	2	RD
RD	2	3 <———>	2	3	TD
SG	5	7 <———>	7	5	SG

Table 11.20   11-Wire Parallel Data-Transfer Cable Pinouts

PC #1	PC #2
2 <———>	15
15 <———>	2
3 <———>	13
13 <———>	3
4 <———>	12
12 <———>	4
5 <———>	10
10 <———>	5
6 <———>	11
11 <———>	6
25 <———>	25

If you plan to use parallel-mode DCC on a frequent basis, consider purchasing a high-speed Direct Parallel Universal Fast Cable from Parallel Technologies, creators of the Direct Cable Connection software for Microsoft (www.lpt.com). This cable also works with third-party remote-control and file-transfer programs, such as LapLink 2000 and PCAnywhere. This cable boosts performance significantly, especially on systems using ECP or EPP parallel ports.

Direct Connect Software

After you have the hardware in place, you need the proper software for the two systems to communicate. At one time, you had to purchase a third-party product (such as LapLink) to do this, but the capability is now part of most operating systems, including DOS 6, Windows 9x, Windows Me, Windows NT 4, and Windows 2000. One computer is designated the host and the other is the guest. The software enables a user, working at the guest machine, to transfer files to and from the host. With Windows, you must specify which folders or drives you will share, and you have the option with Windows 9x and Windows Me to specify a password. Windows NT and Windows 2000 require that you add the guest user to your list of authorized users for the host system.

Setting Up and Using MS-DOS Interlink

In DOS, the software consists of two executable files, called INTERSVR.EXE and INTERLNK.EXE. In the DOS version, you run the INTERSVR program on the host computer. This system can be running a different version of DOS; therefore, you have to copy the INTERSVR.EXE program to it from a DOS 6 machine (using a floppy disk). Select the COM or LPT port to which you have connected the cable. INTERSVR then waits until INTERLNK makes a connection.

On the guest computer, you run the INTERLNK.EXE program from a DOS prompt. As before, you are prompted to select the COM or LPT port to which you have connected the cable. After this is completed, the INTERLNK software establishes the connection with the host computer running INTERSVR. Then, the guest computer mounts the drives from the host in its own file system, assigning them the next available drive letters with Interlink.

Setting Up and Using Windows 9x/Me Direct Cable Connection

On Windows 9x/Me, you click the Start menu and then select Programs, Accessories, Direct Cable Connection (on some systems it might be stored in a Communications folder beneath the Accessories folder). Then, choose the Host option button. You are prompted to select the COM or LPT port to which you have connected the cable.

On the other computer, you select the same Direct Cable Connection menu item in Windows and choose the Guest option button. Again, you are prompted to choose the correct port, after which the software establishes a connection between the two machines. With the Windows Direct Cable Connection, you can either access the shared drive as a folder or map a drive letter to it with Windows Explorer after the connection is established.

Windows 9x and DCC can use parallel, serial, or IR ports. Windows Me can also use a separate IR Link utility for initiating file transfers via the infrared port.

Setting Up Windows NT 4 Direct Connection

Windows NT 4 treats direct connections as a form of dial-up networking that uses a serial cable as a substitute for a modem. Thus, you must use the Modems icon in Control Panel to Install a New Modem: Choose Dial-Up Networking Serial Cable Connection Between 2 PCs from the list of standard modems. Parallel connections are not supported in NT 4.

If you are going to host the connection, you also need to do the following:

- Install and configure NT networking (if not already installed)

- Install and configure remote access services (RAS)

- Install NetBEUI protocol

This process is clumsy and complex. A good visual tutorial for both host and guest setup is available online at J. Helmig's World of Windows Networking Web site:

   www.helmig.com/j_helmig/dccnt4.htm

As an alternative, you might want to use LapLink 2000 or other file-transfer programs with your NT 4 system.

Hosting NT 4 Dial-Up Networking Serial Cable Connections

If you're hosting the connection, log in as Administrator, open the Administrative Tools (common) folder on the Start button, and select Remote Access Administrator.

Open the Server menu and then select Start Remote Access Service. Your server will wait for the connection.

Using NT 4 Dial-Up Networking Serial Cable as Guest

Open the Dial-Up Networking Wizard and create a new connection. For the modem, select the Dial-Up Networking Serial Cable you installed previously. Do not enter a phone number. Click the Server tab and specify PPP: Windows NT as the server type. Next, select NetBEUI as the protocol, select Enable Software Compression, and deselect Enable PPP LCP Extensions.

Enter the username and password required to make the connection to an NT 4 or a Windows 2000 host. If you are connecting to a Windows 9x/Me Direct Cable Connection host instead, you can use any username you want, but enter a password only if the shared resource is using a password for security. After you are connected, you can use the Dial-Up Networking Monitor to check your connection status and speed.

Setting Up and Using Windows 2000 Direct Parallel and Direct Serial Connections

In Windows 2000, you use the same Network Connection Wizard used for other types of network connections to make the link. Most of the network setup work is already done if you also use modem or LAN networking with the computer. Before you start, ensure that the NetBEUI protocol has been installed. Open the Networks icon in the Control Panel, select your current network connection, and view its properties.

To create a connection, click Start, Settings, Network and Dial-Up Connections. Open Make New Connection to start the wizard. If you are prompted for telephone information (area code and outside dialing code), fill in the information before continuing. If you don't fill this in, your connection options are limited.

To set up DCC, click Next on the first screen and then select Connect Directly to Another Computer. On the next screen, select Host or Guest. Then, on the following screen, select the parallel or serial port you want to use (parallel is recommended).

Next, select the user you are granting access to from the list of authorized users. If the user you want to grant access to isn't listed, add him with the Users option in the Control Panel. Click Next and then Finish to complete the connection setup process. The system waits for you to make the connection.

Windows 9x, Me, NT 4, and 2000 systems can use their versions of DCC to connect to each other as either guest or host.

Using DCC

After a connection has been established, you can use the drive letters or folders representing the host system just as though they were local resources. You can copy files back and forth using any standard file management tool, such as the DOS COPY command or Windows Explorer. The only difference is that file transfers will, of course, be slower than local hard drive operations.

DCC is the perfect way to install CD-ROM–based software to older machines lacking such drives. You can install the DCC Host software on a notebook computer with a CD-ROM drive, install the DCC Guest software on a desktop computer, cable them together, and install the software. DCC is also the cheapest network around.

I've also used DCC to run tape backups remotely. I set up the system I wanted to back up as the host and logged in to it as guest with the computer containing the tape backup program. After mapping the remote drive to a drive letter, I was able to back up the files via a parallel LapLink-style cable.

Some users have set up DCC on machines using the TCP/IP protocol and used it for game playing. For other advanced tricks you can perform with DCC, see the following Web site:
www.tecno.demon.co.uk/dcc/dcc.html.

Troubleshooting Direct Cable Connections

As Table 11.21 and the following checklist indicate, several places exist where a Direct Cable Connection setup can go wrong. Use this checklist, and Table 11.21, to make this virtually free "network" work best for you:

- Make sure the same networking protocols are installed on both the host and guest machines with Windows 9x, Me, NT, or 2000. The simplest protocol to install is NetBEUI, and that's what Parallel Technologies (creator of DCC) recommends for a basic DCC mini-network. To configure NetBEUI, all you need to supply is the workgroup name (same for both guest and host) and a unique computer name for guest and for host.

- Use the parallel (LPT) ports for DCC when possible; although serial (COM) or IR port transfers will work, they are unbearably slow. Note that Windows Me refers to IR ports by their COM port alias in DCC, not specifically as IR ports.

- Ensure that both host and guest LPT ports are working correctly, with no shared IRQ problems. Use the Windows 9x/Me/2000 Device Manager to check for IRQ conflicts with the parallel port you're using.

- Make sure the person using the guest computer knows the network name of the host computer (set through the Networks icon in Control Panel, Identification tab). With a simple protocol such as NetBEUI, it might be necessary to enter the name to log in to the host machine.

- If the user you want to connect to your Windows 2000 or Windows NT host computer isn't on the list of authorized users, you'll need to add that user before you set up the direct connection.

- Install the Client for Microsoft Networks on the guest computer.

- Don't print to the printer(s) normally connected to the LPT port while you're using DCC; the printer will be set for offline mode and require you to manually release the print jobs after you re-establish the printer(s). Also, allow any print jobs to finish (or hold them or delete them) on any port you want to use for DCC before you set up your cables.

- Make sure that the host computer is sharing a drive, so that the guest computer can copy files from it or move files to it. The sharing is accomplished in the same way that peer-to-peer network sharing is done on Windows 9x/Me systems; on Windows NT/2000, you specify permissions for authorized users.

- If you don't want to unplug your printer to use DCC, you might want to add a second printer port for DCC use if you plan to use this option frequently.

- Download the DCC troubleshooter from the FAQs and troubleshooting page at Parallel Technologies's Web site: www.lpt.com/faqs1.htm.

Use Table 11.21 to see whether you are ready to connect your computers via DCC.

Table 11.21 Direct Cable Connection–Type Configuration Requirements by Operating System

Operating System	Host Program	Guest Program	Network Components Types to Install	Port Supported	Username Required?	Passwords	Drive	Connects with Other OS Mapping and sharing
MS-DOS 6.x	INTERSVR.EXE	INERLNK.EXE	None	Serial, parallel	No	No	Automatically maps all remote drives	MS-DOS or Windows command-prompt using INTERLNK/INTERSVR
Windows 9x Windows Me	Direct Cable Connection (host and guest)		NetBEUI, MS Network Client	Serial, parallel, IR	No	Optional	Host must specify shares; mapping optional on guest	Windows NT4 or Windows 2000
Windows NT 4	Dial-Up Networking (host and guest)		Modem: direct serial connection, NT Networking, RAS, NetBEUI	Serial	Yes	Yes	Host must specify shares; mapping optional on guest	Windows 9x or Windows 2000
Windows 2000	Direct Parallel or DirectSerial connection (host and guest)		Networking, RAS, NetBEUI	Serial, parallel, IR	Yes	Yes	Host must specify shares; mapping optional on guest	Windows NT4 or Windows 9x

Chapter 12

Operating System Installation and Diagnostic Testing

This chapter covers methods for testing and diagnosing systems and the software you'll use. For hardware tools, see Chapter 13, "Tools and Techniques."

Installing an Operating System on an Empty Drive

Use this section for a quick reference for the procedures you'll follow and software you'll need to install an operating system.

Installing MS-DOS

Prerequisites:

Create a bootable disk (containing COMMAND.COM and hidden files). The boot disk also should contain FDISK, FORMAT, SYS, and MSD, along with Help, Qbasic, and Edit files. Create the bootable disk with FORMAT A:/S on a system with the same MS-DOS version. Then, copy files from the \DOS folder.

Follow these steps:

1. Boot the system with the bootable disk.

2. Run FDISK and create the partition(s) desired. The drive must have an active (which will be C: and bootable) partition; it can also have an extended partition (D: and beyond) that can contain one or more drives.

3. Exit FDISK.

4. Reboot the computer with the bootable disk.

5. Run FORMAT to format drive(s) created with FDISK:

   ```
   FORMAT C:/S formats & copies system files to C:
   FORMAT D: formats D: drive if present; repeat for
   E: & others
   ```

6. Remove the bootable floppy and restart the system from the C: drive.

7. Install the remainder of the operating system files from the disk or other storage device (install drivers first if necessary).

Installing Windows 9x

Prerequisites:

You'll need an Emergency System Disk (create it on a computer with the same OS, or use the bootable disk supplied with the full version). The disk must contain at least COMMAND.COM and hidden files, plus FDISK, FORMAT, SYS, and Edit.

Follow these steps:

1. Boot the system with the Emergency System Disk.

2. Run FDISK and select Large Drive Support if you want to exceed 2GB per drive letter with Windows 95 OSR2.x/98/Me. Create the partition(s) desired. The drive must have an active partition (which will be C: and bootable) and can also have an extended partition (D: and beyond) that can contain one or more drives.

3. Exit FDISK.

4. Reboot the computer with the bootable disk.

5. Run FORMAT to format drive(s) created with FDISK:

   ```
   FORMAT C:/S formats & copies system files to C:
   FORMAT D: formats D: drive if present; repeat for
   E: & others
   ```

6. Remove the bootable floppy and restart the system from the C: drive.

7. Install the remainder of the operating system files from the CD-ROM or Windows 95 disc; install CD-ROM drivers and restart the system. You must provide proof of a previous OS purchase (old Windows disks or CD-ROM) when prompted if you are installing an upgrade version onto a blank drive.

> **Note**
>
> You can also use OEMSETUP from a CD-ROM (called by the setup program on disk) if you want to automate the process with the full (non-upgrade) version.

Installing Windows Me

Prerequisites:

- An Emergency Startup (boot) Disk (EBD) created from another Windows Me or Windows 98 installation

- Hardware drivers (for Me or Windows 98) for any hardware not supported by the drivers on the Windows Me CD-ROM

- The Windows Me CD-ROM drive

Follow these steps:

1. Boot the system with the Emergency Startup Disk.

2. Run FDISK and select Large Drive Support if you want to exceed 2GB per drive letter *and* if any other OS you might install can also use FAT-32. Create the partition(s) desired. The drive must have an active partition (which will be C: and bootable); it can also have an extended partition that can contain one or more drives (D: and beyond).

3. Exit FDISK.

4. Reboot the computer with the Emergency Startup Disk.

5. Run FORMAT to format drive(s) created with FDISK:

   ```
   FORMAT C: formats C: drive
   FORMAT D: formats D: drive if present; repeat for
   E: & others
   ```

6. Restart the system with the EBD; boot files will be installed on the hard disk during step 7.

7. Install the remainder of the operating system files from the Windows Me CD-ROM as prompted. Restart the system when prompted. You must provide proof of a previous OS purchase (such as old Windows disks or a CD-ROM) when prompted if you are installing an upgrade version onto a blank drive.

Installing Windows NT 4.0 or Windows 2000

Prerequisites:

You will need to create setup disks (three or four—it varies with each version) by running WINNT32 from the \I386 folder of the Windows NT 4.0 or Windows 2000 CD-ROM. The computer you use to create these disks doesn't need to be running Windows NT 4.0 or Windows 2000.

Follow these steps:

1. Start the installation process on the target computer by putting Setup disk 1 into the A: drive and restarting the computer; follow the prompts for each additional disk.

2. Put the Windows NT 4.0 or Windows 2000 CD-ROM into the CD-ROM drive on the target computer when prompted and follow the prompts to complete the installation process.

Upgrading an Operating System
Installing to the Same Folder

Installing the new version of an operating system (such as Windows 9x, Me, or 2000) to the same folder as the existing version of Windows upgrades your current copy. You will not need to reinstall applications to use them.

Installing to a Different Folder

Installing the new version of an operating system to a different folder can enable you to *dual-boot* (select which operating system to use at each system startup) your computer. If you want to use your existing applications with the new operating system, you must reinstall your applications to the new folder.

> **Note**
>
> If you are interested in building a computer with more than one bootable operating system, I recommend picking up a copy of *The Multi-Boot Configuration Handbook*, published by Que.

Installing to a Different Partition

Installing the new version of an operating system to a different partition is similar to installing to a different folder, plus it enables you to use a more efficient partitioning method than if you install to the same folder or different folder on the same drive. See information on FAT-32 and NTFS in Chapter 4, "SCSI and IDE Hard Drives and Optical Drives," for details.

Checking for IRQ, DMA, I/O, and Memory Usage
MS-DOS Using MSD

Follow these steps:

1. Start MSD from the \DOS or \Windows folder, or from the CD-ROM if you are using a version of Windows 9x that includes it.

2. To see IRQ usage, select Q from the main menu.

3. View the IRQ listing; items listed as "reserved" are *allegedly* available, unless you see a device driver or device name listed in the right column. Standard IRQs are also listed; however, if the device (serial, parallel, or other port) is absent, the IRQ listed for the device is also free.

Note

MSD is unreliable for detecting IRQ usage by non-standard peripherals, such as sound cards and network cards. If you run MSD within an MS-DOS window under Windows 9x, you will see memory and other information assigned to your DOS session, rather than the full amount of memory and so on.

As an alternative that's also more accurate, use the IRQ detection features in Norton Diagnostics (part of the Norton Utilities or System Works), CheckIt, QA Plus, or AMIDiag (the latest versions are best).

4. To see the I/O Port address usage for serial and parallel ports only, select C(om) for serial ports or L(pt) for parallel ports.

5. To see the conventional memory usage (BIOS chips and UMBs), select M from the main menu. The display on the left shows a visual map of usage; the display on the right lists memory managers in use and memory created by HIMEM.SYS, EMM386.EXE, or equivalents.

Windows 9x/2000/Me

1. Right-click My Computer.

2. Select Properties.

3. Select the Device Manager tab.

4. Double-click the Computer icon at the top of the list of device categories.

5. Select Interrupt Request (IRQ) from the list of choices.

6. The IRQs in use (0–15) are listed along with the devices using them; IRQs not listed are free. A yellow (!) icon indicates devices with conflicts or other problems. A blue (I) icon indicates a PnP (Plug and Play) device that has been set manually.

Note

Use the same procedure for DMA, I/O port address, and memory address detection.

Windows NT 4.0

1. Click the Start button, Programs, Administrative Tools (common), Windows NT Diagnostics.

2. Select the Resources tab.

3. Click IRQ to see the IRQs in use, along with the devices using them; IRQs not listed are available.

4. Click I/O Port to see I/O port addresses in use.

5. Click DMA to see DMA channels in use.

6. Click Memory to see memory addresses in use.

Software Toolkit

Tables 12.1–12.3 list the software tools you should have to perform important tests.

Tip

If you have a CD-R or CD-RW drive and licenses permit, create a CD-R with an entire collection of tools you can take with you.

Table 12.1   Operating System Software and Drivers

Item	Purpose	Notes
Your operating system files on CD	Allows fast reloading to fix numerous problems	Verify exact operating system on computer before reloading.
Bootable disk with CD-ROM driver(s) for each operating system supported	Allows operating system reload when Windows isn't working	Verify exact operating system on computer before reloading.
Standard system image on bootable CD-R	Can be restored in minutes to a system with a standard hardware configuration	Create with Drive Image, Norton Ghost, PowerQuest EasyRestore, or ImageCast plus bootable option in CD-R creation software. Bootable CD-ROM requires boot files onboard, boot CD-ROM first setting in BIOS, and boot-compatible drive.

Table 12.1	Operating System Software and Drivers Continued	
Item	**Purpose**	**Notes**
Windows 98/Me Emergency disk	Has drivers for most CD-ROM drives	Can be used to "cheat" by making a CD-ROM drive available for a Windows 95 installation.
Network card software	Including drivers, test, and diagnostic software	Use to verify proper operation and test network communication.

Table 12.2 includes the most popular testing, maintenance, and reference programs and files found in Microsoft Windows and MS-DOS.

Table 12.2 Testing, Maintenance, and Reference Software Included in Major Operating Systems		
Item	**Name**	**Notes**
MSD.EXE	Microsoft Diagnostics	Found in MS-DOS and Windows 3.1 standard installations and on some versions of the Windows 95 CD-ROM.
		Provides useful information, especially on COM and LPT ports, BIOS and video data, and mouse testing. Offers printer testing that works for laser, inkjet, and even PostScript printers.
		Inaccurate IRQ listings are a major limitation.
WINMSD.EXE	Microsoft Diagnostics	Standard Windows NT system reporting tool.
HWDIAG.EXE	Hardware Diagnostics	Found on OEM CD-ROM versions of Windows 95 OSR2.x.
		Can be downloaded from
		User.aol.com/AXCEL216/osr2.htm
		(the Tricks + Secrets Files database) for Win95 users who don't have it on their CD-ROMs.
		More thorough and accurate than the Windows 95 Device Manager information about hardware drivers and resources. Also lists INF files and Registry keys. Works with all releases of Windows 95.
HWINFO.EXE	System Diagnostics	Similar to HWDIAG.EXE, but for Windows 98.
MSIE32.EXE	System Information	Standard part of Windows 98 and Office 97. Provides information superior to Device Manager reports in Windows 95. Office 97 and newer versions can be used with Windows 95/98/NT4.
		Maintains history of device drivers and links to other repair tools.

Table 12.2   Testing, Maintenance, and Reference Software Included in Major Operating Systems Continued

Item	Name	Notes
Win95rk.hlp	Windows 95 Resource Kit	The entire 1,200+ page text of Windows 95 Resource Kit book is stored on the Windows 95 CD-ROM as a help file in \Admin\Reskit\Helpfile.
		Windows 98 Resource Kit Online is a similar product stored in Tools\Reskit\Help on the Windows 98 CD.
		Both provide large amounts of technical references and troubleshooters not found in the standard help system.
Help.exe	MS-DOS 6.x Help file	Standard part of the MS-DOS 6.x installation.
		Contained on some CD-ROM versions of Windows 95.
		Lists all internal and external MS-DOS 6.x commands along with syntax and usage notes. Most command-line utilities in Windows 9x are similar, so it's still useful to refer to.
		Limited help is available with most DOS or Windows command-line utilities by typing /? after the command.
Scandisk.exe	Scandisk	Standard utility in MS-DOS 6.x, Windows 9x/Me, and Windows NT/2000.
		Performs a check of disk structures and (optional) surface testing.
		Runs automatically in Windows 95 OSR2.x and Windows 98/Me if Windows isn't shut down properly.
		Best used from drive properties sheet in Windows 9x/Me/NT/2000 because it tracks last use. Run before defrag or backup.
Defrag.exe	Defrag	Standard utility in MS-DOS 6.x and Windows 9x/Me/2000.
		Realigns all files into contiguous clusters in full defrag mode. Windows 98/Me offers enhanced options for faster program loading. Run program from the Start button to adjust properties.
		Windows NT 4.0 and earlier must use a third-party defragmenter, such as Diskeeper. Windows 2000 contains a defragger based on Diskeeper.

Table 12.3 lists third-party diagnostic and testing utilities, most of which go beyond what can be done with built-in operating system utilities. Web sites are listed for products that aren't widely found at retail locations.

Table 12.3 Third-Party Test and Diagnostic Utilities		
Program	**Uses**	**Notes**
Norton Utilities	Hardware testing, data protection, data recovery, system information, system speedups, anti-virus; defragment and disk testing routines significantly better than standard Microsoft utilities	Best buy when purchased as part of System Works Professional, which includes many other programs; loopback plugs are available for serial and parallel port testing.
AMIDiag (www.ami.com)	Hardware testing, system information; burn-in test routines included for stress testing of new equipment	From the makers of the AMI BIOS; are loopback plugs available for serial and parallel port testing.
Win CheckIt 6.5 (www.checkit.com)	Hardware testing, system information; burn-in test routines included for stress test of new equipment; for Windows 9x/Me/NT	Can be used to gather information from multiple PCs and analyze reports at a single PC; loopback plugs are available for serial and parallel port testing.
TestDrive (www.msd.com)	Floppy drive testing and diagnostic utility	Provides thorough information, especially when used with the appropriate Accuride Digital Diagnostic Disk.
SpinRite (www.grc.com)	Hard disk testing and data recovery	Dynastat Data Recovery, extremely accurate at recovering data from damaged drives; same vendor offers Trouble in Paradise tester for Zip drive media.
AntiVirus Available from Trend Micro, Norton, DrSolomon, McAfee, and others	Detect, clean, and prevent viruses and attacks	Use against program, macro, data, and Web-based viruses; use more than one for maximum protection.

Chapter 13

Tools and Techniques

General Information

Use this chapter as a checklist to help you select the equipment you need to solve computer problems more quickly and easily. Most of the items in the following lists have been mentioned in other chapters. Use these tools along with the "how-tos" in Chapter 12, "Operating System Installation and Testing," to help you get ready for battle with computer problems—and win!

Hardware Tools and Their Uses

Compare your toolbox's contents to the items listed in Table 13.1; if you are missing some items, sooner or later you'll wish you had them. Add them now. The list is divided into sections, enabling you to customize the toolkit for the types of service tasks you typically perform.

Table 13.1 Basic Hardware Tools Everybody Needs

Item	Purpose	Notes
Phillips-head and flat-blade screwdrivers #2 size for most jobs	Opening and removing cases and screws	Magnetic tips are okay if you keep them away from floppies and backup tapes! Discard worn screwdrivers. Use #1 size screwdrivers for attaching and detaching cables.
Hex-head drivers (assorted sizes)	Opening and removing cases and screws	
	Tightening cable connectors on cards	Use in place of screwdrivers whenever possible.
Needle-nose pliers	Removing and inserting jumper blocks; removing cables; cutting cable ties; straightening bent pins	Most flexible tool in the basic toolbox; often omitted from low-cost "basic" toolkits; buy assortment of different sizes, offset heads, and so on for flexibility.
3-claw parts retrieval tool	Grabbing small parts such as jumpers and screws from motherboard	It's better than disassembling a PC to find a single screw!
Tweezers	Removing and inserting jumper blocks; picking up parts too large for parts retrieval tool; holding small parts for use	Typical set found in low-cost tool set, normally useless; replace with one or both of these: eyebrow tweezers from drugstore or hemostat clamps from medical supply store.

Table 13.1 Basic Hardware Tools Everybody Needs Continued

Item	Purpose	Notes
Small flashlight	Illuminating dark places in case	Can be combined with magnifier; for bench use, get arm-mounted magnifier with light.
File	Gently trimming edges on drive faceplates or case edges	Get file with a very fine "tooth" and use it sparingly.
Wire cutter or stripper	Fixing damaged power cables or cutting away bad connectors	Check gauges to make sure your stripper can handle the small wires inside a PC; never cut a wire unless the power is unplugged (not just turned off—because of power-management features in newer systems).
ESD (electrostatic discharge) protection kit	Attach wrist strap to you; cable to ground; unplug system before working inside	Comprises a mat for parts and the wrist strap for you; metal plate on wrist strap must be comfortably tight on your wrist to ground you properly.
Soldering iron	Used on conventionally soldered (not surface-mounted!) chips that have bad solder joints	Practice, practice, practice on "dead" boards before you solder a board that's worth fixing.
Toothpick or thin wire	Probing the depth of screw holes	Helps you avoid damaging a drive by using a mounting screw that's too long.

Tools of the Trade—Drive Installation

Table 13.2 provides a list of tools and parts you'll need to install disk drives.

Table 13.2 Disk Drive Installation Tools and Parts

Item	Purpose	Notes
Floppy drive cable	Used as replacement for suspected failures	Some newer Super I/O chips support drive A only. Use known, working rather than new and unknown. Use a 5-connector cable if you need support for 5" drives.
IDE hard drive cable (40-pin)	Used as replacement for suspected failures	Should be no more than 18" for use with UDMA drives. Check spacing between first and second drive connector if you want to use master and slave on drives in non-adjacent bays. Use known, working rather than new and unknown.

Table 13.2	Disk Drive Installation Tools and Parts Continued	
Item	**Purpose**	**Notes**
IDE hard drive cable with blue end (40-pin, 80-wire)	Used as replacement for suspected failures	Required for UDMA/ATA-66; high-quality for all other drives. Blue end to motherboard.
SCSI ribbon and SCSI external cables	Used as replacement for suspected failures	Use 25-pin, 50-pin, or 68-pin, depending on device needs. Use known, working rather than new and unknown.
Mounting screws	Used to attach drives to drive bays	Keep spare screws from existing or scrapped-out systems. Use the shortest screws that work because overlying long screws can destroy a drive.
Y-cable power splitters	Enables single power connector to run two drives	Examine carefully. Buy splitters with high-quality construction and wire the same gauge as power supply.
Mounting frame	Puts 3.5" drives in 5.25" bay	Standard with most 3.5" retail-pack hard drives; save spares.
Digital Multimeter (DMM)	Tests power going to drive and cable continuity	Test new and unknown cables before using them.
Spare battery for DMM	Keeps tester working	Keep in original blister packaging so it won't short out.
Jumper blocks	Used to adjust IDE drive configuration for master, slave	WD drives use the same jumpers as motherboards and add-on cards; some Maxtor and Seagate models use a smaller size.
Rails	Used for mounting 5.25" drives to some cases	Check compatibility because rail types vary—two rails per drive.

Tools of the Trade—Motherboard and Expansion Card Installation

Table 13.3 provides a list of helpful tools when installing motherboards and expansion cards.

Table 13.3	Motherboard and Card Installation Parts and Tools	
Item	**Purpose**	**Notes**
Stand-off connectors	Holds motherboard off bottom or side of case	Use existing standoffs if in good condition. Buy the same size if they must be replaced.
Slot covers	Covers rear of case openings for card slots without cards	System cooling is affected if these are missing. Keep spares from scrapped systems, or when adding cards.

Table 13.3 Motherboard and Card Installation Parts and Tools Continued

Item	Purpose	Notes
Jumper blocks	Used to adjust motherboard and add-on card configurations	Buy long-handled jumper blocks for easier configuration changes.
Digital Multimeter (DMM)	Tests power going to motherboard and expansion slots	Use power supply case as ground.
Outlet tester	Quick plug-in tester for bad ground, other wiring faults	Finds real cause of "inexplicable" lockups and system failure—bad power.
POST testing card	Used to diagnose bootup problems	Use BIOS POST code tables[1] along with board.
IRQ/DMA testing card	Used to diagnose IRQ and DMA usage and problems	Can be combined with POST features on some models.
Spare Pentium, Pentium II, K6, other CPUs	Used to test motherboard when no POST codes appear	Salvage low-speed versions from retired "junk" PCs. Be sure you jumper host system appropriately and rejumper after re-inserting original CPU.
Spare memory modules	Used to test motherboard that produces memory errors during POST	Salvage compatible small-size types from retired "junk" PCs. Two 4MB 72-pin SIMMs and one 16MB SDRAM DIMM can test most common PCs.

1. POST codes (also called hex codes) for popular BIOS versions are provided on the CD-ROM supplied with Upgrading and Repairing PCs, 12th Edition, and are also available from the Web sites of BIOS, system, and motherboard vendors.

Tools of the Trade—External Device and Networking Installation

Table 13.4 provides a list of tools and parts you'll need to install external devices and network cables.

Table 13.4 External Devices and Networking

Item	Purpose	Notes
Loopback plug for serial port	Used to test serial (COM) ports and cables	Buy or build to match your favorite diagnostic software (see the following). Buy or build 25-pin version as well as 9-pin if you want to test modem cables or if your systems have 25-pin serial ports.

Table 13.4   External Devices and Networking Continued

Item	Purpose	Notes
Loopback plug for parallel port	Used to test parallel (LPT) ports and cables	Buy or build to match your favorite diagnostic software (refer to Chapter 12). Can aid in detection of IRQ usage.
IEEE-1284 parallel cable	Known, working spare for all types of parallel printers	Buy 10' cable to have extra distance in tricky cabling situations.
"Silver satin" phone cable	Known, working spare for modems and all-in-one units	Carry 10'–15' at at least (it's small!).
RJ-45 network cable Category 5	Known, working spare for Ethernet, Fast Ethernet, and Token-Ring networks	Use along with hub to test card and port. Use two pieces at 15'–25' to make an impromptu network.
5-Port Ethernet hub 10/100 speed	Known, working connection for RJ-45 cable	Attach spare cable to hub, check connection with lights.
USB cables and hub	Known, working spares for USB devices	Use powered hub. Have at least one "A" to "A" extension cable and at least one "A" to "B" device cable.
RS-232 breakout box	Analyzes serial signals for use in cable-building and troubleshooting	Allows prototyping of a serial cable.
Device-specific cables	RS-232 modem, SCSI, parallel or serial switchbox, others	Allows isolation of device-specific problems.

Tools of the Trade—Data Transfer

Use Table 13.5 to prepare to pull vital data from systems.

Table 13.5   Data-Transfer Tools, Parts, and Supplies

Item	Purpose	Notes
Parallel data-cable (LapLink or Interlink type)	Used with Interlink, Direct Cable Connection, or LapLink to move files without a network	Parallel transfer is preferred because of speed advantage over serial.
Null-modem serial cable (LapLink or Interlink type)	Used with Interlink, Direct Cable Connection, or LapLink to move files without a network	Previous parallel version preferred. Carry this one as a fallback or for use with Windows NT.

Table 13.5	Data-Transfer Tools, Parts, and Supplies Continued	
Item	Purpose	Notes
Drives and media		Select from the following, depending on the drive technologies you support:
		3.5" floppy
		3.5" SuperDisk
		Zip 100 CD-R
		CD-RW
		DVD-ROM
		DVD-RAM
		SyQuest SparQ
		Etc.
Tape backup cartridges	Carry two of each magnetic device, and one of each optical device you support for use as a backup for vital data.	

Tools of the Trade—Cleaning and Maintenance

Table 13.6 provides a list of supplies you should keep on hand for cleaning and maintaining PC hardware.

Table 13.6	Cleaning and Maintenance Supplies	
Item	Purpose	Notes
Floppy drive cleaning kit	Removes gunk from read/write heads	Use wet-type cleaner.
		Not for use on SuperDisk drives!
		Works best when software-driven with a program, such as TestDrive.
SuperDisk LS-120 Cleaning kit	Removes gunk from read/write heads of SuperDisk/LS-120 drives only	Use Imation-brand or Imation-approved kits.
Tape drive cleaning kit	Removes gunk from read/write heads	QIC models also can be used with QIC-wide and Travan.
		Consult drive manufacturer for service interval.
Endust for Electronics	Effective surface cleaner for monitor cases, monitor glass, keyboards, and other PC part	Blue and silver can. Never spray directly on object to be cleaned!
		Spray on lint-free cloth till damp, then wipe.

Table 13.6	Cleaning and Maintenance Supplies Continued	
Item	**Purpose**	**Notes**
Electronic contact cleaner	Stabilant 22a, CAIG ProGold, CAIG CaiLube MCL (contact vendors for product use details)	Great for lubricating and protecting contacts on card slots, disk drive connectors, and so on.
ESD-safe vacuum cleaner	Eliminates dust and gunk instead of blowing it around	Ensure unit is designed for computer use.
Canned air	Used to clean out dust from power supplies, keyboards, and cases	Hold can at recommended angle; spread newspapers under and behind what you're cleaning to catch the junk you remove.
Foam or chamois cleaning swabs	Used for drive-head and contact cleaning	Use in place of cotton swabs, which shed.
Silicone sprays	Lubricates moving parts	Check label. Spray on swab and apply sparingly to item. Don't spray item directly.

Chapter 14

Connector Quick Reference

Serial Ports and Cables

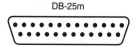

DB-25M 25-pin serial port.

DB-9m 9-pin serial port.

DB-25f 25-pin serial cable.

DB-9f 9-pin serial cable.

Parallel Ports

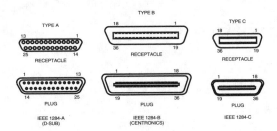

The three different types of IEEE-1284 parallel port connections. Type A receptacle (DB-25m) is used on computers; Type B receptacle is used on most printers. Some HP LaserJet printers use both Type B and Type C receptacles.

SCSI Ports

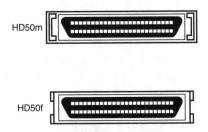

The SCSI HD-50m cable connector (top) and HD-50f receptacle (bottom) are the most common types of external SCSI ports used today.

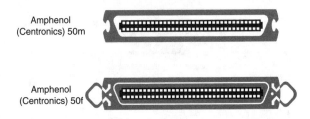

The traditional (Amphenol/Centronics) 50m cable connector (top) and 50f receptacle (bottom) are still widely used for external SCSI devices.

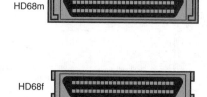

HD68m

HD68f

Wide SCSI HD-68m cable connector (top) and HD-68f receptacle (bottom) are used for Wide SCSI external devices.

USB and IEEE-1394 (FireWire)

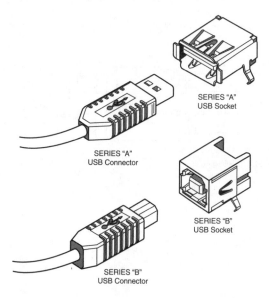

SERIES "A"
USB Socket

SERIES "A"
USB Connector

SERIES "B"
USB Socket

SERIES "B"
USB Connector

USB Type A and Type B ports and cables. Use a Type A to Type B cable to run between USB hubs and most USB devices.

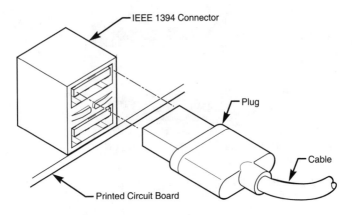

The standard 6-wire IEEE-1394 (FireWire, i.Link) connector, receptacle, and cable.

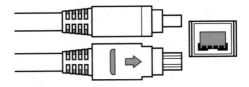

Some IEEE-1394 devices use a four-wire cable and receptacle instead, omitting the power lines.

Video Connectors
Video Ports

Video Card Connectors

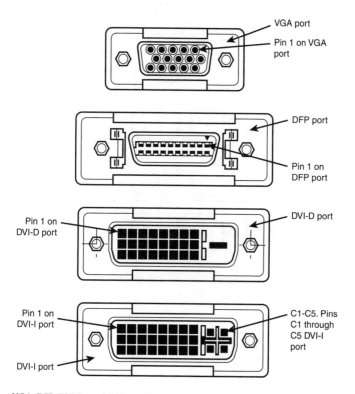

VGA, DFP, DVI-D, and DVI-I video receptacles (top to bottom).

Video Cables

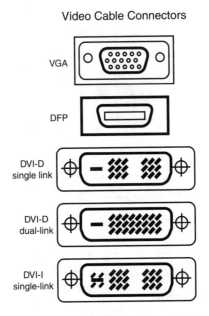

VGA, DFP, DVI-D single link, DVI-D dual link, and DVI-I video cable connectors (top to bottom).

Sound Card Ports
Sound Card External Ports

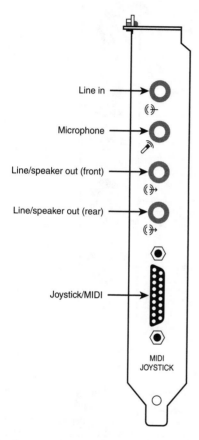

Speaker out, microphone, dual line-in, and MIDI/Joystick port (top to bottom) are found on typical sound cards of all types.

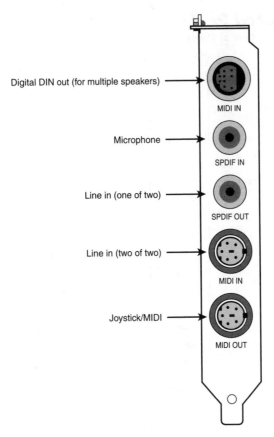

Digital DIN out (for multiple speakers)

Microphone

Line in (one of two)

Line in (two of two)

Joystick/MIDI

MIDI IN

SPDIF IN

SPDIF OUT

MIDI IN

MIDI OUT

Some or all of these ports—digital DIN, SPDIF in, SPDIF out, MIDI in, and MIDI out (top to bottom)—can be found in various combinations on advanced sound cards. They can be mounted on a daughtercard bracket (shown here), attached to the rear of the sound card itself, or mounted on a box connected to the outside of the computer.

Sound Card Internal Connectors

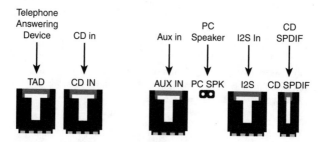

Typical internal sound card ports include, from left to right, TAD (telephone answering device for use with modems), CD in (for playing music CDs through the sound card speakers), Aux in (for connecting other devices), PC SPK (for playing PC speaker beeps through the sound card's speakers), I2S in (for playing DVD audio), and CD SPDIF (for playing digital audio from CD-ROM drives with SPDIF output).

Network and Modem Ports and Cables
RJ-45 Port and Cable

An RJ-45 port, typically used for UTP Ethernet/Fast Ethernet.

An RJ-45 cable connector, typically used for UTP Ethernet/Fast Ethernet.

RJ-11 Port and Cable Connector

RJ-11f

An RJ-11 port, used for modems and other telephone-wire applications. Often found in pairs (one connecting to the telephone network, the other acting as a pass-through to a normal telephone).

RJ11m

An RJ-11 cable, used to connect modems and other telephone-based devices.

Older Network Connectors

DB-15f

A DB-15 connector used for Thick Ethernet (10BASE-5) networks; usually found on the rear of a network card along with an RJ-45 or a BNC connector.

BNC

The BNC connector, used by Thin Ethernet along with a T-adapter. The adapter is used to connect the cable to the network card.

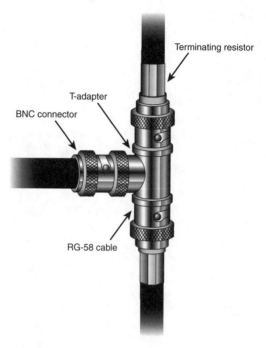

The BNC connector with T-adapter, resistor, and BNC (RG-58 Thin Ethernet) cable.

Index

W

X-Z